NO PROPHETS

NO PROPHETS

THE FIGHT TO SAVE DEMOCRACY FROM CHRISTIAN NATIONALISM

JARED HUFFMAN

W. W. NORTON & COMPANY
Independent Publishers Since 1923

Printed in the United States of America
First Edition

Manufacturing by Lakeside Book Company
Book design by Beth Steidle
Production manager: Lauren Abbate

ISBN 978-1-324-13048-2

W. W. Norton & Company, Inc., 500 Fifth Avenue, New York, NY 10110
www.wwnorton.com

W. W. Norton & Company Ltd., 15 Carlisle Street, London W1D 3BS

Authorized EU representative: EAS, Mustamäe tee 50, 10621 Tallinn, Estonia

10 9 8 7 6 5 4 3 2 1

For everyone who refuses to bow

I have a foreboding of an America in my children's or grandchildren's time . . . when the people have lost the ability to set their own agendas or knowledgeably question those in authority; when, clutching our crystals and nervously consulting our horoscopes, our critical faculties in decline, unable to distinguish between what feels good and what's true, we slide, almost without noticing, back into superstition and darkness.

—Carl Sagan, *The Demon-Haunted World* (1995)

CONTENTS

FOREWORD

AT A TIME OF INTENSIFYING THEOCRATIC ATTACKS ON our democracy and the freedom it protects, America needs badass patriots unafraid to get into some good trouble.

To my utter delight, I recognized one of those patriots in my very first year of Congress. I was elected to the US House of Representatives on Tuesday, November 8, 2016, the same night Donald Trump was elected president, when he kicked off MAGA's authoritarian demolition derby against all constitutional boundaries and values.

Exactly one year after election night, November 8, 2017, Congressman Jared Huffman of the California North Coast became the first member of Congress in history to publicly describe himself as a Humanist, someone who places the needs, ideals, and potential of humanity first, without the requirement of supernatural guidance or religious orthodoxy. In an interview with *The Washington Post* and then speaking in lots of other outlets, he set himself at odds against the surging forces of Christian nationalism that had made a deal with the devil of right-wing political extremism—corruption, lawlessness, the mobilization of hatred and contempt, the glorification of wealth and power, the violation of the rights of women, ceaseless war against working people and the poor. In the darkness of those days of the first Trump administration, Jared Huffman's existential and intellectual coming-out announcement was thrilling to behold.

The day after I read the article about him, I hurried to find Jared on the House floor, reintroduced myself (we had met earlier in the year but rarely saw each other as we didn't serve on the same committees) and congratulated him on this bold move. We began to talk about our heroes of humanist history—Einstein and Spinoza, Ben Franklin and Thomas Jefferson, Bertrand Russell and John Dewey, Christopher Hitchens and Zora Neale Hurston, and Kurt Vonnegut, who is Jared's great favorite humanist writer, and Thomas Paine, who is mine, the political hero who my wife Sarah and I had named our son after.

I delighted in Jared's company, and we would often stay talking on the floor long after votes were over. I found him to be a true intellectual pilgrim, a creative and iconoclastic thinker seeking the truth. But Jared is, above all, a public servant and someone completely serious about defending our constitutional democracy even as he takes time to laugh at the cosmic absurdities of our current political situation. We shared an irreverent sense of humor. I had finally found a colleague who could appreciate all of my jokes collected out on the road, like this one, which was the first I told him:

St. Peter is up in Heaven and walking down the hallway when he passes God's office, only to find God burying his head in his hands. "What's wrong?" St. Peter asks, "You look really upset."

"I *am* really upset," God says, "I'm in love with an atheist and she doesn't even know I *exist*."

Over the subsequent months, our friendship focused on a powerful idea that kept growing stronger: We needed to create a caucus in Congress to defend and promote the Enlightenment principles being dragged through the mud by Donald Trump and MAGA polemicists. We needed a political arena, no matter how tiny—we thought it would indeed be just him and me and our then-colleague Jerry McNerney from California—where we could advance all the besieged humanist principles in the world that oppose the political worship of wealth, power, cruelty, and domination in the name of God.

I wanted to call it the Tom Paine Caucus but, amazingly, we found after talking to colleagues that, even more than two centuries after publication of *The Age of Reason*, Paine's name is still too controversial. So, I gave in to Jared's candidate for our group name, the "Freethought Caucus." And he agreed to help me pass the Thomas Paine Memorial Act, my bill honoring Tom Paine with a memorial statue on federal land in the capital city, which we indeed got passed in 2022 and which President Biden signed into law in January of 2023.

In 2018 we launched the Freethought Caucus with four organizing principles: to defend the Jeffersonian "wall of separation" between church and state; to promote the passage of public policy based on reason, evidence, and scientific knowledge; to oppose discrimination against people based on their religious beliefs or nonbeliefs; and to provide a forum for dialogue among members of Congress on matters of ethics, morality, and their personal spiritual and religious journeys.

Despite our fears that it would just be us, the Freethought Caucus now has an amazing thirty-two members, which is more than the right-wing Freedom Caucus. We have found a large number of members (all Democrats, alas) with the will and desire to challenge the proliferating violations of the separation of church and state engineered by a MAGA-run government. Our members also have the intellectual breadth and historical consciousness to situate Christian nationalism alongside the other forces of unreason—like political corruption, racism and anti-Semitism, misogyny, conspiracy theory, pseudoscience and disinformation—that threaten to destroy secular democracy and its achievements. And, like Jared, they have the strength of character and empathic intelligence to try to understand why so many people are turning to religious fanaticism and extremism in the first place.

I know that I never would have had the bravery or single-minded focus to create the Freethought Caucus myself, so we are fortunate that God, Providence, or the good people of California's Second District—depending on your perspective—rose to the historical occasion and sent Jared Huffman to Congress.

On any given day, whether MAGA is trying to ban "blasphemous" books, restore compulsory prayer to public schools, or plaster religious art in US military facilities, Jared provides muscular and eloquent defense of Jefferson's "wall of separation" between church and state. He is expertly qualified to debunk and derail the theocrats by virtue of his broad study of American constitutional history and his personal immersion in American religious life.

One of the joys of this book is Jared's effortless dismantling of the profuse myths and fallacies advanced by Christian nationalists on a seemingly daily basis. He is not intimidated by their dogmatic appeals to scripture or historical fallacies about the founders' purported determination to create a Christian republic. Jared knows he finds kindred spirits in the founders of America, who were Enlightenment liberals like James Madison, Thomas Jefferson, Ben Franklin, and the pamphleteer of radical democracy, Tom Paine. They were so far from being theocrats and Christian nationalists that Jefferson was constantly denounced as an "atheist" and an "infidel."

But significantly, I have found that, even with all his impressive polemical energy and dangerously logical argumentation skills, Jared always seeks to understand, never to vilify, ridicule, or embarrass religious people, religious beliefs, or religious communities. His own remarkable winding spiritual odyssey—from his upbringing in Independence, Missouri, in the Reorganized Church of Jesus Christ of Latter-Day Saints in the 1960s and '70s to his unprecedented declaration of his secular humanism and atheism as a member of Congress in 2017—is a story of swimming towards personal understanding, philosophical reason, and unjaded compassion. Readers of all faith perspectives will appreciate how this book exposes the bizarre fallacies and vices of theocratic politics and politicized religion, while taking care never to disparage faith itself.

Even amid our most ferocious daily struggles against extremist Christian nationalism, Jared models the same kind of personal tolerance, kindness, and gentleness that Ben Franklin, Thomas Jefferson, and James Madison displayed in the eighteenth century. Like those rationalist founders, Jared understands that the antidote to dogma and irrationalism is not humiliation, but rather the restoration of the democratic gifts of reason and common sense that are the true glory of American culture.

This deep well of decency and compassion also gives Jared the moral clarity to confront hard truths without flinching. This book does that by aggressively linking the rise of Christian nationalism with other authoritarian forces roiling American society. The Ranking Democratic Member of the Committee on Natural Resources, Jared is the pro-science, pro-climate rescue, pro-environment leader our country needs.

By "coming out" as a nontheist in politics, Jared Huffman has shown guts and a remarkable comfort in his own skin—and in his own mind and heart. There's a lot to learn in this powerful book, on everything from the underappreciated role of Christian nationalism in the January 6, 2021, insurrection, to the way Christian Zionism is distorting foreign policy and empowering the far right in Israel, to what it's really like to stand up against violations of the First Amendment perpetrated by your own friends and colleagues in government.

There are humanists who love "humanity" in the abstract but have no real time for human beings in the particular. And then there are humanists who truly love humanity and people both, and show it by fighting for freedom and justice every day. That's Congressman Jared Huffman. Long may he run.

Jamie Raskin
January 5, 2026

NO PROPHETS

INTRODUCTION

THE CROSS AND THE COUP

"CHAIRMAN JEFFRIES, *YOU ARE NOW LIVE*!" THAT'S HOW the 9 a.m. Democratic Caucus meeting began on the morning of January 6, 2021. The singsong voice of Ernestine Dawson introducing our chairman, Rep. Hakeem Jeffries, over Zoom had become a fixture for House Democrats during the pandemic. This meeting was about the important constitutional responsibility we would discharge that day: certifying the 2020 presidential election results.

I was logged in from the bedroom of my rowhouse four blocks from the Capitol. My two housemates, Rep. Mike Levin from southern California and Rep. Greg Stanton from Phoenix, Arizona, were Zooming from other rooms in the house. That's how it worked in the nadir of COVID: Members of Congress flew thousands of miles to talk to each other on computer screens from inside the same house.

Democrats were upbeat that morning. We had come through the election with our House majority intact and had just received more good news: Both Reverend Rafael Warnock and Jon Ossoff had won their Senate elections in the Georgia runoff, a huge rebuke to Donald Trump. We would have a majority in the Senate, just barely, fifty-fifty, with Vice President-elect Kamala Harris breaking any ties. And of course,

Joe Biden would soon be the forty-sixth president of the United States, ending a Trump presidency that every Democrat (and secretly many of our Republican colleagues) viewed as nothing short of a disaster.

After a round of encomiums for Nancy Pelosi, whom we had reelected as Speaker of the House three days earlier, our leadership team gave the rundown on how the day would go. Speaker Pelosi and Vice President Mike Pence would gavel in the joint session of Congress around 1:00 p.m. The House and Senate would then separate into our respective chambers to begin the proceedings. We knew the House Freedom Caucus would object to the electoral results from Arizona, Michigan, Nevada, Pennsylvania, and Georgia—maybe more. It wasn't a serious challenge. Trump's conspiracy theories and claims of a stolen election had already been swatted down by state officials and the courts. But if even one senator backed an objection, it would trigger a separate debate and vote for each contested state, making it hard to predict when the final certification vote would happen.

The bigger question that day was what to expect from thousands of MAGA loyalists whom Trump had summoned to Washington. For two months, the Trump campaign had been stirring up rage through "Stop the Steal" rallies, protest marches, and all manner of bellicose threats. Most Democrats were focused on the future, looking forward to certifying the election so we could all move on. But I couldn't ignore two disturbing patterns in the Trump team's refusal to concede and their ongoing mobilization.

First, the rhetoric was lurid and violent: extreme even by Trumpian standards. The "Stop the Steal" rallies featured chants of "victory or death," open calls for revolution, and the thuggish presence of militia groups like the Proud Boys and Oath Keepers.

Second, the religion dial was cranked to eleven. These weren't political protests in any normal sense; they were megachurch revivals. Firebrand pastors delivered apocalyptic sermons. Speakers invoked violent Bible stories, labeled Biden a "demon" and "Antichrist," and cast their mission to keep Trump in power as a holy war. One event was so surreal it made national headlines: the "Jericho March" on December 12. That day, thousands of MAGA faithful marched around the Capitol, Supreme Court, and Department of Justice, blowing traditional ram's horn trumpets called "shofars" in a reenactment of the biblical siege of Jericho. Then they gathered on the National Mall for the "Let the Church ROAR!" rally, where pastors shared the stage with Trump surrogates like Trump's former national security advisor, General Michael Flynn, and MAGA gadfly Mike Lindell, aka the My Pillow Guy. The incendiary rhetoric pouring out of these protests and saturating social media was worrisome to my fellow House Democrats. We talked about that. But somehow my colleagues either didn't notice or didn't care about the way religion, specifically Christianity, was woven throughout the violent invective.

I sure did. You see, I've got a complicated relationship with religion. I grew up as a devout Christian, lost my religion in college, drifted for years, and eventually found clarity in Humanism—a moral framework that emphasizes human reason and agency. Humanism affirms our responsibility to lead meaningful, ethical lives based on compassion and rational inquiry without the inducement or fear of an afterlife. It is sometimes described as "good without God." In 2017, I "came out" as a Humanist, the only one to ever serve in Congress. In so doing, I also became the only member of Congress dumb enough to publicly admit I don't believe in God.

My first four years in Congress were a crash course in just how eroded Jefferson's "wall of separation" between church and state had become. Then came Trump, the billionaire narcissist who improbably won the support and adoration of millions of conservative Christians and proceeded to open the theocratic floodgates by elevating fringe religious zealots into powerful positions. By the morning of January 6, 2021, however, I wasn't just cursing these religious encroachments and puzzling over Trump's appeal to devout Christians. I was focused on the rising menace to democracy he was inflaming: Christian nationalism.

Experts define Christian nationalism as the fusion of Christian religious and cultural identity with right-wing politics, rooted in a narrative of America as a "Christian nation." It has been called the "connective tissue" that bonds Trump' disparate MAGA elements together. And the MAGA Christian nationalism Trump stoked wasn't an innocent combination of gauzy patriotism and nice Christian values. It seethed with grievance and hatred.

I saw it everywhere. Trump knew that raw Christian nationalism had won him the presidency, and he spent four years feeding the beast with policy and personnel moves, incendiary rhetoric, and media spectacles—like the one on June 1, 2020, when he marched the White House press corps to nearby St. John's Episcopal Church minutes after federal law enforcement had forcibly cleared a Black Lives Matter protest. Holding a Bible aloft while the cameras rolled was his silent but unmistakable Christian nationalist battle cry.

After Trump's election loss, the MAGA Christian nationalist movement fumed with a volatile combination of religious fervor, anger, and betrayal. In their rhetoric and rallies I could plainly discern something more than just political passion: There was a deeply held conviction, however disconnected from reality, that Biden and the Democrats were trying to cheat God's plan.

Few in the media or Congress seemed troubled by the threat of Christian nationalism, but outside the Beltway, secular watchdogs and First Amendment advocates had been sounding the alarm for months. One progressive advocacy group, People for the American Way, had a digital tracking initiative called Right Wing Watch to monitor and expose far-right extremism.

Right Wing Watch was how I knew about the pyromaniacal preaching of Christian nationalist pastors like Trump's White House spiritual advisor, Paula White, and how conservative Christian media platforms were brimming with the QAnon conspiracy theory—the notion that Trump is fighting a secret cabal of satanic, pedophile liberal elites—and becoming echo chambers of bloody prophecy and militant religious fantasy. Among the unsettling examples in the months leading up to Election Day: Pastor Rick Joyner, the charismatic leader of the Christian media network MorningStar TV, claimed God had revealed to him that America was being "seeded" with military veterans trained in urban warfare ready to join Christian militias for the coming civil war. Televangelist Jim Bakker told his huge internet and satellite TV audience that if Biden wins, "we're gonna have a revolution" with Christians flooding the streets. And Catholic priest Frank Pavone, the combative leader of Priests for Life, tweeted that the election was "a spiritual battle—no less than a civil war."

A month before the election, as violent Christian nationalist rhetoric escalated, I tried (not nearly hard enough, in hindsight) to spotlight this national security threat by convening a congressional briefing. I invited my colleagues to hear from investigative journalist Katherine Stewart, whose book *The Power Worshippers* offers a chilling autopsy of Christian nationalism's century-long evolution and its combustible new iteration under Trump. Only one of my colleagues attended.

My heightened concern relative to others in Congress was probably because of my lived experience with the danger of unchecked religious extremism. I'd seen once-rational people, friends of mine, driven to brutality, even murder by the force of their beliefs. To me, it seemed obvious that religious violence was brewing.

Eighteen days before our joint session meeting, my worries deepened when Trump posted an ominous late-night tweet: "Big protest in D.C. on January 6th. Be there, will be wild." Trump's call to action quickly went viral. Hashtags like #wildprotest, #Jan6, and #donotcertify began spreading on social media. Details emerged about a coordinated series of rallies and marches culminating in the "wild" protest at the Capitol. There were even slick brochures and a user-friendly "MAGA Rally Map Guide" for protestors.

This was the dark cloud hanging over our January 6th caucus meeting, especially as we turned to the topic of security. I considered the US Capitol a fortress, but I was grateful when several colleagues spoke up to voice concerns about safety. I had been worried enough to tell my staff to work from home just in case. Our Democratic majority leader, Steny Hoyer, did his best that morning to calm caucus members' nerves and field questions. But specifics were scarce. All he could offer was a general assurance from Capitol Police: Extra security measures were being implemented, members should use the tunnel system to get from their offices to the House chamber to avoid protestors, and keep an eye on email and text messages throughout the day for updates. There was no assessment of any actual threats, and certainly nothing about the religious violence I feared.

I got a lot more information from my Twitter feed than from the Caucus meeting itself. That's how I learned that the kickoff protest at the Ellipse, near the White House, was heating up. Twitter was already buzzing about the warm-up acts, each more incendiary than the last.

Pastor Paula White set the mood with an opening prayer questioning the election results and asking God to "give us a holy boldness in this hour." Flanked by a row of American flags, she implored the Almighty to "overturn" the forces aligned against Trump.

As our Caucus meeting wrapped up around 10:30 a.m., I began my short walk to the Longworth office building. Within a block from my house, I could already see the promised Capitol Police presence: Officers and barricades were everywhere. So were protestors. I waded through a stream of people in MAGA regalia, grateful for my heavy wool topcoat, which made me less recognizable as a member of Congress.

Arriving at my office on the fifth floor of Longworth, I settled in for what I thought would be a day of catching up on work-related reading while waiting for votes. My plans were soon interrupted by text messages from Capitol Police alerting me and my colleagues that "suspicious devices" had been found, and evacuations ordered in some areas near the Capitol. By 11 a.m., the noise outside was rattling my windows. On the street below, I could see throngs of people festooned with MAGA hats and jackets carrying religious posters, banners, and flags. Sirens wailed, airhorns pierced the air, and the low, rhythmic blast of shofars seemed to be ringing out from every direction.

I recognized a flag several protestors were waving above the crowd: It featured a white field, green pine tree, and the words "An Appeal to Heaven." I first encountered this flag in 2018, when a cadre of charismatic evangelical prophets calling themselves the New Apostolic Reformation convened an "Appeal to Heaven" conference in Washington. The prophetic conclave was timed to coincide with ceremonies honoring the late Billy Graham, one of the most influential evangelical Christian leaders of the twentieth century. Right Wing Watch posted footage of the bizarre ceremony where these prophets took turns beseeching God to bring ruin and destruction on their "Antichrist" enemies: liberals, abortion rights supporters, Muslims, nonbelievers. At one point, "secular humanism" was added to the divine hit list by a speaker who repudiated "weak, limp-wristed, cowardly Christianity" and urged Americans to embrace "the Lord as a man of war." Were these the same "Appeal to Heaven" people marching past my office?

My colleague Rep. Adam Kinzinger (R-IL) was just a block away in the Rayburn building. Like me, his windows faced west, toward the swelling crowd. For Kinzinger, an evangelical Christian attuned to the spiritual undercurrents of the mob, the moment struck deep. For months he had followed the far-right rhetoric on social media, the QAnon fervor, and the swirl of right-wing Christian prophecies. He knew violence was coming. He even tried to warn his Republican colleagues during a conference call on January 1st, but GOP Leader Kevin McCarthy brushed him off with a curt dismissal: "Next caller."

When Kinzinger looked out his window on January 6th, he felt something he couldn't shake. "I just felt like this darkness that I have never felt in my life before. And I would describe it as a spiritual darkness, just like this oppression. I've never felt it before, and I've been to war," he later told me. The trumpeting of shofars was part of it. "I mean, who the hell would think to bring a shofar unless you believe this is a prophetic moment where the people of the Lord are rising up," he said. He recognized that the crowd was staging a Jericho March.

Like most Christians growing up, Kinzinger and I both learned the story of Joshua and the Battle of Jericho in Sunday school. It is taught as a tale of faith and obedience, where God instructs Joshua to march his army of Israelites around the walls of the Canaanite city while blowing shofars. God then rewards Joshua with a miracle: The walls collapse, and the Israelites triumph. When I spoke to Kinzinger while writing this book, I asked him about the part they leave out in Sunday School—the aftermath, where God commands Joshua to loot the city's gold and slaughter every living thing, "both man and woman, young and old, ox and sheep, and ass, with the edge of the sword." And to burn it all afterward. Kinzinger laughed uneasily. "I forgot that part," he said. "Glad I didn't think about it at the time."

By noon on January 6th, the crowd around the Capitol had thickened, and reports from the Ellipse rally grew darker. Even before Trump took the stage, media outlets were reporting a surge of protestors flooding down the National Mall toward the Capitol. I couldn't stomach watching Trump's speech live, but the internet lit up with excerpts, including his final incendiary directive: "We fight. We fight like hell, and if you don't fight like hell, you're not going to have a country anymore. So, let's walk down Pennsylvania Avenue."

Minutes later, all hell broke loose. Trump's shock troops slammed into the west side of the Capitol. From a block over and five stories up, the noise was deafening. I had to shout into the phone for my wife to hear me. I told her I needed to "keep my head on a swivel." Somehow, that didn't reassure her.

Text alerts from Capitol Police poured in: outer barriers breached, pipe bombs found at both Republican and Democratic headquarters nearby, and evacuations underway in a nearby building. A (thankfully false) rumor on Twitter claimed that rioters were roaming the halls of my office building. Then came a chilling directive from Capitol Police: We were to shelter in place, lock doors, avoid windows, silence electronics, and remain quiet.

When Vice President Pence posted his letter affirming the electoral count would proceed, I hoped it might cool the chaos. Instead, it poured gasoline on the fire. Near one of the towering Christian crosses in the crowd, protestors erected gallows and began chanting "Hang Mike Pence!" The shock troops pushed against lines of police in riot gear desperately trying to secure the west entrance to the Capitol.

Inside the House chamber, the joint session debate was underway. Outside, the MAGA mob was trying to stop the election certification through brute force. Insurrectionists scaled the scaffolding on the Capitol's west side that was set up for President-elect Biden's inauguration, smashed through doors and windows, and within minutes overwhelmed riot police and streamed into the building. For the first time since the War of 1812, the United States Capitol was breached.

The Senate and House abruptly recessed as police frantically tried to slow the attackers long enough to evacuate members of Congress, staff, and media. Watching these events unfold on TV while hearing the chaos through my office window was surreal. Colleagues texted grim updates from the House chamber, where they'd barricaded the doors as the mob tried to break through. Then came the report of shots fired just outside the chamber in the Speaker's lobby. That report would turn out to be a fatality: Insurrectionist Ashli Babbitt was shot and killed by Capitol Police.

Those were the darkest hours of the day: a three-hour stretch when the insurrectionists effectively seized control of the Capitol. I had no idea if reinforcements were coming, if more rioters were en route, or if, having sacked the main Capitol building, the mob would storm through the tunnels and deliver the Jericho treatment to Canaanites like me.

Perhaps most unsettling was the total silence from Trump. No statement. No condemnation. No call for peace. No tweets of any kind. Was he coordinating with the attackers? Would he arrive at the Capitol as promised, perhaps to declare martial law, as some in his circle had urged? And where was the military? Why the uncharacteristic restraint from Capitol Police in the face of a violent assault on the seat of government? Trump had spent years courting the loyalty of law enforcement and the military. Was there coordination? Were elements within those institutions sympathetic to the coup? Or was there something about the crowd itself—its flags, its Christianity, its whiteness—that tempered the response?

By 4:30 p.m., my worst fears had begun to ease. Police reinforcements and the National Guard were finally arriving, and their combined presence was helping wrest parts of the Capitol back under control. Then, at last, Trump surfaced, posting a video message on Twitter. Like an arsonist returning to the blaze with a teacup of water, he offered a limp plea: "Go home, and go home in peace." But not before repeating his lie that the election had been stolen and showering the insurrectionists with affection: "We love you."

By sunset, the insurrection was effectively over, and police were removing the last rioters from the Capitol. At 6:30 p.m., Speaker Pelosi sent me and the rest of our colleagues an email decrying the attack on democracy, laying blame squarely on Trump, and announcing that Congress would reconvene that evening to certify election results when the Capitol was finally cleared. It was vintage Pelosi, who will go down as the greatest Speaker in history because of her steely resolve, brilliant political instincts, and keen sense of history. Even before the Capitol was totally secure—before crews had begun to clean up the broken glass, blood, and feces left in the rioters' wake—she knew the truth of that day, especially Trump's culpability, must be recorded and preserved for history. Equally important, she knew we needed to proclaim which side had won, that democracy prevailed. I wasn't surprised to see the way Pelosi, who is deeply religious, closed her email that evening, by referencing the Catholic celebration of January 6th as the Feast of the Epiphany and urging all of us to "pray that this instigation to violence will provide an epiphany for our country to heal."

At 11 p.m., I walked through the tunnel that had been used to evacuate my colleagues a few hours earlier, past the battered door of the Speaker's lobby where there was still broken glass and blood on the floor, and into the House chamber where I voted to certify the Arizona results. A little after 2:30 a.m., I cast my final vote of the night to certify the Pennsylvania results. The 2020 presidential election was officially over.

If you've lived through a traumatic event, you may know how its meaning can evolve over time. Days or months later, after the adrenaline fades, your mind pieces together what actually happened. Combat veterans often describe PTSD this way, as a creeping reckoning that arrives after the body is safe, but the mind is still catching up. This is how trauma sometimes unfolds—the experience keeps revealing itself long after the event is over.

That's how January 6th is for me. If you'd asked me that night what had happened, I would've pointed the blame squarely at Trump. He was, without question, the proximate cause. He was not only the spark that lit the dry kindling, he was also the one who piled it up, doused it with kerosine, and stood back watching it burn.

But if you ask me now, with the benefit of everything I've learned and reflected on since, my answer is more complex. Trump is still the primary culprit, but there was a lot more going on than just one man's imperious ego and the cultlike devotion of his followers. There's a deeper, more unsettling truth. The January 6th insurrection wouldn't have happened without legions of fervent Christian nationalist believers, and it turns out they weren't just following Trump—they were *leveraging him* for a religious agenda they truly believe in and are willing to do anything for.

Some details I barely registered in real time—the "Appeal to Heaven" flags, the shofars, the huge wooden crosses, the rioters praying with their hands aloft as mayhem raged. These things now feel like flashing indicators of something far more profound: January 6th was not just an attack on the Capitol that nearly upended the transfer of presidential power. It was a rupture that exposed the Christian nationalist movement as an existential threat to our safety, our fundamental rights, and our democracy. That movement never conceded defeat. And its volatile fusion of right-wing politics, faith, and fury shapes our current moment even as most Americans still don't understand the central role it played on January 6th, much less the greater danger it poses now.

There's a quote attributed to novelist Sinclair Lewis that has always haunted me. "When fascism comes to America, it will be wrapped in the flag and carrying a cross." On January 6, 2021, something eerily close to that vision descended on our Capitol, festooned in stars and stripes, brandishing crosses, and violently shattering our centuries-old tradition of peaceful power transfer. Democracy survived the assault, and we were granted a second chance.

But let's not kid ourselves. The damage was done, and this threat was never just a one-off. Especially now, with Trump back in the White House waging what feels like a slow-motion sequel to the insurrection. "Wrapped in the flag and carrying a cross" isn't just chilling prose; it's the playbook. This time, we may not get a second chance.

THIS BOOK CONFRONTS a danger we failed to see coming, a deepening threat that our institutions remain either too complacent or too compromised to resist. Political leaders across the spectrum quietly abetted its rise; many now work openly to accelerate its advance. Still, our public discourse falters, unable or unwilling to even name it.

January 6th should have been a national wake-up call to the shocking power of Christian nationalism. Instead, America, including many of my colleagues in Congress whom the mob wanted to kill, went back to sleep. Half a decade later, we still haven't reckoned with the reality of that Christian coup, driven by a militant movement that rejects pluralism, constitutional democracy, and peaceful coexistence. Since 2021, that movement has grown stronger, more organized, and more determined than ever to achieve its goals.

No Prophets argues that extreme Christian nationalism is now America's most dangerous political movement. Its theocratic, authoritarian ringleaders, once dismissed as fringe, now wield mainstream power, and they're using it to dismantle secular democracy from within. From a frontline perspective, I'll show how this threat has advanced much further than most people realize. Indeed, it will be hard at this point to stop it from turning America into something unthinkable for most of us—something our Enlightenment-era founders fought against and built Constitutional walls to protect us from. But I wouldn't write this book if the fight wasn't still winnable.

Defeating extreme Christian nationalism starts with a clear-eyed understanding of the movement: its origins and the theology of supremacy and dominion that drives its religious architects. That's where we begin in the first few chapters, including my own entry point studying the progenitor of today's movement under the tutelage of a renowned professor who wrote the book on the "New Religious Right" of the 1980s. We'll trace how, in barely a generation, right-wing Christians morphed from waging a rule-bound culture war within the system of democracy into today's scorched-earth insurgency that actively seeks to destroy it.

Chapter 2 reveals how unchecked prophetic Christianity—including self-declared prophets and apostles who claim direct revelations from God about elections, candidates, and America's national destiny—pushed me into the fight for church-state separation. This book's title, *No Prophets*, evokes the inherent volatility of this religious variant, and the madness of Trump elevating its fanatical leaders from the fringe of American religion into the political mainstream, and astonishingly, into positions of trust and influence in our government. I grew up experiencing the tragic consequences when prophetic belief goes off the rails, as it invariably does. Informed by that experience and lessons throughout history, I could not just stand by hoping the powder keg doesn't explode.

Chapter 3 spotlights the theology and power structures of the three ascendent religious factions that make Christian nationalism much more than a political movement. We'll profile their religious architects and unravel the absolutist beliefs—rejected by most Christians—that put them on a collision course with democracy. Then in Chapter 4 we'll examine the Christian nationalist movement's main strategies and tactics, especially the relentless promotion of fabricated history about

America's founding. We'll explain why these myths are so pernicious as we dissect and refute them.

Then begins perhaps the hardest and most urgent part of our reckoning with Christian nationalism. Waking from America's sleepwalk into theocracy requires crossing one of the most stubborn taboos in our national discourse: the unwillingness to scrutinize Christian extremism with the same intellectual rigor we apply elsewhere. Christian privilege—our cultural reflex to presume all things "Christian" are good—operates as both a sword and shield for the Christian nationalist movement, easing its advance and protecting its strongholds. Christian privilege and deference thereto are the default settings of our institutions and the political leadership of both parties. This is why urgent warnings fail to penetrate. Like the one Katherine Stewart delivered in a congressional briefing in October 2020, attended only by Rep. Jamie Raskin and me. It's why the letter Raskin and I sent to President-elect Biden six weeks before the insurrection, warning that Christian nationalism posed a national security threat, received no response. And it's why the House Select Committee investigating January 6th chose to deliberately erase a central element of the insurrection from its final report. Chapter 5 takes us behind the scenes to reveal that untold story—one of the most consequential political cover-ups in recent history and a profound security failure. We'll go on to examine the persistence and terrible cost of Christian privilege and reckon with the urgent need to confront it notwithstanding the discomfort of doing so.

Chapter 6 takes us inside the US Capitol, the supposed citadel of secular democracy, for an unvarnished look at what I call the shadow theocracy. We'll see the expanding reach of Christian nationalism inside the highest levels of our government. The project to dismantle secular democracy and enshrine biblical doctrine as policy is far more entrenched than most Americans realize, as we'll see from the leaders, groups, and networks that are advancing the theocratic agenda every day in Washington, amplifying parallel theocratic initiatives at the state and local government levels.

We'll zoom in on Israel and Christian Zionism in Chapter 7 to show how our foreign policy is increasingly warped by biblical prophecies, and how that distortion carries huge geopolitical consequences.

We'll see that Christian Zionism is not only a glimpse of biblical governance in action; it is also a double-edged sword for the Jewish people, and a rumbling fault line within the MAGA Christian nationalist coalition where unwavering support of Israel by Christian Zionists coexists uneasily with the virulent anti-Semitism that permeates other right-wing Christian factions.

At several points in the book, we discuss the significance of rapid cultural and demographic changes, which is essential context for understanding the Christian nationalist threat. Religious extremism is shaking the foundations of our republic at a time when America is becoming not only more ethnically and racially diverse, but also dramatically less religious. Currently, one in three Americans identify as nonreligious. You might expect waning religiosity to weaken theocratic momentum, but instead, it's accelerating it. This paradox is also an explanation. As right-wing Christians lose cultural dominance, they radicalize. Their shrinking influence becomes a rallying cry for conquest and restoration. They see pluralism and secularization not as progress, but as an existential threat. Decline breeds desperation. And desperation breeds extremism.

Some of that desperation and extremism is aimed at modernity itself. A century after the Scopes Monkey Trial, America finds itself relitigating basic questions of education, evidence, and reason. The uneasy truce that has prevailed between Christianity and the Enlightenment for the past 250 years is in serious jeopardy and the consequences are daunting—not just for democracy, but for the health, safety, and prosperity of future generations. Chapter 8 examines this unraveling driven by right-wing Christian dogma and weighs the societal cost of our national backslide on public education, science, research, and critical reasoning.

There is light at the end of the tunnel—hope, if you like, though I prefer just a clear-eyed, unyielding resolve to prevail. The final chapter examines the path forward, showing how the seemingly unstoppable threat of MAGA Christian nationalism can be defeated. We can still save democracy. We can repair the crumbling wall of separation between church and state before it fails. And in doing so, we can begin to heal the religious and political fractures ripping this country apart.

But first, we must venture boldly into the chaotic intersection of religion and politics with our eyes wide open and ask: What exactly is going on here? And, more important, how do we stop Christian nationalism from not only causing more violence, but also destroying America as we know it? To answer those questions, we must talk about religion like any other subject, without special animus, but without special immunity from scrutiny. That's harder than it should be in this country. But buckle up. We're heading straight into that intersection.

CHAPTER 1

NOT YOUR PARENTS' CULTURE WAR

ELEMENTS OF CHRISTIAN NATIONALISM HAVE BEEN around for a long time, including the belief that America is divinely chosen, that our laws should reflect Christian values, and that white Christians deserve cultural dominance. But the term itself was rarely used before the 2000s, when it started surfacing in academic journals, progressive religious critiques, and a prescient book, *Kingdom Coming*, by journalist Michelle Goldberg who, in 2007, sounded an early alarm about a rising Christian nationalist movement in America's heartland. After Trump's 2016 victory, sociologists and political commentators began to realize he had harnessed something that demanded closer scrutiny—and a label.

Two groundbreaking books in 2020 helped introduce the term "Christian nationalism" into public discourse. Investigative journalist Katherine Stewart's *The Power Worshippers* revealed the coordination and financing behind the Christian nationalist movement. And sociologists Andrew Whitehead and Sam Perry, in *Taking Back America for God*, showed, through national survey data, how strongly Christian nationalist ideology correlates with support for policies and norms that privilege Christians.

Still, few Americans had heard about it until the insurrection. Only after that, starting with the Public Religion Research Institute's nationwide survey in 2022, did we begin to measure its dimensions, and the data has held steady ever since. About 30 percent of Americans embrace Christian nationalism, but among Republicans that jumps to a majority, 53 percent. Zooming in on those Republicans sharpens the picture: 55 percent embrace "dominion" theology, the belief that Christians should control all aspects of society; more than 60 percent want America to be officially declared a Christian nation and to have laws based on Christian values; and more than a third endorse violent insurrection "to save our country."

How did this happen? How did right-wing Christianity become so extreme, theocratic, and open to violence as a political strategy, when barely a generation ago it was waging a rule-bound culture war within the system of democracy? This chapter charts that evolution, beginning with the Moral Majority of the 1980s and tracing the cultural and political shifts that forged today's MAGA Christian nationalist movement. The story begins in Santa Barbara.

UC Santa Barbara in the 1980s felt like the counterculture's afterparty: sun-drenched, restless, and still echoing defiance. Palm trees swayed over a serene campus where students surfed at Campus Point between (or in lieu of) classes. On the surface, it was idyllic. But beneath the serenity, you could still feel the cultural quakes of the '60s and '70s. A decade earlier, UCSB had been a frontline campus in what some called America's great unraveling. Students marched against the Vietnam War, demanded racial and gender justice, challenged puritanical norms, and torched symbols of establishment power. In 1970, antiwar activists clashed with police and set fire to the local Bank of America at the edge of campus—a dramatic act of rebellion seared into campus lore. By the time I arrived as a freshman in the fall of 1982, the flames were long gone, but you could still smell the smoke in the carpet.

I stepped off the bus in Santa Barbara as a devoutly religious eighteen-year-old from Independence, Missouri, thinking mainly about the postcard-perfect campus and the scholarship that had landed me a spot on UCSB's top-ranked Gaucho volleyball team. I wasn't yet aware that I'd also stepped into one of the more volatile intersections in American cultural and political life, a fault line where Reagan-era conservatism was clashing with the counterculture idealism of the California coast.

The UCSB campus community, including a teaching assistant in my first political science class who casually told us she'd thrown the first brick through the BofA window, didn't want to admit that America was lurching rightward. But just a few miles east in the Santa Ynez Mountains sat Ronald Reagan's western White House. Two years before I arrived on campus, the Gipper had galloped into Washington with a posse of fundamentalist Christians calling themselves the Moral Majority. They filled a void in America's soul that Vietnam had bled dry. Assassinations, race riots, and Watergate had scorched the nation's conscience. There was no trust in government, and then came inflation, malaise, and a stalled Cold War under Jimmy Carter. By 1980, the left was exhausted, and the right was furious—perfect conditions for a conservative counterrevolution.

Of course, much of this was lost on me as a wide-eyed freshman adjusting to my new surroundings. But by the winter of my junior year, the culture shock of UCSB had worn off. I was soaking up the political and cultural complexity around me and for the first time, I found myself caring almost as much about school as I did about volleyball. That shift had a lot to do with a religious studies professor named Walter Capps.

Professor Capps didn't just teach about religion and politics; he made the collision compelling. A seminarian and Yale-trained scholar, he was soft-spoken, probing, and profoundly humane. He taught us to dissect ideologies, to challenge their champions and critics, and he welcomed all sides into the lecture hall. His courses were also legendary for the constellation of high-profile guest speakers he attracted.

Capp's flagship class on the Vietnam War's impact on American religion and culture became a national sensation, drawing praise from members of Congress, television news anchors, and public intellectuals. I took the Vietnam course as a sophomore, and by junior year I was eager to enroll in another of his signature offerings: Religious Studies 153, *Religion and Politics in America Today*. The course generated buzz when it debuted two years earlier, cotaught by Capps and former presidential candidate George McGovern, and featuring guest appearances from ideologically diverse luminaries like Eugene McCarthy, Jerry Brown, Paul Weyrich, Cal Thomas, and Robert Billings.

In the 1985 iteration of the course, Capps and his guests dove deep into what he called "the New Religious Right," a movement that was rapidly reshaping American politics. Our reading list spanned the spectrum from GOP strategist Richard Viguerie and evangelical firebrand Francis Schaeffer to academic analysts like Erling Jorstad and George Marsden.

No figure cast a longer shadow over this movement than Rev. Jerry Falwell Sr., the charismatic televangelist who founded the Moral Majority, a political organization that became synonymous with the New Religious Right. Falwell was a virtuoso communicator and, although we didn't use the term back then, a full-throttle Christian nationalist.

He began preaching in the 1950's as a segregationist and opponent of civil rights. By 1976, when he launched the Moral Majority with a fifty-state "I Love America Tour," Falwell had rebranded his message into a more genial form of bigotry. Racially segregated religious schools, for example, were defended in the name of "religious liberty" instead of overt racism. His preaching distilled the Moral Majority's war on America's alleged sins: court rulings that curtailed school prayer and condoned abortion, the rise of feminism, sexual permissiveness, homosexuality, liberal media, and foreign policy that coddled godless communists. Falwell championed a vision of America rooted in obedience to biblical authority and conformity with traditional values, placing him in tension with Enlightenment principles like individual rights, rational inquiry, and free thought. Indeed, he railed against modernity and "secular Humanism" as threats to the Bible that were corrupting the nation's soul.

While Falwell seethed at liberal politicians and journalists, he was equally scathing toward fellow Christians in the ecumenical movement—those who wanted to bridge historic schisms between denominations and promote "big tent" Christianity. To Falwell, ecumenicalism was a Trojan horse for doctrinal compromise, cultural decay, and political surrender. He demanded purity, especially on abortion, feminism, and family values. These weren't just theological positions; they were strategies to advance the one ecumenical goal Falwell embraced. He sought to forge a powerful coalition between conservative evangelicals and Catholics, a "moral majority" capable of reshaping American politics and culture from the ground up.

I found Jerry Falwell's politicized preaching appalling. As a twenty-one-year-old, I had spent most of my life in and around churches where politics were kept out of the sanctuary. In the faith community where I grew up, subjects like abortion, school prayer, and Supreme Court rulings were simply never discussed, not from the pulpit, and not even among congregants in my experience. It would have been unthinkable. Which is why Falwell's brash fusion of Christian theology and public policy felt so jarring.

I also recoiled at Falwell's hellfire absolutism and his condemnation of anyone outside his belief system. The recent death of my father had shaken my faith in the supernatural tenets of Christianity; I ultimately abandoned those beliefs. But the ethical teachings of Jesus Christ as I understood them—the values of love, humility, compassion, forgiveness, nonjudgment, and grace—still drove my moral compass. Falwell's preaching struck me as the antithesis of those values.

My main takeaway from Capps's course was that the New Religious Right was not a spiritual revival but a political machine, one that cloaked its ambitions in scripture and wielded faith for partisan ends. Falwell, with his booming voice and southern charm, was persuasive to many. But to me, especially at that time, newly estranged from faith, skeptical of religious dogma, but still steeped in the values and sensibilities of my Christian upbringing, the entire performance felt deeply offensive.

Professor Capps, ever the dispassionate intellectual, let the material speak for itself. He showed Falwell's sermons and speeches, posed probing questions, and urged us to grapple with the societal implications of the New Religious Right. But reviewing the UCSB archives of Capps's writing from that era makes clear that his restraint in the classroom masked a deeper concern about the movement and its corrosive influence on public life.

In a 1982 essay, Capps wrote about his visit to Lynchburg, Virginia, where he interviewed Falwell and other Moral Majority leaders and attended a sermon at Liberty University. True to form, Capps presented Falwell's remarks with minimal editorializing. But every so often, he exercised the writer's prerogative by offering a quiet rebuttal, a pointed observation, or a subtle critique. For example, Capps wrote critically of Falwell's fixation on abortion and sexual norms as a defense of "male dominion and the supremacy of patriarchal order."

One of the most compelling critiques to emerge from Capps's writings on Falwell centers on their opposing narratives about the Vietnam War. For Falwell, America's defeat was divine punishment: a consequence of secularism, moral decay, and the abandonment of our covenant with God. His prescription was clear. We needed to reset the nation's moral compass, restore the covenant, and rebuild our military might to ensure we never again lose to "demonic" communists.

Capps saw something else entirely. He viewed Falwell as a product of Vietnam, a figure born from the national disillusionment and existential drift that followed. He argued that the academic and religious establishments had underestimated Falwell, dismissing him as a fringe figure rather than reckoning with the real moral anxieties his movement tapped into. Falwell's theology may have been simplistic and flawed, Capps argued, but he had keen instincts. Falwell correctly sensed vulnerability in the uneasy alliance between rationalism and Christianity that had prevailed since the eighteenth-century Enlightenment. That truce, born from the scars of Europe's bloody religious wars and America's own colonial theocracies, was deemed unbreakable, but Falwell was making inroads toward prying it apart.

Perhaps most viscerally, given the ever-present specter of nuclear annihilation during the Cold War, Capps was appalled by Falwell's apocalyptic rhetoric and cavalier posture toward global destruction. That, along with Falwell's other moral and theological shortcomings, led Capps to conclude that the Moral Majority was doomed to fail because it would simply scare too many Americans. He believed that Falwell and the New Religious Right were deeply troubling but ultimately transitory—too antithetical to America's founding principles to endure, too dismissive of individual rights and intellectual freedom to thrive. By demeaning and alienating most people, Capps predicted, the Christian right wing was planting the seeds of its own demise.

That era of Christian nationalism was clearly different than what we're living through today. While some of the Moral Majority's rhetoric resembles MAGA Christian nationalism, it never seemed to Capps or to me that they were trying to overthrow democracy. Capps hated their warmongering, but he believed that it was the policy, not the movement itself, that threatened national security.

Indeed, Falwell and other Moral Majority stalwarts framed their efforts as a mirror image of the left's own playbook from the 1960s and '70s. They used the same tools of grassroots mobilization, legal advocacy, and cultural persuasion to further their conservative Christian vision. Falwell disclaimed any interest in theocracy, insisting he simply wanted to steer a wayward culture back toward moral clarity, using the levers of political influence. He touted his friendship with Senator Ted Kennedy, seemingly an affirmation that, for all their extreme positions, Falwell and his allies were intent on working within the system of democracy.

Falwell even invited Kennedy to address the students and faculty of Liberty University. Kennedy's October 3, 1983, speech—delivered after dining with the Falwell family in their home—was one of the most impactful course materials from Capps's class. Standing before a staunchly conservative evangelical audience, the liberal Catholic fearlessly defended church-state separation, condemned book burning, and reminded the crowd of the fragile nature of religious liberty: "Today's Moral Majority could become tomorrow's persecuted minority." On abortion, he didn't flinch, telling the pro-life audience, "The proper role of religion is to appeal to the conscience of the individual, not the coercive power of the state." His thunderous conclusion: "In short, I hope for an America where neither 'fundamentalist' nor 'humanist' will be a dirty word, but a fair description of the different ways in which people of goodwill look at life and into their own souls. I hope for an America where no president, no public official, no individual will ever be deemed a greater or lesser American because of religious doubt—or religious belief."

The Liberty University audience warmly applauded, and Falwell praised Kennedy for his sincerity and courage. That kind of grace across ideological lines feels like a relic of a more democratic era.

The New Religious Right of the 1980s was many things, none of them good in my view. Falwell and the Moral Majority were brash, combative, and wrong. Their agenda was backward-looking, morally coercive, and steeped in righteous absolutism. But they were trying to win within the system, not burn it down. At least in the 1980s.

Capps's seminal work, *The New Religious Right: Piety, Patriotism, and Politics*, was published in 1990. Seven years later, after an unexpected win in the 1996 midterm election, he found himself serving in Congress, but only for a few months. Capps died suddenly of a heart attack at Dulles International Airport. I never had the chance to reconnect with my former professor. But I did have the privilege of serving in Congress alongside his widow, Lois, who carried forward his legacy with grace and conviction. For that, I'm deeply grateful.

Capps's prediction about the New Religious Right was correct. The Moral Majority was disbanded just before his book was published. The movement fragmented, and by the early 1990s, it had collapsed. But it wasn't because they were too extreme, as Capps had imagined. It was the sudden implosion of the Soviet Union and the end of the Cold War that brought them down. Up to that point, America's external enemy—the godless Soviets—gave the movement coherence and urgency. When the Cold War ended, that ideological scaffolding vanished.

Republican presidential candidate Pat Buchanan tried desperately to revive the old magic at the GOP convention in August 1992, with his fiery "culture war" speech, but the moment had passed. The speech failed to register in the new political terrain. That fall, Bill Clinton won the presidency, ending twelve years of Republican rule and signaling that the country was ready to move on from both the Cold War and the culture war it had fueled. Right-wing Christians were no longer in power; their political movement had crumbled. But the Christian nationalism of that era didn't totally disappear. In the 1990s, vestiges of the fallen New Religious Right began evolving to meet the moment.

BY 1993, church attendance was plummeting. The staunchest pro-choice president since *Roe v. Wade* was in the White House and his wife, a career-minded Ivy League lawyer, was unapologetically redefining the role of First Lady. Americans were warming to gender equity,

LGBTQ rights, and multiculturalism as a surge of immigration from Latin America, Asia, and the Caribbean brought demographic and cultural shifts. Throughout the long Cold War, America's monolithic white Christian identity had held steady: The nation was 76 percent white and 90 percent Christian. By the end of the 1990s, however, the percentage of Christians had dropped 10 points, religiously unaffiliated "nones" were rising fast, and suddenly Hawaii was no longer the only state where whites were not the majority: California joined the list. Texas and New Mexico would follow just four years later.

In the face of these changes, the fractured Christian right scrambled for new strategies. Their rules-bound culture war began morphing into an aggrieved insurgency. With the Soviet Union gone, their moral panic turned inward toward domestic enemies. Government, portrayed as demonic and evil, joined liberal culture as the new foil. Guns became sacred, and violence was increasingly justified, if not sanctified.

Critical milestones in this transitional phase of the movement were the deadly confrontations between white Christian extremists and federal agents at Ruby Ridge, Idaho (1992), and Waco, Texas (1993). Ruby Ridge is where white separatist Randy Weaver barricaded himself, his family, and a friend in a remote Idaho cabin after refusing to appear in court on federal weapons charges. Weaver embraced a theology known as Christian Identity that was spreading among militia groups at the time. It exalts racial purity, apocalyptic readiness, and a conspiratorial belief that the federal government is satanic. His standoff with US marshals resulted in the death of a deputy marshal along with Weaver's wife and fourteen-year-old son before Weaver and his friend, both seriously wounded, ultimately surrendered.

Waco was even more deadly. It involved a Christian sect known as the Branch Davidians at their heavily armed compound. The group's leader, self-declared prophet David Koresh, founded the communal sect based on his belief that God had chosen him to usher in the Bible's end-times. When federal agents attempted to serve a warrant for illegal weapons, Koresh and his followers saw it as the beginning of an apocalyptic showdown foretold by scripture. A gunfight erupted, killing four agents and six Branch Davidians. The ensuing fifty-one-day standoff ended in a catastrophic fire, killing seventy-six Davidians including Koresh, twenty-five children, and many who had been shot or trapped inside.

These tragic flashpoints were mythologized into persecution stories, recast by right-wing Christian leaders not as tragic consequences of radical defiance but as proof of an evil secular government at war with faith and freedom. Ruby Ridge and Waco became battle cries that catalyzed the Patriot Movement, a white supremacist militia movement that fused conspiracism and antigovernment narratives with Christian nationalism. At its peak in the mid-1990s, the Patriot Movement swelled to hundreds of militias with tens of thousands of members. In 1995, after one of these militiamen, Timothy McVeigh, bombed a federal building in Oklahoma City, killing 168 people, including nineteen children, the "Patriot" name was tainted with domestic terrorism and fell out of favor. But the militias and their ideology endured, metastasizing into groups—including Oath Keepers, Three Percenters, and Proud Boys—that would become woven into the fabric of today's MAGA Christian nationalism.

The political work of the New Religious Right continued under the auspices of various GOP groups, including new political and legal organizations that focused less on popular persuasion and more on litigation, novel legal theories, and long-game constitutional battles premised on securing a conservative religious majority on the Supreme Court. Mobilizing Christian voters became the work of decentralized faith networks rather than the top-down structure of the 1980s.

This decentralization mirrored a broader transformation within evangelical Christianity itself: a shift from denominational authority to a sprawling, entrepreneurial religious landscape. Across American Christianity, traditional denominations were shrinking, and churches were closing. But independent charismatic ministries, led by innovative and enterprising pastors, were finding ways to grow.

This trend caught the attention of an evangelical scholar, C. Peter Wagner, the Professor of Church Growth at the Fuller Theological Seminary in southern California. In 1996, he launched a network of churches and ministries called the New Apostolic Reformation (NAR), which quickly began to transform evangelical Christianity. NAR combined a decentralized, nondenominational growth model with militant, charismatic theology rooted in the imperative of Christian dominion over all parts of society, including government. NAR preached that political adversaries are demons who must be vanquished through mass mobilization and "spiritual warfare": targeted prayer and worship campaigns. The list of NAR's demonic enemies was familiar: abortionists, the LGBTQ community, public education, secularists, liberals: essentially the same groups targeted by Falwell's Moral Majority. But NAR brought an ethos of conquest, not persuasion, and it explicitly advocated theocratic takeover.

Thanks in significant part to the growth of NAR-aligned churches and online ministries, the militant antidemocracy ethos of the emerging Christian nationalist movement began to intensify during the 2000s, especially after Barack Obama's 2008 election. For many, the Obama presidency felt like a time when America's founding principles of equality and liberty for all were finally being realized. But those of us who saw the moral arc of the universe bending toward justice missed the fact that millions of our fellow Americans saw it differently: They saw a Christian nation under siege from within.

We also failed to notice that the atomized remains of the New Religious Right were radicalizing into what would soon be called the Christian nationalist movement. Beginning in the 1990s and increasingly in the 2000s, growing numbers of right-wing Christians rejected pluralism and church-state separation outright, breaking with democracy and increasingly embracing political violence as an option. The explosive growth of NAR, with its theology of demonization, conquest, and theocratic ambition, was a catalyst. Throughout these years, the seeds of extremism that would forcefully erupt on January 6, 2021, were germinating. Most of us just didn't see it.

One of the senior henchmen of right-wing Christian politics saw this dangerous transformation unfolding from the inside. Colonel V. Doner helped propel the New Religious Right to its peak of power in the 1980s and remained a key GOP strategist for the next two decades. Doner was more than just a campaign guru: He was a true evangelical believer who worked at the highest levels, from Falwell and Ronald Reagan to Pat Robertson and Sarah Palin, constructing and guiding the right-wing Christian political machine.

But as his movement edged toward what would become today's MAGA Christian nationalism, Doner's conscience began to stir. He grew increasingly unsettled by the movement's fixation on dehumanizing enemies and its neglect of core Christian teachings, including love, mercy, and compassion. He saw how volatile theology fused with militant rhetoric was starting to ignite real-world violence, including murders of abortion providers.

Then came September 11, 2001. When Islamic jihadists carried out their deadly attacks on the United States, Doner saw something hauntingly familiar: religious absolutism, the demonization of enemies, and a righteous lust for violence. It was, to his horror, a mirror image of the Christian political movement he had helped construct. Yet instead of reckoning with the parallels, right-wing pastors were urging Christians to *emulate* the intensity and all-in dedication of the jihadists. Doner recounts a chilling example of a prominent youth pastor urging peers to indoctrinate an army of "spiritual suicide bombers" for Christ to make young Christians just as violently fanatical as Islamic jihadists.

He traces his moral reckoning in his book *Christian Jihad*, which chronicles the escalating radicalization and warns—nearly a decade before the January 6th insurrection—of a movement that had traded democracy for dominion and was sanctifying violence to that end.

I didn't know about Doner and his story until I was researching this book in 2024, but reading *Christian Jihad* carried me back to the New Religious Right I had studied at UCSB. I realized that even though we didn't use the term then, Prof. Capps's course was all about the 1980s variant of Christian nationalism. He predicted that movement would collapse, and it did, albeit for reasons he hadn't anticipated. But he surely would have been dismayed to see it metastasize over the next two decades into something much more virulent.

Imagine what Capps's course, *Religion and Politics in America Today*, would be like if he were still alive and teaching. Without a doubt, it would focus on MAGA Christian nationalism, tracing how this extreme antidemocracy insurgency evolved from the ruins of a movement that seemed radical in the 1980s but now looks almost quaint. Capps would leave the contrasts and contradictions for us to grapple with. With scholarly detachment, he would present the evidence, including material from the experts and faith leaders we'll meet later in this book, and maybe he'd bring some of them in as guest speakers. Capps's gift was the discipline of inquiry, not certainty, so he would ask probative questions and leave the answers to us.

He would likely pose the same final exam question he asked my class in 1985. That deceptively simple question outlived the professor and his course, and now it belongs to all of us: "Is the involvement of religious groups in politics a good or a bad thing? Discuss."

I don't remember how I answered it in 1985, but I know my answer today: It depends.

If religious groups engage in politics while respecting democratic norms—following the law, peacefully bringing their values into the public square, and accepting that in a democracy you don't always get what you want—that's a healthy democracy, whether I agree with their views or not. But if they reject the democratic order and seek to impose their religion on others through the coercive power of government, then it's not just bad, it's dangerous and anti-American.

I'll stake my grade on that. But this exam is still in progress, and history is doing the grading.

CHAPTER 2

BREAKING FAITH

"ALRIGHT, WHO'S GOING TO HOLD THE BIBLE?" SPEAKER John Boehner asked as the C-SPAN cameras rolled.

I froze.

It was January 3, 2013, my first day in Congress. After weeks of orientations, training sessions, and soaking up advice from senior members and veteran staffers, I thought I was ready for anything. But no one warned me about religion. Suddenly, this closeted Humanist had two seconds to answer Boehner's Bible question for the swearing-in photo op.

Up to that moment, everything had gone smoothly. I had given Boehner a bottle of my homemade "Steelhead Syrah," a nod to his love of red wine from my Sonoma County district. "You've got the right idea," he said with a smile. "I'll drink it!"

Perfect. Nailed it.

But somehow, as I was waiting in the photo line with my wife Susan, children Abby and Nathan, older brothers Tim and Jim, and my eighty-three-year-old mother Phyllis, I failed to notice that the colleagues ahead of me were all posing with their hand on a sacred text. I would later learn that most of them had put a lot of thought into it. Rep. Tulsi Gabbard, the first member of Congress to identify as Hindu, used the Bhagavad Ghita. Others honored their faith traditions with a family Bible or Torah, and a few used the Constitution.

I hadn't thought about it at all. With Boehner's question hanging in the air, I glanced at my devout Christian mother who was beaming with pride. Mom knew I stopped going to church a long time ago, but not the full extent of my nonbelief. I didn't want to hurt her feelings, so I stammered a response to Boehner: "Um, I will."

Which made no sense—no one holds their own Bible while being sworn in. Plus, I didn't have one. Undeterred, Boehner's staffer produced a large white Bible for families who didn't bring their own. Boehner pressed, "You do *want* to use a Bible, right?"

Another awkward glance at Mom. "Um . . . sure."

And then my wife Susan took the wheel. Our daughter held the huge Bible, and I sheepishly put my hand on it. The photo was taken. The Huffmans were ushered out. It was all over in less than a minute.

On the bright side, Boehner liked my wine and Mom was happy. But this rookie mistake left me feeling sullied and hypocritical. It was my first clue that even though I had been done with religion for many years, it was not done with me.

As I would soon learn, Christianity is woven into the rhythms, routines, and ceremonies of the supposedly secular citadel of Congress. Each day begins with public prayer led by taxpayer-funded chaplains, always Christian, in the House and Senate, unless the prayer is given by preapproved guest clergy. Many committees open their hearings with sectarian Christian prayer, a tradition embraced by chairmen of both parties with no regard for how non-Christians on the committees, the staff, or in the audience might feel about it. Pastors from quasi-official Capitol ministries roam the halls each day, greeting and evangelizing to members and staff. Members of Congress, mostly Republican, but including some Democrats, go out of their way to profess their faith, including nudging peers to attend the various Bible studies and prayer services that happen daily under the dome of the Capitol. For the first time in my public life, it seemed like everyone—colleagues, the Capitol Hill press corps, advocacy groups, and research organizations like the Pew Center—wanted to know *my* religion.

Only a few close friends and family members knew about my complicated journey from being a devout Christian to a nonreligious Humanist. I wanted to keep it private, partly because I wanted to keep my job. America had come a long way in recent years, but polling still showed that being an atheist (which a Humanist technically is) was politically radioactive. Only one person in the long history of Congress, Rep. Pete Stark, in 2007, admitted to being an atheist. He was defeated five years later, not necessarily because of his atheism, but it surely didn't help.

So, for my first four years in Congress, I declined to answer questions about my religion and swallowed my discomfort at the public religiosity all around me. Making waves about religion wasn't what I came there to do. I wanted to work on water, environmental, and climate policy, the stuff I knew best from my time as an environmental attorney at the Natural Resources Defense Council and my work in the state legislature. That was where I thought I could make a difference.

Two things happened in 2017 to change my calculus. First, my sweet mother died. I no longer needed to worry about upsetting her if my Humanism became public. Second, and the real moral breaking point for me, Donald Trump became president of the United States, and the floodgates of religious encroachment into government opened in a way that made my previous concerns seem trivial.

Pundits still ponder how Trump clinched the presidency in 2016 despite losing the popular vote to Hillary Clinton by nearly three million votes. In my view, his embrace of raw Christian nationalism was a decisive factor. A landmark study by sociologists Andrew Whitehead, Samuel Perry, and Joseph Baker found that Christian nationalist ideology—the belief that America is and should remain a Christian nation—was one of the strongest independent predictors of support for Trump.

Trump weaponized Christian nationalism like no one before him. His "Make America Great Again" narrative promised a return to a mythic past where white Christians reigned unchallenged and encouraged them to take back their power. That message landed with force in key swing states like Pennsylvania, Michigan, and Wisconsin, where white evangelicals turned out in droves, enabling Trump to narrowly flip states that hadn't gone Republican in decades.

I didn't see it coming. I knew Trump was pandering to the religious right, but I thought Christians would see right through his bravado. What I didn't know, however, was that Trump had a secret weapon: prophets.

Centering his campaign on Christian nationalism was only part of his success. The bigger reason Trump won the GOP nomination and went on to win the general election with a staggering 81 percent support from white evangelicals was the huge bet he placed on a faction of charismatic evangelicals led by a cadre of prophets previously dismissed as fringe.

You'll recall the New Apostolic Reformation (NAR) from the previous chapter. This decentralized prophetic network was launched by C. Peter Wagner in 1996 during a time of great turmoil and change for American Christianity. The New Religious Right had just collapsed and thousands of churches were closing each year, especially Protestant denominations which lost nearly five million members (a 9.5 percent decline) during a decade in which the US population grew by twenty-four million. Yet NAR's network of nondenominational charismatic evangelicals rapidly expanded, including massive online ministries that attracted millions of followers.

One of the high-profile prophets aligned with NAR was a platinum blond televangelist, Pastor Paula White. Her show, *Paula White Today*, was a high-octane blend of revival-style preaching, "prosperity gospel" fundraising grifts, and lifestyle branding featuring advice from wellness "experts" and Christian beauty tips. In the early 2000s, White's rising profile as the "Oprah of the evangelical world" caught Trump's eye, and he invited her to Trump Tower. The two became friends, and soon White was hosting celebrity prayer meetings in Trump's Atlantic City casino. In the early days of Trump's presidential campaign, White, through her connections with NAR, arguably won Trump the presidency by facilitating a prophecy that would spread like wildfire among evangelicals: the Cyrus anointing.

It came at a time of desperation and dismay for right-wing Christians. On June 26, 2015, the Supreme Court legalized same-sex marriage in the landmark *Obergefell* decision. After decades of trying and failing to build a religiously conservative Supreme Court, this was the lowest point yet. Stopping America's slide into sinful secularism, right-wing faith leaders concluded, required a bully. And Paula White had one for them. She reached out to the prophets of NAR and arranged a meeting where Trump convinced them he was the bully they needed.

But even with the prophetic authority NAR wielded with millions of evangelicals, getting devout Christians to back Trump was a big ask. He was a preening billionaire who didn't attend church, bragged about his sexual exploits, mocked the disabled, and claimed he'd never asked God for forgiveness. Mainstream conservative Christians were already rallying behind religious candidates like Ted Cruz, Mike Huckabee, and Ben Carson. The prophets needed something big to flip the script.

That's when prophet Lance Walnau claims to have had a revelation that God was anointing Trump to be a modern-day King Cyrus. In the Bible, Cyrus was the unlikely pagan ruler whom God chose to deliver the Jews from Babylon. Walnau prophesied that God was doing it again with Trump: using a flawed, secular ruler to restore the divine destiny of his chosen people. Walnau relentlessly promoted this prophecy in videos, media appearances, and even a book entitled *God's Chaos Candidate*. Soon dozens of other prophets validated the Cyrus anointing, including NAR's influential founder, C. Peter Wagner. Thanks to NAR's massive online prayer network, the prophecy went viral.

And so it came to pass that millions of evangelicals shed their reservations and got behind Trump. And lo, even the "grab 'em by the pussy" scandal was explained away by the prophets: God was "humbling" the new Cyrus for the great work ahead. Which, they reminded evangelicals, included stacking the Supreme Court with religious conservatives. NAR apostle Dutch Sheets put it bluntly: "You're not voting for a personality. You're voting for that Supreme Court."

After getting to the White House on this improbable path, I thought Trump would pivot. I expected him to ditch the prophets and the extreme religious agenda he had promised to support in favor of some modicum of political normalcy. It's one thing to weaponize Christian nationalism to win a close election, but surely no president would *govern* that way.

Wrong again. Days after taking the oath of office, he delighted evangelicals with his Supreme Court nomination of Neil Gorsuch, whose evasive testimony in his Senate confirmation hearing presaged the vote he would cast to overturn *Roe v. Wade* five years later. Trump served right-wing Christians more catnip by filling his cabinet with religious extremists: evangelical Mike Pompeo as secretary of state; Muslim-hating General Mike Flynn as national security advisor; and Ben Carson, a neurosurgeon and devout Seventh Day Adventist who considers evolution satanic, as secretary of housing. For attorney general, he chose a white nationalist homophobe, Jeff Sessions, who promptly cited the Bible to justify hard-line anti-immigrant policies. Calvinist billionaire and church school crusader Betsy DeVos would squeak through her Senate confirmation to be secretary of education, but her hostility to public education was so controversial that two Republican senators voted "no," forcing Vice President Pence to break a tie. And for director of the Environmental Protection Agency, Trump chose Scott Pruitt, a climate change denialist who justified his pro-polluter agenda by pointing to the Bible's mandate for humans to take "dominion" over the earth. Keeping my Humanism secret in the face of mounting religious encroachments had been hard enough for my first four years in Congress, but now Trump and Pruitt were bringing the Bible into my policy lane.

My tipping point was the prophets. Trump lifted NAR-aligned prophets from the margins of American Christianity into powerful White House fixtures with breathtaking influence over his reshaped Republican Party. This sea change was perhaps best summed up by President George W. Bush's former chief of staff Andy Card: "The rug of American politics used to have more rug than fringe. Today, the rug seems to have little rug and a lot of fringe."

Charismatic prophet Paula White, who delivered one of the *six* prayers at Trump's inauguration (a presidential record) became a White House regular as Trump's "spiritual advisor." She publicly boasted of connecting Trump to nearly four hundred religious leaders and surrounding him with men and women of God "to make sure that door and that access continues for people of faith." Another fanatic Trump lifted from the fringe was Dutch Sheets, the NAR kingpin who was tasked with leading a team of prophets in a fifty-state mobilization of evangelical support for Trump's agenda. It was dubbed "POTUS Shield"—a two-fer acronym referring not only to Trump but also to NAR's vision of establishing God's "prophetic order of the United States."

By the summer of 2017, my reckoning was unavoidable. Seeing wild-eyed prophets wielding presidential-level power and influence was disturbing in a very personal way. You see, I grew up embracing prophetic Christianity. I know its pull. I also know its peril.

I was raised in the Reorganized Church of Jesus Christ of Latter-Day Saints (RLDS), an offshoot of Mormonism. It was a loving, supportive faith community headquartered in my hometown of Independence, Missouri. The RLDS church of my youth, like the evangelical prophets surrounding Trump, embraced what the Greeks called *charismata*, manifestations of the Holy Spirit: prophecy, speaking in tongues, healing, and other miracles. It was not the full "holy roller" experience where people are "slain in the spirit" and fall to the ground after being touched in faith-healing revivals, or like the charismatic Pentecostals of Appalachia where believers handle poisonous snakes as a test of faith and divine protection. But in RLDS churches it was not uncommon for a presiding elder or priest to stand before the congregation and deliver what they claimed were direct words from God.

For example, I was attending church while home for Christmas during my freshman year of college when I learned, mid-sermon, that I was being called to the priesthood. The presiding elder at our East Alton RLDS congregation paused dramatically, his voice shifting into something solemn and otherworldly: "I call my son Jared Huffman to be ordained to the office of teacher in the Aaronic priesthood." Then, reclaiming his own cadence, he sealed the moment with the familiar phrase: "Thus sayeth the Lord." This kind of divine interruption wasn't unusual. At church reunions or prayer meetings, worshippers were sometimes so moved that they would stand up and start speaking gibberish. At that point, a church leader usually "interpreted" the utterance as a message from God, translating babble into revelation. I didn't just believe in these prophetic phenomena—I thought they were awesome.

But I also know what happens when prophetic Christianity turns dark. When people claim exclusive access to God's voice—what mental health professionals might call auditory hallucinations, a hallmark of schizophrenia—and when others believe them without question, the consequences can be deadly. That's how my former high school basketball teammate ended up helping murder an innocent family in a "blood sacrifice" to please God.

Richard Brand was a solid defender and ball handler on our Chrisman High School basketball team, and like most people I grew up with, he was RLDS. While I was at UCSB falling away from the church, he was completing an engineering degree in Missouri and apparently becoming more religious. About the time I was taking Prof. Capps's course, he went on a pilgrimage many RLDS people aspire to sometime in their life: to the sacred temple in Kirtland, Ohio. That's when he met an RLDS tour guide named Jeffrey Lundgren.

Both Brand and Lundgren were disillusioned with the church's recent decision to ordain women into the priesthood. Lundgren was obsessed with prophecy and claimed to have discovered a "chiastic" method of interpreting scripture: judging a verse's authenticity by cross-referencing the ones above and below it. After he was fired from the temple for embezzlement, Lundgren declared himself a prophet and founded a new "true" church built around his chiastic theology.

This was a familiar pattern in my youth. The RLDS was open to direct prophecy, an inheritance tracing back to prophet Joseph Smith Jr.'s revelations in the 1820s, which formed the theological foundation of the LDS movement. This tradition had always offered fertile ground for eccentric spinoffs and self-anointed visionaries. Prophetic belief is like volatile genetic material: In its healthiest form, it animates churches with vitality—a living sense that God still speaks to us. But like unstable DNA, it invites mutation. Inevitably, inspiration blurs into delusion, and under pressure, prophetic fervor becomes dangerous.

Lundgren's prophetic startup was convincing enough to attract a small band of followers, including my former teammate, Richard Brand, and Greg Winship, another RLDS acquaintance from Independence. They moved into a farmhouse outside of Kirtland, signed over their paychecks to Lundgren, and began calling him "Dad."

Among Lundgren's followers were Dennis and Cheryl Avery and their three young daughters. Unlike the others, the Averys declined to live communally with the rest of the congregation, a choice that didn't sit well with "Dad." Lundgren's paranoia swelled into apocalyptic fever. He ordered the men to undergo firearms training and dress in military fatigues, preparing for a divine mission. Then came a new revelation: They were to sell their possessions and retreat into the wilderness to build Zion. The group, including the Avery family, began making plans. But there was a catch. Lundgren told select followers that he'd received a chilling command from God: Before Zion could be built, they had to make a blood sacrifice. God, he claimed, wanted the Averys dead.

Richard Brand could have stopped it. He could have called the police, broken ranks, and saved five innocent lives. But like the others, he believed Lundgren spoke for God and that disobedience meant damnation. So, he went along.

On the night of April 17, 1989, the Averys were invited to Lundgren's farmhouse. Dennis Avery was led to a nearby barn, where Brand and others bound and gagged him. Greg Winship revved a chainsaw to muffle the sound of Lundgren shooting Dennis repeatedly with a .45. The same ritual was repeated for Cheryl Avery and their daughters—ages fifteen, thirteen, and seven. Each time, Brand did the binding. Winship ran the chainsaw. The bodies were buried. Lundgren was convicted in 1990 and executed six years later for orchestrating the murders, and Brand and Winship served twenty-one years in prison for their roles.

Newspapers across the country carried the story of the chilling prophetic cult murders with headlines such as "Ohio Cult Leader Charged in Slayings of Family of Five" (Associated Press), "Bodies of Five Found in Ohio Barn; Cult Leader Held" (*The New York Times*), and "Cult Prophet Accused of Mass Murder" (*The Washington Post*). The RLDS community was shaken by the tragic, misplaced loyalty of the Averys, who were decent, devoted people of faith, and the way Lundgren, Brand, and Winship not only betrayed their trust, but also betrayed the very faith they thought they were honoring.

Less tragic but no less unsettling is the story of my high school friend Jordan Smith. Jordan was RLDS royalty: a distant relative (or so he told me) of founder and first prophet Joseph Smith Jr. We lost touch after high school, and while I was at UCSB Jordan plunged into prophetic obsession and conspiracy theories. According to newspaper reports, his research and interpretation of scripture led him to believe

Communists would soon invade Missouri with chemical weapons. He also believed God had anointed him to heal the schism between three rival LDS-based churches in Independence: the RLDS, the Mormons, and the Church of Christ Temple Lot, a small restorationist offshoot that occupied a sacred plot of land in the center of town where Joseph Smith Jr. had prophesied the Saints should build their temple. Jordan began attending all three churches, alarming congregants with his bizarre prophecies and warnings about God preparing to "cleanse" the Temple Lot church site.

On New Year's Day, 1990, he broke into the Temple Lot church wearing war paint, barricaded the doors, and called police claiming he had weapons and grenades. After a one-hour standoff, during which he lit the church on fire, he agreed to surrender on one condition: that he be allowed to perform a Native American dance on the front stoop of the burning building. Jordan danced as the church burned. He was later convicted of arson and burglary and spent five years in prison for crimes he sincerely believed God told him to commit.

So I have history with prophetic Christianity. I've felt the emotional pull of what I once believed were prophetic experiences. And I've seen ordinary people who I grew up with in Missouri driven into bizarre and terrible acts by prophetic beliefs. These aren't isolated episodes. History is chock-full of charismatic prophets leading credulous believers into violence and mass death: the fourteenth-century Flagellant movements during the Black Death plague, where prophetic leaders drove frenzied mobs into self-harm and violent persecution; the Münster Rebellion of 1534–35, when prophets seized a German city, imposed polygamy, and awaited the apocalypse before being slaughtered; and in my own lifetime, the Charles Manson "Helter Skelter" murders in 1969, the Rev. Jim Jones's mass murder-suicide in 1978 that killed nine hundred of his followers in Guyana, the deaths of more than seventy Branch Davidians under prophet David Koresh in Waco in 1993, and the thirty-nine mass suicides of prophet Marshall Applewhite's "Heaven's Gate" followers in 1997, to name a few. The pattern is immutable: When charismatic extremists claim direct prophecy from God and others credulously believe them, tragedy follows.

Which is why, by the summer of 2017, the ascendance of prophets in Trump's orbit, paired with the Christian nationalist takeover that was reshaping so many federal agencies and policies, was my moral breaking point. I knew that inviting apocalyptic prophecy into the highest reaches of our government was playing with fire. Trump either didn't know or didn't care about the disastrous results that invariably flow from entrusting and empowering unhinged prophets. Either way, America's White House is the last place prophets should be calling the shots, yet there they were in the Oval Office: surrounding the president, anointing and prophesying over him, boasting of their newfound influence, and exalting the prophetic destiny of our "Christian nation" now that America's own King Cyrus was enthroned.

As I knew from Professor Capps's class, Christian nationalists had been trying for decades to take over the Republican Party. The first wave surged during the Reagan-Bush years but never quite got there. But the ambition didn't die; it gradually metastasized into the MAGA Christian nationalist movement. By the summer of 2017, under Trump, the mission was finally accomplished. The GOP and Christian nationalism were one and the same. And now this new religious-political entity had won the presidency, both houses of Congress, and was on the verge of controlling the Supreme Court.

My fellow Democrats, meanwhile, seemed incapable of even naming, much less confronting, Christian nationalism head-on. We were being urged by political advisors to become more publicly religious to better compete with Republicans for the Christian vote. I heard it time and again in our Democratic Caucus meetings, and from campaign gurus who gave us strategic advice at our caucus retreats. That seemed insane to me, like a theocracy arms race. Trump was shredding church-state separation before our eyes, Christian extremism was breaching the firewalls of governance, and Democrats' answer was to be more publicly religious?

It was finally time to step out of my lane and speak out against Christian nationalism and the GOP's empowerment of unhinged religious extremists. And yet, doing that while continuing to tiptoe around my own religious views felt just as hypocritical as when I put my hand on Speaker Boehner's big white Bible at my ceremonial swearing-in. So, I began contemplating a decision that would change everything:

What if I simply told the truth? What if I publicly admitted I don't believe in God?

Call it coincidence or providence, but just as all of this was weighing on my mind, I received a candidate questionnaire from the Center for Freethought Equality, a secular advocacy group. I'd gotten questionnaires from Humanist and atheist groups before and always ignored them. But this moment felt different. I decided to fill it out truthfully. A few days later, I got a call from Roy Speckhardt, the executive director of the American Humanists Association.

It turns out I had been on their radar for the past two years, ever since they noticed my awkward encounter with comedian Stephen Colbert on "The Colbert Report," the show he hosted before taking over "The Late Show" on CBS. Colbert blindsided me by zeroing in on the "unspecified" answer I had given to a religion questionnaire, pressing: "Come on, grow a pair. What is it? Are you an atheist?" "I don't know," I replied, squirming like I was strapped to a lie detector and the needle was starting to twitch. He let me off the hook with a wink and a comic zinger: "I'll just put you down for 'heathen-slash-hell-bound!'" Most people laughed it off, but the secular community saw the needle twitching.

And now that I had finally responded to their questionnaire, they were eager to know: Did I really mean what I said in my answers? Would I accept the Freethought Equality PAC endorsement, stigma and all? Would I consider publicly acknowledging my nonbelief in God? Yes, yes, and probably yes again, I told them. But before going public, I wanted to do some vetting.

My wife, brothers, senior staff, and a few trusted political advisors all told me the same thing: This was a terrible, career-wrecking idea. That was solid political advice. According to the Pew Research Center's 2014 survey, being an atheist in politics was still a third rail. "No other trait," Pew explained, "including being gay or having never held elected office, garnered a larger share of people saying they'd be less likely to support the potential candidate." But with everything happening under Trump, I could no longer exalt caution over principle by hiding my beliefs.

Nearing my decision, I wanted to have two final meetings with people who happened to both be devout Catholics. The first was Nancy Pelosi. I owed her a heads-up, since she was keenly focused on winning back the House majority in 2018 and my coming out as a Humanist was the opposite of what experts were telling Democrats to do. I braced for admonishment, but to my great relief, she told me that she knew a little about Humanism and thought it was "beautiful." Green light.

My final meeting was with House Chaplain Father Pat Conroy. I consider congressional chaplains unnecessary and unconstitutional. James Madison thought so, too. He fought against the congressional chaplaincy for years, writing in his post-presidential Detached Memoranda that it was "a palpable violation of equal rights, as well as of Constitutional principles." But after more than a century of debate, the Supreme Court finally ruled in 1983 that having a legislative chaplain does not violate the Constitution. While I disagreed with the congressional chaplaincy in principle, I liked Father Pat. I respected his Jesuit intellectual curiosity. I appreciated that he didn't proselytize and that his ecumenical prayers respected non-Christians. And it helped that Father Pat was relatable—a fellow guitar player who jammed with me after hours at our Democratic Caucus retreats.

I expected him to be annoyed and maybe offended. But Father Pat listened politely as I told him what I planned to do. He said that he might not agree with me, but if Humanism is what I believe, and I'm comfortable going public with it, I should do it. He went even further, saying that he wished more members would just be honest about what they believe and don't believe. I hadn't sought Father Pat's blessing, but it felt like I had gotten it anyway.

The last thing was to roll out my decision in a dignified way through a serious national journalist who understood the terrain. I chose Michelle Boorstein, *The Washington Post*'s respected religion writer. Her story ran on November 9, 2017, under the headline: "This Lawmaker Isn't Sure that God Exists. Now, He's Finally Decided to Tell People." And just like that, an unexpected chapter in my political career opened.

The next day on the House floor, my friend Jamie Raskin—a constitutional law scholar and a rising star in his first congressional term—sought me out. He commended the moral clarity of my decision and expressed that he shared my concern about creeping theocracy. We began brainstorming a congressional coalition to defend church-state separation. A few months later, the Congressional Freethought Caucus was born and our work began, none too soon.

The ascendancy of MAGA Christian nationalism in 2017 was my crucible: the moment I recognized that the prophetic extremism that ensnared people I grew up with had followed me to Washington. It was no longer a fringe phenomenon with spectacular reappearances throughout history: It was a clear and present danger inside American government that I was compelled to confront.

I knew that my unconventional leap of non-faith was the principled thing to do, but it also turned out to be a surprisingly good political move and a critical first step. It allowed me to fight theocratic threats publicly, authentically, and fearlessly, and it brought me into coalition with Raskin, our new Freethought Caucus allies, and advocacy groups fighting from the outside to defend secular democracy. But taking that fight to the next level would require me to understand the threat of MAGA Christian nationalism with greater clarity and look beyond the spectacle of fanatics in the Oval Office. I needed to examine the deeper currents including the theology and the religious architects shaping this ascendant movement. That is where the next chapter takes us.

CHAPTER 3

THREE ROADS TO THEOCRACY

BY 2021, I THOUGHT I KNEW A LOT ABOUT RELIGIOUS extremism. I'd studied the New Religious Right in college, seen childhood friends swept into violence by prophetic Christianity, watched Trump mainstream fringe prophets, and for three years I'd co-led the Congressional Freethought Caucus through briefings and events about threats to religious freedom, including Christian nationalism. But in the aftermath of January 6th—with Trump temporarily in exile, licking his wounds in Mar-a-Lago—I needed to know whether the forces of religious extremism that had fueled the insurrection had receded. Was January 6th a final spasm of a fading movement or a glimpse of something more organized, enduring, and dangerous?

My search for information led me fifty miles east to Baltimore, to Dr. Matthew Taylor, the senior Christian scholar at the Institute for Islamic, Christian and Jewish Studies. Taylor is not just a blue-chip theologian; he's also a lifelong Christian who worked as an evangelical minister for a decade. Like me, amid the chaos of the insurrection, he recognized religious images and expressions that left no doubt that this was a distinctly Christian coup. But Taylor was also able to discern sights and sounds of charismatic worship that were familiar from his many years of evangelical ministry and study. His scholarly interest was especially piqued by the ecstatic fervor that permeated the crowd. It felt like a Pentecostal revival but pulsing with violence. Taylor describes it as "charismatic revival fury."

Thousands of Christians don't randomly converge on the Capitol with that ethos, coalesced around one violent, common cause. Yet the media and the political establishment seemed oblivious to this critical aspect of the insurrection. Taylor took it upon himself to investigate, to follow the theology, identify the principal theological architects of the insurrection, and assess whether it was a one-time religious convulsion or an early tremor portending worse upheaval to come.

Since January 6th, Taylor has emerged as a go-to religion expert on MAGA Christian nationalism. He speaks at forums across the country, explaining the extreme beliefs, theocratic ambitions, and potent mobilization strategies that fueled the January 6th insurrection and continue to supercharge the movement, including a briefing for the Congressional Freethought Caucus. That's how we met and how he became my unofficial theology teacher.

Taylor and other leading religion experts warn of three ascendant Christian supremacist subcultures that power the MAGA Christian nationalist movement. These three factions are working together, for now, and their escalating radicalization poses an imminent threat to pluralism and democracy. With the help of these experts, this chapter delves into these three groups, their religious scaffolding, and the ringleaders behind this threat.

We've already encountered the biggest and most powerful of the three factions: the charismatic evangelicals and prophets of the New Apostolic Reformation (NAR). But two others round out the threat: radical traditionalist Catholics (Rad Trads), and the Communion of Reformed Evangelical Churches, also known as the Theo Bros. Each has its unique doctrines, priorities, and tactics, but all three are rooted in Christian supremacism and dominion theology: the belief that God has chosen Christians to seize and hold power above all others. These groups are united in their opposition to church-state separation, disdain for pluralism, fear and disgust over demographic changes and "woke" liberal culture, and devotion to Trump. As you'll see, NAR was the most deeply embedded in the insurrection, but all three are major players in a Christian nationalist movement that is determined to secure a religious chokehold on American democracy.

An important disclaimer before we wade deeper into the fraught subject of religion: The vast majority of Christians reject the extreme beliefs and radical individuals we are about to discuss, even if they belong to the same religious denomination. For example, the first subculture we'll examine is Catholic, and as a proud graduate of a Jesuit law school who has been married to a Catholic for over thirty years, I'm definitely not worried about Catholics writ large. But violent religious movements whose leaders point people in a dangerous direction must be understood, so let's take a closer look.

THE RAD TRADS OF CATHOLICISM

We all have our peccadilloes, and one of mine is loving the Kansas City Chiefs. I left my hometown of Independence, Missouri—a stone's throw from Arrowhead Stadium—more than four decades ago and have lived in Marin County, California, for over thirty years. I root for Bay Area sports teams now, except when they play the Chiefs.

So, it was painful to see the Chiefs' superstar kicker and three-time Super Bowl champ Harrison Buttker make headlines in May of 2024 for his misogynistic, homophobic, and authoritarian commencement speech at Benedictine College in Atchison, Kansas. Buttker's rant patronized women and scolded society at large for straying from true Catholic moral teachings. Buttker railed against the "diabolical" feminist lies the female graduates had been fed and he mansplained that the highest female fulfillment comes from marriage and motherhood. He went on to denounce LGBTQ rights and Pride Month as deadly sins, and lambast abortion, IVF, surrogacy, euthanasia, DEI and more, blaming these societal "disorders" on moral failings, including the "delusional" leadership of so-called fake Catholics like Joe Biden. He closed with the "hard truth" that Catholics must stop trying to be so nice and refocus on unapologetic adherence to traditional Catholic doctrine.

Buttker's jeremiad to the Benedictine graduates, and his other public claims of being "persecuted" by wrongheaded church reforms, make him a textbook example of the archconservative traditional Catholics who turned out in droves for Trump in each of the past three elections, even when he faced a Catholic. I doubt that Buttker would ever trade his football uniform for black tactical gear and storm the Capitol. But at the radical margin of traditional Catholicism, there are many who would. This is where we kick off, if you will, our examination of the first of three extreme religious subcultures that are shaping the Christian nationalist movement: radical traditional Catholics (Rad Trads).

Rad Trads are part of a lineage of firebrand Catholic extremists who have long decried secular democracy and scoffed at church-state separation. The most famous proto-Rad Trad is Father Charles Coughlin, the Nazi-loving "radio priest" who, from 1926 to 1940, inflamed up to thirty million listeners a week with his Sunday broadcasts. Father Coughlin declared democracy "doomed" in 1936: "It is fascism or communism. We are at the crossroads. I take the road to fascism." Two years later, he defended Hitler's Kristallnacht rampage during which 267 synagogues were torched, seven thousand Jewish-owned businesses were destroyed, and thirty thousand Jews were arrested, praising the Nazis for their restraint. "When we get through with the Jews of America, they'll think the treatment they received in Germany was nothing," he railed.

Father Coughlin's successors have taken his Depression-era blueprint of nativist Christian nationalism, anti-Semitism, and fascist flirtation, and updated it for the modern age. Echoing Buttker's tirade, today's Rad Trads seethe with stern social conservatism, rigid patriarchy, and nostalgia for a mythic past when Catholics reigned supreme.

For Rad Trads, the trouble started with the Vatican II reforms of the 1960s that modernized Church practices by promoting openness to the contemporary world and dialogue with other faiths. While most Catholics embraced these reforms, Rad Trads view them as betrayals of sacred tradition. They view ancient rituals such as the Traditional Latin Mass and female veiling as the purest expression of Catholic identity untainted by modern compromise.

Critical to Rad Trads' worldview is the core belief of "integralism"—essentially a Catholic version of dominion theology. Rooted in the ancient model of church-state fusion dating back to the Roman Empire, integralism holds that Catholic authority must be enthroned as the governing order. While most mainstream Catholics rejected integralism long ago, Rad Trads have revived it as a post-liberal alternative to pluralism and secular democracy.

Rad Trads are a small minority of American Catholics, but it's hard to pin down their numbers because the ecosystem is murky, the label itself is mostly used by outsiders and rarely embraced by those it describes, and boundaries between violent extremism and ordinary traditionalists can be blurry. In some cases, Rad Trad hallmarks like female veiling and devotion to the Traditional Latin Mass are just benign expressions of piety. But there's nothing benign about the integralist ideology, anti-Semitism, and extreme conspiracism that flourishes in dozens of Society of St. Pius X (SSPX) chapels that function as incubators and hubs of Rad Trad extremism. That's why SSPX has drawn scrutiny from experts, watchdog groups, and the Vatican itself. Recognizing the breakaway sect reflects poorly on Catholicism writ large, the Vatican places SSPX in a disfavored limbo status it calls "irregular," just short of formal schism.

But the Vatican's wariness of Rad Trads hasn't stopped them from gaining traction through traditional Catholic networks. The ascent of Rad Trad sympathizers into mainstream politics helps pave the way—figures like Vice President J. D. Vance, Steve Bannon, Supreme Court puppet master Leonard Leo of the Federalist Society, the Heritage Foundation's Kevin Roberts, firebrands Kellyanne Conway and Sebastian Gorka, and influencer Candace Owens, not to mention the far-right Catholic majority on the Supreme Court. Rad Trad influence also spreads through the prolific splenetic commentary of nearly a dozen organizations that the Southern Poverty Law Center tracks as part the Rad Trad hate group network, including groups like Christ or Chaos and Tradition in Action.

The most unmistakable manifestation of Rad Trad influence, however, is the annual Catholic Identity Conference (CIC) in Pittsburgh, Pennsylvania. CIC is organized and sponsored by the Remnant Foundation, a sprawling media matrix that reaches hundreds of thousands of people each week through the twice-monthly Catholic newspaper *The Remnant*, its video and broadcasting arm Remnant TV, and its Remnant Press publishing house.

In barely a decade, the CIC has grown from a niche symposium into a major flagship exhibition that showcases and amplifies Rad Trad power, attracting high-profile speakers from around the world, selling out with nearly one thousand attendees, and reaching countless others online. The CIC doesn't bother with nuance: The conference's website greets viewers with the pixelated cosplay of Crusader Knights kneeling to receive the Traditional Latin Mass, and agenda titles like "HIDE YOUR KIDS: The Devil's War on the Christian Family." Inside the conference, presenters lament the moral decay of Vatican II, promote antigovernment conspiracy theories, demonize secular education and climate science, and extol the greatness of Donald Trump. Keynote speakers include MAGA Catholic firebrand Steve Bannon and Archbishop Carlo Maria Viganò, a radical priest who was excommunicated after he declared Pope Francis an imposter installed by Satan.

The surging political reach of Rad Trads was on display at a larger gathering in 2024: the Conservative Political Action Committee conference, where Bannon welcomed the incendiary Catholic culture warrior Jack Posobiec to the stage. "Welcome to the end of democracy!" Posobiec thundered. "We are here to overthrow it completely." The crowd roared, Bannon smiled approvingly, and Posobiec continued: "We didn't get all the way there on January 6, but we will endeavor to get rid of it and replace it with this, right here," holding up his clenched fist.

Posobiec wasn't joking. Rad Trad faith leaders tried unapologetically to overthrow democracy on January 6th after stoking religious violence throughout the 2020 presidential campaign. They were called out for it by mainstream Catholics like Jesuit James Martin, who penned an essay rebuking the "alarming number" of radical Catholic priests and bishops who had fanned the flames. He specifically denounced Archbishop Viganò, who called the election an "apocalyptic" spiritual war and warned a Biden victory would trigger a "near-Satanic age." Rad Trad incitement, in Martin's view, led many violent rioters to believe they were waging a "fight for life, for morality—for God." There was no contrition, however, in the priests name-checked by their fellow

Catholics. Two years later, Archbishop Viganò was still at it, calling for Catholics to fast and pray in solidarity with the January 6th rioters who were being unfairly prosecuted.

Perhaps the most powerful vector of Rad Trad influence is the subculture's expansive online reach. Father Martin's essay alluded to this, criticizing Rad Trad priests for "aligning with self-appointed social media champions of 'real Catholicism'" in inciting insurrection.

Professor Lauren Griffin, a religion scholar from Louisiana State University who studies this aspect of Rad Trad culture and influence, warns against underestimating it. "Power flows from a lot of places," Griffin told me. "We're attuned to looking at Catholics on the Supreme Court or to the powerful Catholics that meet with Trump, and certainly that has influence on power. But it's a mistake to sleep on the culture that is downstream of that stuff and all this energy and traction that is happening online." Griffin tracks Rad Trad activity on familiar platforms like Facebook, TikTok, and Instagram, as well as in the subterranean realms of 4Chan and Reddit, where she sees Rad Trad influence growing fast among younger generations.

The most prominent architect of Rad Trad extremism online is unabashed neo-Nazi agitator Nick Fuentes, who entered public life in 2017 as a teenage participant in the Charlottesville "Unite the Right" white supremacist rally. Fuentes found right-wing celebrity as a prolific live-streamer and provocateur who repackages bigotry and fascism in a youthful, flippant aesthetic. His penchant for hate speech got him banned from mainstream social media on multiple occasions, but he still reaches hundreds of thousands of followers, many of whom dub themselves "Groypers," each week with his "America First" podcast and his live-streaming platform, "cozy.tv." Through these channels, he brings Rad Trad ideas to the masses.

A self-described integralist, Fuentes openly calls for a Catholic theocracy to replace democracy. "Yeah, the track record of democracy? Not so good. Catholic autocracy? Pretty strong. Pretty strong record. Catholic monarchy? Catholic monarchy, and just war, and crusades, and inquisitions? Pretty good stuff." In 2022, he urged a "white uprising" to install Trump as dictator, disband Congress, and permanently end elections.

Fuentes' radicalism is typically cloaked in memes, euphemisms, and sarcasm. But with his frequent glorification of authoritarians, mocking of victims, and declarations of "Groyper Wars" against his enemies—including the late right-wing activist Charlie Kirk and other Republicans he deems insufficiently reactionary—it is no wonder that real-world violence swirls around him. He featured prominently in the bloody Charlottesville rampage. He promoted and showed up with a cadre of Groypers for the January 6th insurrection, and during the mayhem Fuentes shouted encouragement over a megaphone as a cluster of Groypers joined the riot waving a green "Kekistan" flag: a parody Nazi banner born from one of Fuentes's alt-right memes. It may have happened again on September 10, 2025, when Kirk was murdered by a chronic internet dweller who reportedly trafficked in Groyper memes.

Fuentes is the most infamous Rad Trad influencer, but Professor Griffin tracks many others. Like Fuentes, they use memes to call for a Catholic monarchy and often shroud their violent messages in nihilistic humor. These junior varsity influencers don't make headlines like Fuentes, but there are dozens of them, and their viral posts regularly reach hundreds of thousands of followers. Such is the power of Rad Trads' online reach. For every boomer attending a Traditional Latin Mass in real life, there's a millennial woman in an online chat group exalting female veiling, and a zoomer (a Gen Z young adult) on a discussion board casually endorsing monarchy or Nazism. Professor Griffin and other experts warn that Rad Trad extremism, rhetoric that sacralizes violence, corrodes democratic norms, and desensitizes audiences to hate and brutality, is coursing through online circles, with inevitable real-world consequences.

In 2023, the FBI—whose hiring, culture, and investigative priorities have long skewed in favor of conservative Christians—identified Rad Trads as a security concern. After noticing the spate of violent white nationalists gravitating to Rad Trad online communities, the bureau briefly considered recruiting informants in some churches where the Traditional Latin Mass is offered, just as they have done many times in fundamentalist mosques as a counterterrorism tactic. The internal memo that floated the proposal took pains to describe Rad Trads

("RTC's" in bureau parlance) as a small minority "separate and distinct" from most traditionalist Catholics.

The FBI memo was never acted upon. That's not because it lacked merit, but because it was leaked, triggering a right-wing political backlash led by the pugnacious Catholic League, a self-described watchdog for Catholic "civil rights." The Catholic League accused devout Catholic President Joe Biden of harboring an "anti-Catholic cell group" in the FBI, fueling a performative partisan dogpile that included a letter from twenty Republican state attorneys general. The FBI cowered and withdrew the memo.

But the FBI was not wrong in its original assessment of Rad Trad subculture as a breeding ground of radicalization and violence. Since 2023, experts warn that this Christian nationalist subgroup has gotten stronger, drawing disillusioned young conservatives with the promise of tradition, ritual, and militant community. Nick Fuentes is back on Twitter/X, reinstated in May 2024 to the delight of his one million followers. In October 2025, he was platformed for a mainstream conservative audience on *The Tucker Carlson Show* podcast, where his anti-Semitic bile reached nearly twenty million viewers across social media platforms.

Rad Trads are clearly on the rise. From their CIC conferences to their media archipelagos; from the "irregular" chapels of SSPX to the backrooms of the Heritage Foundation, the Federalist Society, and the White House itself; from the digital underworld to fanatical priests preaching violent revolution and theocratic arsonists like Fuentes and Jack Posobiec—Rad Trads are keeping the spirit of Father Coughlin alive and well, and spoiling for a fight with secular democracy.

RECONSTRUCTIONIST THEO BROS

Defense Secretary Pete Hegseth doesn't do subtlety. He wears his Christian nationalism on his sleeve, literally. His right biceps feature the Crusader battle cry, *Deus Vult* (Latin for God wills it) and a favorite neo-Nazi slogan as of late. Further down his arm is a "kafir" tattoo, Arabic for infidel, in case you were wondering what he thinks about

Christian-Muslim reconciliation. Bursting from his right pectoral is the Jerusalem Cross, the Crusader battle emblem symbolizing Christian dominion and the mission of spreading Christ's word to the four corners of the earth. The "cross fit" jokes write themselves.

The Crusades is Hegseth's template for living, fighting, and governing. In his book (you'll never guess the title, *American Crusade*), he says if you like Western civilization, "thank a Crusader." Christians "don't want to fight," he writes unconvincingly, "but, like our fellow Christians one thousand years ago, we must." If Christians fail to vanquish Islamist and leftist ideology, Hegseth predicts the collapse of civilization.

Despite his penchant for theatrics and provocation, I was skeptical when news began spreading on the morning of May 21, 2025, that Hegseth was hosting a "Secretary of Defense Christian Prayer & Worship Service" in the Pentagon auditorium during working hours for the entire staff. The Pentagon is a buttoned down, rules-based institution with mountains of policy binders and ritualized operating procedures that aren't just followed—they're saluted. In its eight-decade history, no one ever had the audacity to do something like this. It wouldn't just cross the line of church-state separation; it would be a drunken cannonball in the deep end of the constitutional pool.

Which was apparently Hegseth's point. At 9 a.m. on the morning of May 21, 2025, he sent an email inviting all twenty-six thousand military and civilian employees of the Pentagon to join him at 10:30 a.m. for the "Secretary of Defense Christian Prayer & Worship Service" in the main auditorium. The invite was subtly decorated with a stained-glass bald eagle flanked by an American flag.

The Christian prayer service, broadcast live on internal Defense Department networks, started with Hegseth leading the standing-room-only audience of "voluntary" attendees in an opening prayer. Without a trace of interfaith humility, he began with "King Jesus" and ended with, "It is in the name of our Lord and Savior, Jesus Christ, that we pray. And all God's people say amen." A Pavlovian chorus of "Amen" rose from the attendees, including generals.

Hegseth then handed things off to Pastor Brooks Potteiger, whom he had brought in from his home church in Goodlettsville, Tennessee, to deliver the sermon. Potteiger's sermon packed explosive charges.

After decreeing that President Trump was "sovereignly appointed," he informed Pentagon staff of the new chain of command under Trump and Hegseth: God keeps the launch codes, and "Jesus is sovereign over Tomahawk and Minuteman missiles, strategy meetings, and war room debriefings." Potteiger closed by praying that Hegseth's new *monthly* workday prayer service would spread similar Christian gatherings and influence across "our nation's capital and down throughout this great nation."

By 11:02 a.m. church was over, long before any First Amendment lawyer could get a court order. As I would soon learn, the Pentagon prayer service had the Communion of Reformed Evangelical Churches (CREC)—the second religious subculture in our unpacking of Christian nationalist theology—written all over it.

Hegseth's journey to CREC began back in 2022, when he was still a Fox News co-host. He had grown tired of New York City and wanted to move his family to someplace more aligned with his political and religious values. He wanted his children to attend a classical, Christian school that rejected "progressive" education and instead followed the medieval Christian model of Trivium and Quadrivium, where kids learn Latin and the Bible is integrated into every subject. Hegseth and his wife Jenny prayed for such a place, and he says God led them to Goodlettsville, Tennessee. The kids were enrolled and "biblically saturated" at the nearby Jonathan Edwards Classical Academy. The Hegseth family began worshiping with Pastor Potteiger at the Pilgrim Hill Reformed Fellowship, part of the CREC network.

Founded in 1998 by Pastor Doug Wilson, CREC has grown from a single congregation in Moscow, Idaho, into a bustling nationwide network of more than 160 conservative Protestant churches—"kirks" in Wilson's parlance. At approximately twenty thousand members nationwide, CREC is a relatively small Christian denomination, but it has been growing steadily and punches far above its weight politically.

CREC's distinct religious culture mixes hardcore biblical rigor, blood-and-soil nationalism, and swaggering masculinity. Its leaders include dozens of mostly millennial male pastors, authors, and influencers who, like Wilson, usually sport beards, a symbol of biblical masculinity, cultural resistance, and traditional values. Their ethos, amplified through slick media strategies and powerful alliances in the tech world, has garnered CREC the nickname "Theo Bros," as in "theological bros." It's a nom-de-snark sobriquet so fitting that Wilson himself sometimes uses it.

What sets CREC apart from other Christian denominations is its fusion of Reformed Calvinist theology with militant cultural politics. Unlike Christian traditions that emphasize universal grace, inclusivity and reconciliation, CREC frames Christianity as a political tribe and a cultural fortress to be defended. Biblical literalism, strict patriarchal authority, and nationalist identity are central articles of faith.

Wilson didn't invent CRECs underlying theology; he repackaged it from Reconstructionism, a mid-twentieth century movement led by Rousas John (R. J.) Rushdoony, the most influential right-wing theologian you never heard of. In the 1950s and 1960s, most of the attention in right-wing Christianity was on charismatic televangelists like Rev. Jerry Falwell Sr. and Rev. Billy Graham. But at that time, Rushdoony was laboring behind the scenes on a radical new framework to anchor biblical law in all aspects of life and transform society into the Kingdom of Heaven on earth, or "Christendom." He called it Reconstructionism.

Reconstructionism's first principle is Christian dominion, the idea that Christians should have total control, not just influence, over all dimensions of modern life, especially government. Rushdoony saw Christian domination as a biblical mandate based on the passage in Genesis 1:28 where God directs Adam and Eve to be fruitful, multiply, and subdue and rule over everything on earth. Rushdoony took that message literally and built a framework to bring society into alignment with Old Testament law. Toward that end, he proposed three spheres of "government," all led by men.

Starting at the bottom, the men in charge of "civil government" oversee a diminished state that serves the minor function of enforcing the Bible's civil laws, like stoning sinners to death for the crimes of idolatry, adultery, and sabbath breaking. Above that is the sphere of "church government," which is charged with more important functions like worship, doctrine, and spiritual discipline. Then the big one:

"family government," where husbands and fathers rule over the family's economics, welfare, charity, and all moral and religious instruction, including education.

The endgame for Reconstructionism is to build Christendom in America, then globally. To Reconstructionists, Christendom is not a metaphor, but an actual earthly kingdom where the Bible dictates every institution, law, and cultural norm. To get there, they seek to build decentralized, family-centered enclaves that gradually expand and merge into a global Christendom. Unlike other branches of Christianity that envision a rapture or great upheaval triggering Christ's return ("premillennialism"), Reconstructionists are "postmillennial." They believe that the gradual building of Christendom will yield a golden age (the "millennium") after which Christ will return and claim the throne.

Rushdoony rejected democracy, separation of church and state, and any notion of religious neutrality in the law as schemes to dilute Christian power. While vague on the mechanics of theocratic government, he was emphatic on one point: No human king should be crowned in Christ's absence. Jesus was already king, just ruling remotely until the Second Coming. Rushdoony offered little guidance beyond a kind of theological placeholder: Trust the process, stay the course, and don't ask too many questions.

Reconstructionism profoundly impacted protestant Christianity for two decades. Conservative Christians embraced concepts like the dominion mandate, governing spheres, and policies like opposing no-fault divorce. The "classical" Christian school movement, homeschooling, and eventually the parental rights movement all drew ideological scaffolding from Reconstructionism. But by the 1980's, Rushdoony's extreme and violent ideas—like ending democracy, banning unions, repealing civil rights, and imposing the death penalty for biblical infractions—proved too much for most conservative Christians. They wanted to wage culture war within the system of democracy, not burn it down. The Reconstructionist movement splintered, and most of conservative Christianity ghosted Rushdoony and moved on.

But not Doug Wilson. The bookish contrarian gave Reconstructionism a makeover and dressed it up for the twenty-first century. Wilson kept the core theology, but rebranded Reconstructionism to have softer edges. Wilson preached a less menacing "mere Christendom," disguising the path to Christian dominion with an aesthetic of restraint and emphasizing that CREC's parallel societies would grow gradually. Nothing to see here folks, just bearded white kirkers with large families minding their own business and buying land for Old Testament covenant clusters.

For the first two decades, Wilson's build-out of CREC hewed to this approach. Their founding enclave in Moscow, Idaho, expanded to include several kirks, "classical" Christian schools, a publishing company (Canon Press), a seminary (New Saint Andrews College), and numerous affiliated businesses. But outside of Idaho, CREC was virtually unknown until 2007, when Wilson catapulted himself from obscurity into national right-wing Christian stardom in the most ironic way.

Firebrand atheist Christopher Hitchens, fresh off his #1 bestseller *God Is Not Great,* invited challengers to debate religion's value. Wilson got the gig. Their exchange landed in *Christianity Today,* followed by a multicity debate tour and a widely acclaimed 2009 documentary *Collision,* which showcased their intellectual jousting and the unlikely friendship they formed. When Hitchens complimented Wilson as one of his most formidable opponents, conservative Christians swelled with pride: They'd found a faith warrior who could hold his own against the arch-heretic. Suddenly Wilson was the Christian Right's most literate brawler.

At which point, Wilson ditched the gradualism and seized the moment, using the exposure from Hitchens to plant new kirks around the country and surge the size of CREC. He would do it again during the COVID pandemic, leveraging media coverage of his militant defiance of public health protections into a dramatic increase in church attendance and CREC expansion.

Wilson traffics in the same radical theology as Rushdoony: citing scripture to justify slavery, opposing voting rights for women, and advocating criminal punishment for gays, heretics, and "sabbath breakers." But he's careful to cloak his fanaticism in ambiguity and sophistry. Wilson coyishly presents himself as not a racist, just a "paleo-confederate" who thinks slavery got a bad rap; not a misogynist, just a "biblical sexist" who believes women should not vote or hold positions of authority;

and not an authoritarian theocrat, but a "theonomist" and "theocratic libertarian" who just thinks government should police speech, sex, and religious beliefs. He downplays his opposition to pluralism and democracy by claiming he is merely trying to reclaim America's "Puritan past."

Wilson advocates officially making the US a Christian theocracy by codifying the Apostle's Creed in the Constitution and requiring all public office holders be Christians. He knows these changes would be a tumultuous break from our constitutional order: "Reformations never happen to the polite background sound of golf applause," he says. But would it be violent? Wilson chuckles: "that depends on the bad guys." Despite this collision course with democracy, and despite CREC's accelerating growth and soaring political influence, Wilson continues to assure us there's nothing to fear in his radical societal prescriptions.

But even as Wilson downplays the stakes, he pursues a relentless campaign of culture capture that he aims to achieve by promoting a face-lifted, hipster Reconstructionism through CREC's many enterprises and expanding network of kirks. Toward that end, Wilson deploys a cadre of mini-me bearded protégés as messengers—men who are equally comfortable sipping cold brew, quoting Kant and Kierkegard, or live-streaming sermons on female submission and quietude. They fill the manosphere with content designed to make adherence to ancient biblical mandates look cool and intellectual.

A prime example is Joel Webbon, who projects pastor-scholar vibes from a wingback leather chair in a book-filled study while streaming monologues that call Judaism a "parasitic religion" and wax nostalgic for Jim Crow segregation. In July of 2025, Webbon dedicated an episode of his YouTube show streamed to 123,000 followers to defending Trump's coverup of the Epstein files, arguing without evidence that Epstein was an Israeli agent trying to blackmail Trump and other politicians. Another Wilson acolyte is the Princeton scholar Stephen Wolfe, whose book, *The Case for Christian Nationalism,* was proudly published by CREC's Canon Press. Wilson and these surrogates have succeeded in making their regressive ideas seem palatable to many, including some very influential allies.

CREC has not only projected its influence into the Department of Defense; it has also developed a powerful bromance with Silicon Valley. You might think tech titans who made their fortunes in a culture of artificial intelligence and transhumanism would have nothing in common with biblical purists. But the Tech Bros share the Theo Bros' anti-woke positions, hatred of taxes, support for monarchy, and approval of Trump. Like Wilson and his bearded protégés, they style themselves as bold thinkers who are re-engineering society to suit their vision. Indeed, the Tech Bros' latest futuristic fever dream of "network states" like the crypto-utopia of Prospera in Honduras and techno-libertarian "freedom cities" like Praxis in Greenland, mimic CREC's model of parallel society enclaves. Their concept of bespoke high-tech cities in America has been endorsed by Trump, who wants to donate or sell off public land to make it happen.

The Theo-Tech bromance is attracting a lot of money from MAGA-pilled tech billionaires like Peter Thiel and Marc Andreessen. In this strategic convergence of creed and greed, tech heavyweights are pouring money into CREC-aligned media platforms and businesses, including Christian startups like southern California's "Gundo Bros," who boast a hypermasculine mix of high-tech military software and manufacturing, pumping iron, and praising Jesus.

Perhaps the most audacious Tech Bro-Theo Bro collaboration is the New Founding project, funded by Andreessen. The vision is to buy up real estate and take over local governments to establish enclaves for white Christians who embrace dominion theology, patriarchy, and biblical law. One of its flagship efforts is the proposed Highland Rim community in Tennessee, less than one hundred miles from Pete Hegseth's home in Goodlettsville. Controversial CREC pastor Andrew Isker ("This country belongs to Jesus, not the Jews") has already relocated there to help jump-start the enclave. New Founding CEO Nate Fischer, who has extensive ties to CREC, claims a "birthright to lead Western civilization into the digital age." Exalting authoritarianism as the answer to America's cultural decline, he has tweeted that "national divorce must be on the table. . . . The only question is whether it happens peacefully." His codirector, Josh Abbotoy, goes further: "America is going to need a Protestant Franco." Longtime residents of Highland Rim are alarmed, fearing their bucolic community is being transformed into a staging ground for Christian nationalist ambitions.

Like the other two Christian supremacist factions examined in this chapter, the Theo Bros fueled religious passions in the 2020 election by framing it in apocalyptic terms and questioning the legitimacy of the results. But unlike Rad Trads and NAR who were active promoters and participants in the insurrection, there is no evidence connecting Pastor Doug Wilson, CREC, or any prominent Theo Bros to January 6th. Which is striking, given their contempt for democracy and political alignment with the rioters.

But religion scholars who study the Theo Bros, like Dr. Julie Ingersoll at University of North Florida and Dr. Bradley Onishi at University of San Francisco, have a likely explanation. The insurrection—a conspicuous top-down coup fueled by premillennialist fervor—wasn't the Theo Bros' style, at least not back in early 2021. Wilson had spent forty years growing a different theology and different brand: a movement that gradually advances Christian takeover of society and government and tries to avoid scaring people. His postmillennialist Reconstructionism was designed as a slow-brewed theological kombucha, not a Molotov cocktail.

The Theo Bros' absence on January 6th should not be mistaken for moderation, much less absolution as a dangerous ongoing threat. There are plenty of reasons they are one of the most dangerous Christian nationalist factions, starting with their unwavering determination to replace democracy with white nationalist theocracy and the fact that their influence is far greater than their numbers.

The vast reach of the Theo Bros' Reconstructionist theology is sometimes hard to see. The protestant Christian school movement, for example, which now includes almost thirteen thousand private schools, along with homeschooling and the parental rights movements, all sprang from Reconstructionism. These movements are upending state and national education policies. "Their power has never been rooted in their size," Ingersoll explains. But when you hear people using terms like "civil government," "spheres of authority," or "building God's Kingdom,"

Ingersoll says they're echoing Reconstructionism whether they know it or not.

Finally, Wilson's nothing-to-see-here gradualism shouldn't fool anyone. CREC is hugely ambitious and increasingly powerful, and no amount of coyness can obscure its mission of an authoritarian Christian takeover. Wilson is a world-class opportunist. And now he's breathing the rarified air of power and seizing his biggest opportunity yet. Wilson headlined the National Conservative Conference in 2024 and was profiled by CNN and *The New York Times* in 2025. With the financial clout of his Tech Bro alliance, and with America's most famous Theo Bro, Pete Hegseth, running the Pentagon and force-feeding CREC theology to the military, Wilson's "mere Christendom" is morphing into something far more aggressive. Wilson has begun describing his plans with a wink, still talking about the theocratic takeover of America as a long-term project, but leaving the door open for a rapid move—"We're not talking about the next ten minutes."

We should never underestimate CREC's sophistication. For example, Pete Hegseth probably thinks he chose CREC's Pilgrim Hill as his kirk, through prayer and careful consideration. But it was CREC's algorithms and a proprietary tool called Hotspot Project that brought him into the fold. The Theo Bros developed this strategic church planting system using data and modeling to identify places with the most ideological demand and cultural appetite for a new kirk. Pastors like Brooke Potteiger use Hotspot Map to plant kirks where they have the best chance of taking root.

And so it came to pass in 2021 that the Hotspot system pointed Potteiger to Goodlettsville, where he planted Pilgrim Hill. He then followed the CREC playbook by cultivating relationships with a nearby "classical" Christian school and families steeped in dominion theology, and *voila*. The algorithm predicted someone like Hegseth would come along.

The alliance with Hegseth says a lot about where CREC is going. Wilson's extreme theology and aims are being operationalized into real-world power at the highest level of government. For years Wilson masked his theocratic battle plan in literary allusions and theological nuance. But Hegseth lays it bare. He has always been a Christian nationalist crusader, but now he is Wilson's flashy new battle standard, heralding the Theo Bros' pivot from "mere Christendom" to *Deis Vult* opportunism.

That's definitely how it looked on July 13, 2025, at the launch of ChristKirk DC, a church plant unlike anything Wilson had done before. This spot, situated four blocks from the Capitol on Pennsylvania Avenue, wasn't chosen by the proprietary Hotspot system. There's no serious appetite for a kirk in the progressive bubble of DC. But Wilson wasn't chasing congregants; he was planting a flag and signaling intent. This was a cultural and political beachhead in the heart of American "civil government" that would serve as an outpost for big things to come.

If a theocratic takeover is coming, maybe Wilson and his bearded Theo Bro disciples won't be the ones in tactical gear storming the Capitol. They steered clear of direct violence on January 6th. But they've evolved since then and so have the circumstances. With newfound power, CREC is ditching the pretense of gradualist restraint and accelerating their advance to Christendom. Now that they are a major national player, CREC intends to be in Washington when the dust settles, and Christian nationalism is enthroned. They're jostling for position with both Rad Trads and the powerful prophets of NAR, the faction that the Southern Poverty Law Center calls "the greatest threat to American democracy that most people have never heard of." That underappreciated threat is the final stop on our Christian nationalist theology tour.

THE NEW APOSTOLIC REFORMATION

On New Year's Day 2021, five days before the insurrection, apostle Dutch Sheets delivered a prophetic revelation to his three hundred thousand YouTube followers. In a dream, Sheets was part of an army of "prayer warriors" mounted on horseback and waiting for God's command. God reached down from Heaven to flick open the dome of the United States Capitol building. "We then heard a cavalry bugle playing the signal to charge and we began moving toward the Capitol, not at a full gallop, but at a steady determined fast trot. As we started, on the ground in front of us, written in white letters, were the words *Don't Stop*." Sheets interpreted the message for his followers: God is coming to purge government.

Like most of the insurrectionary prophecies Sheets had been churning out since Election Day, this one didn't directly tell people to storm the Capitol and overturn the election. But the implications were unmistakable. As Dr. Matthew Taylor wrote, "no single Christian leader did more to mobilize Christians for the insurrection than Dutch Sheets."

Sheets is arguably the most influential operative in the Christian nationalist movement. He is both a leader and an embodiment of the largest and most powerful part of the Christian nationalist coalition: the New Apostolic Reformation. When Taylor warns that the Capitol rioters weren't just angry citizens but religious zealots—true believers radicalized by leaders who abhor pluralism, valorize violence, and are intent on overturning democracy—it is NAR that alarms him most.

NAR is a sprawling, fast-growing, and decentralized network of evangelical faith leaders whose theology is wildly different than the Rad Trads or Theo Bros. It is built on a platform of charismatic worship steeped in revelations, miraculous healings, and speaking in tongues. NAR's vast army of "prayer warriors" consider themselves active combatants in a cosmic battle between God and Satan, with the fate of humanity hanging in the balance. Through a type of violent worship they call "spiritual warfare," NAR believers aim to activate God and his team of angels to defeat Satan's agents they see operating all around them in politics, culture, and society.

The intensity and militancy of NAR's theology is reflected in the movement's uncompromising goals and tactics. While Theo Bros tinker with parallel society models and Rad Trads pine for ritual purity and Catholic monarchy, NAR is moving fast. Prophetic leaders are summoning angels, slaying demons, and mobilizing millions of evangelicals with the urgency of true believers who know time is short and the stakes are cosmic.

The name "New Apostolic Reformation" highlights the centrality of prophets and prophecy in their theology. Unlike traditional churches,

NAR elevates self-declared prophets whose visions guide the movement's priorities, strategies, and political engagement. Apostles like Dutch Sheets are the top leaders, sitting atop a prophetic governing body called the *Ekklesia,* a Greek term loosely translated as the "called out" assembly. NAR believes God has vested the *Ekklesia* with special spiritual gifts and charged them to take the baton of leadership from the first-century apostles originally chosen by Jesus. God is working through the *Ekklesia,* NAR believes, to prepare Christians for a global end-times revival.

This concept of reviving the apostolic order ahead of Christ's return traces to a post-World War II Pentecostal movement known as Latter Rain, which inspired C. Peter Wagner, then a professor at the Fuller Theological Seminary, to make it a centerpiece of the new nondenominational church growth model he was brainstorming. Wagner launched NAR in 1996, brashly declaring it "the most radical change in the way of doing church since the Protestant Reformation." Wagner's protégé Dutch Sheets describes his apostolic role with similar immodesty. "God has prepared and positioned Kingdom ambassadors to wield His influence and shape our national destiny . . . to partner with Him by making bold governmental decrees, strongly supporting Godly leaders, strengthening the church, and releasing divine strategy for re-igniting a prayer movement that will shift our nation toward righteousness."

In addition to prophecy, NAR's other theological cornerstone is its unique model for achieving Christian dominion: the Seven Mountains Mandate. Unlike the Rad Trad vision of integralism, which subordinates government to the church and embeds Catholic moral teaching into laws, or the Reconstructionist model of three biblically governed spheres, NAR's approach is sweeping and tactical. It divides society up into seven key domains of influence—the "mountains" of religion, family, education, media, arts and entertainment, business, and of course government—and directs Christians to conquer all of them. The Seven Mountains Mandate isn't just theology: It's a battle plan.

NAR wants all of this to happen fast. Unlike the Theo Bros, NAR isn't waiting patiently for Christ's return while building a patchwork of enclaves. That kind of small-bore gradualism is not enough. NAR's premillennial and accelerationist theology demands urgent pursuit of the higher prize: global Christian dominion.

Like other evangelicals, NAR teaches that humanity's destiny will be decided in the upheaval of the end-times, culminating in Christ's glorious return. This is why NAR believers often view pandemics, wars, natural disasters, political unrest, and other calamities with ecstatic anticipation. Unlike some evangelicals, NAR does not believe in a rapture that will sweep Christians up to Heaven before global chaos ensues. Rather, NAR embraces an activist, triumphalist vision in which taking dominion is seen as a prerequisite for Christ's return. In other words, Christians aren't waiting for God to act; he's waiting for them to start conquering the Seven Mountains.

As you've probably surmised, NAR's theology leaves no room for America's constitutional order. The Seven Mountains Mandate and the supreme power of God's *Ekklesia* are inherently antidemocratic. Sheets makes his theocratic agenda crystal clear. He rails against church-state separation as an "unbiblical" scheme to undermine the *Ekklesia* and warns that the coming theocracy will require totalitarian measures, at least at first, "while people are learning truth, integrity, honor, and how to make decisions." Once the *Ekklesia* finishes the process of purification and assimilation, Sheets assures us that some liberties will be restored; he just doesn't say which ones.

It's hard to overstate the centrality of demon hunting in NAR's worldview. The constant imperative to identify and vanquish satanic forces permeates their conception of Christian daily life and shapes every challenge and encounter. Virtually anyone or anything that upsets them is deemed to be under demonic influence. And any person or thing associated with Team Satan must be crushed.

Among the demonic networks flagged for destruction by NAR apostle Chuck Pierce, for example, are psychic hotlines, fortune telling, and "secret societies" like Elks, Shriners, and Oddfellows clubs. He also includes "those who practice any form of false religion—including Mormonism, Islam, Jehovah's Witnesses, Hinduism, Eastern religions, Native religions, Christian Science, and Bahai." Apostle Cindy Jacobs warns of demonically possessed antique furniture, while others namecheck demonic novels by Stephen King. In this fantastical paranoid milieu, conspiracy theories like QAnon are readily absorbed, and occult motifs often bleed into NAR's practices of mapping and hunting of demons, creating a supernatural miasma that looks like madness to outsiders.

This "demons are everywhere" theology empowers NAR's *Ekklesia* because, it turns out, the Bible doesn't say much about confronting demons beyond just casting them out. The field is wide open for prophets to concoct elaborate protocols to purge demonic influence. One of them is a process called "spiritual mapping" whereby the *Ekklesia* leads or authorizes a kind of supernatural detective work to chart out hidden networks of demonic influence. The process can target anything, including individuals, movements, government agencies, geographical areas, and even objects. Once a person or thing is identified as demonic, NAR's prayer warriors launch "spiritual warfare attacks" to break Satan's control. This is war, so it gets nasty. NAR apostle Mary Glazier, a key spiritual advisor to Sarah Palin, gleefully describes how she identified a witch applying for a job as chaplain in the Alaska prison system, and then activated local prayer warriors to bring suffering and injury to the poor woman.

If you're hearing echoes of the Puritans' Salem witch trials, there's nothing wrong with your ears. Theologian Dr. Steve Snow characterizes NAR's "demonological theory of everything" as a contemporary twist on America's age-old practice of religious scapegoating straight from the lineage of Puritans, who demonized and sometimes executed accused witches, heretics, and Native Americans.

NAR's galvanizing theology, coupled with its decentralized, nondenominational structure, has produced explosive growth. Ever since bursting onto the scene in the mid-1990s, NAR has kept growing while mainline churches and denominations continue to wither. Experts estimate that over three million Americans now attend NAR-aligned churches in the US, millions more worldwide, and NAR's online reach is much greater. Many of NAR's apostles and prophets command hundreds of thousands of followers online, and some of their megachurches have millions.

But NAR is also rigged to explode. This movement franchises

the power of direct prophecy across a sprawling web of independent actors, in a fantastical vortex of conspiracism and paranoia, with no guardrails. My lived experience and myriad examples throughout history show how prophetic belief can mutate into violence and tragedy. To protect against this, traditional denominations have clear lines of authority, a formal ordination process for pastors, and mechanisms like de-credentialing and excommunication if things go off the rails. But NAR is like a loose association of prophetic freelancers. Sheets and his *Ekklesia* claim sweeping divine authority, but they have virtually no structural controls over NAR's vast nondenominational network of independent churches and ministries. Apostles and prophets are affirmed through relational networks and mutual recognition. The only formal authority is a theological peer-review group known as the Apostolic Council of Prophetic Elders that meets occasionally to seek consensus on major prophecies.

Experts like Onishi consider this prophetic free-for-all inherently dangerous. "The most volatile form of religion," he warns, "is the one that says the divine can speak to a human being directly, right now, at any given moment. If revelation came in the past, or only to one person once every few decades, there's less volatility. But if apostles in Pensacola, prophets in Baton Rouge, or someone in rural Arkansas hears directly from God and tells their followers, 'God has told me we need to do this,' the volatility is built into that kind of structure."

But that same loosely structured network, pulsing with prophetic intensity, produces a political potency that sets NAR apart from other MAGA religious factions. Its enormous prayer network flexes power for the GOP like nothing else in American religion, capable of instantly reaching millions of dedicated believers and compelling not only votes but also mass mobilization. That's how NAR musters huge turnouts for events like Jericho Marches. And it's why, Onishi believes, the presence of so many prophetic Christians at the Capitol on January 6th "was not an accident."

NAR began showcasing this political power back in 2000, when Dutch Sheets barnstormed the country and activated the network for George W. Bush. When the results of that election hung in limbo awaiting the Supreme Court's ruling on the Florida recount, Sheets issued a dramatic prophecy from the White House grounds, and he and Peter Wagner later cowrote a book, *Destiny of a Nation*, claiming that prophecy and their intercessory prayers had put Bush in the White House. In the razor-close 2000 election, NAR may well have made the difference, but through their mobilization of evangelical voters, not their mystical powers.

By the time of Trump's reelection campaign twenty years later, the MAGA Republican Party had fully embraced NAR as a power player. Their Cyrus anointing and huge evangelical mobilization had propelled Trump to an improbable victory in 2016, and Trump had delivered on that investment with a 6–3 conservative religious majority on the Supreme Court. Evangelical voters were primed for battle, thanks to NAR's nationwide POTUS Shield initiative. Emboldened by all this momentum, dozens of NAR *Ekklesia* issued prophetic decrees that God would deliver a reelection victory to Trump.

When Election Day exposed these prophecies as fantasies, NAR did not pause for self-reflection. There was no reckoning, no repentance for the sin of false prophecy their own scripture condemns so harshly. Instead, they doubled down for Trump, insisting the world, not their prophecy, was wrong. And over the next two months, they revealed the qualities that make them such a unique ongoing threat: militant theocratic ambition, formidable mobilizing power, total integration with Trump's MAGA political operation, and a prophetic belief system that is both unshakable and infinitely adaptable.

Sheets and other prophets immediately went to work activating NAR's huge prayer network, certain they could bend the outcome back to God's will. Sheets issued new prophecies with the usual unsubtle metaphors, like the dream one of his friends had that he shared with his followers on November 11, where left-wing activists were spinning blue plates on sticks and boasting about serving America a "blue plate special." Then Trump ordered a spiritual sniper to shoot the plates, causing them to turn red and shatter into the shapes of Georgia, North Carolina, Pennsylvania, and Arizona.

Throughout November and December, as Trump's legal teams flooded the courts and his political operatives strong-armed local officials to block certification of the election results, Sheets spearheaded

NAR's parallel religious blitzkrieg. Sheets' calendar—aligned with Trump's legal and political pressure campaign—was the battlefield: Georgia on November 21, Michigan on November 22nd, Arizona on November 23rd, Wisconsin on November 24, Nevada on November 29, New Mexico on November 30, Pennsylvania on December 1, and then back to Georgia on December 13.

At each stop, there were Jericho Marches and huge revival-style prayer meetings live-streamed to hundreds of thousands on Facebook and YouTube. Sheets was joined on the tour by other NAR prophets who stoked audiences into religious frenzy with sermons and prophecies seething with violence. Including apostle Don Lynch, who told the Arizona audience the fight for Trump was like the test of courage God posed for David in the Bible when he commanded the beheading of the fallen Philistine giant, Goliath. "Put your foot on his chin and expose the neck," screamed Lynch to rapturous applause. "I say, Finish this! . . . For God says, 'No chicken legged Philistine is going to become the most powerful political leader in the world!'"

As weeks passed without a miracle, NAR's organizing turned to the huge final Jericho March and protest at the Capitol on January 6th. Believers were urged to not just continue waging spiritual warfare against judges and election officials, but also to be physically present in Washington on that day. Thousands of them, led by dozens of NAR *Ekklesia*, made the trek and showed up at the Capitol on that fateful morning.

But not Dutch Sheets. The NAR apostle who spearheaded this massive buildup and mobilization, who chummed the water for nearly two months, stayed home in South Carolina on January 6th. According to Taylor, who has combed through Sheets' statements and broadcasts from this period, his absence was almost certainly shaped by a prophecy from his close ally, NAR apostle Chuck Pierce, who decreed that Trump's election victory would not be settled until January 18. For Sheets, prophetic cues like the "don't stop" directive and the "blue plate special" revelation pointed to Congress' January 6th election certification vote as a significant waypoint. But Pierce's date-specific prophecy marked January 18 as the true Jericho moment, and the lesson from the book of Joshua is clear: Follow God's instructions to the letter. So on the morning of January 6th, Sheets delivered his usual online sermon, praying for angel armies to break the demonic forces aligned against Trump, and then he watched the drama at the Capitol unfold from a distance.

Even more surprising than Sheets skipping the insurrection was the role he played as an unlikely peacemaker on January 6th. When the violence began, several prominent NAR apostles at the Capitol phoned Sheets and asked him to share his prophetic guidance with the crowd. In that moment, he could have easily lit the powder keg he had created, sending hundreds, perhaps thousands of adrenaline-filled protestors storming into the Capitol building. Yet at 2:24 p.m., Sheets uncharacteristically preached restraint: "We declare peace over the Capitol grounds this day." Sheets ended up doing far more to quell the violence than Trump, who would take two more hours to finally post a video message telling rioters to go home.

To be clear, apostle Dutch Sheets did not suddenly have an epiphany about mercy and reconciliation. In the years since the insurrection, he has never once shown remorse or contrition for his role in setting that deadly attempted coup in motion. Nor has he tempered the vitriol in his preaching. He simply thought January 6th was too soon because NAR takes its prophecies seriously and literally.

When Taylor began his investigation after January 6th, he knew about NAR because its founder, C. Peter Wagner, had taught at Taylor's alma mater, the Fuller Theological Seminary. Taylor initially dismissed NAR as a fringe curiosity: loud, eccentric, theologically unruly, but not a real threat to anyone. But after finding NAR's fingerprints all over January 6th, discovering its vast following and the reach of its political connections, Taylor realized NAR is no longer fringe; it has grown powerful and dangerous.

In barely one generation, NAR reshaped the right-wing religious landscape, fueling a turn toward militancy and explicit theocratic ambition, while adding formidable political muscle. Its sprawling network and digital mobilization tools now function as a parallel religious-political universe that is larger, and can be activated much faster and more intensely, than the shrinking churches and ossified denominational structures it eclipsed.

That universe is also a cauldron of radicalization. NAR's volatile theology and unchecked prophetic franchise system has created a petri dish for fanaticism free of doubt and detached from rationality. When prophecy tilts toward violence—as it often does with spiritual warlords like Dutch Sheets and his *Ekklesia* demonizing adversaries, sacralizing slaughter, and glorifying decapitation—true believers are not easily deterred by legal consequences or democratic norms. Especially when they see themselves as warriors in a cosmic battle carrying out direct instructions from the Almighty.

NAR played a leading role in the explosion of religious violence on January 6th. Inevitably, until more Americans learn to recognize dangerous radicalization, not just in foreign deserts and mosques, but here at home among some Christians, more religious bombs will explode.

One of them detonated in Minnesota on June 14, 2025. According to investigators, Vance Boelter, an erstwhile evangelical pastor, suited up in tactical gear, impersonated law enforcement, and launched a shooting spree targeting several pro-choice politicians. Two people, State Representative Melissa Hortman and her husband, Mark Hortman, were killed and two others were wounded.

This wasn't random violence; it was spiritual warfare with an assault weapon. Boelter was indoctrinated into NAR's gospel of demonization and spiritual warfare years earlier at Christ for the Nations Institute (CFNI) in Texas, where Sheets had graduated and later been welcomed back as executive director. Leaders and graduates of CFNI often cast abortion and its supporters as demonic evils, and CFNI teaches "violent prayer" as a Christian duty. Indeed, the institute's main lobby displays this quote from founder Gordon Lindsay like a battle cry: "Everyone ought to pray at least one violent prayer each day." When CFNI learned the Minnesota murderer was one of its graduates, a statement condemning the killings was quickly issued. "This is not what we teach," CFNI explained, and "violent prayer" is just a metaphor.

NAR's theology is taking American Christianity by storm. While the country overall is becoming more secular, many of those who remain Christians are starting to echo NAR's teachings whether they know it or not. In a recent survey, 42 percent of American Christians agree "God wants Christians to stand atop the Seven Mountains of

Society," and 61 percent believe in "modern-day apostles and prophets." Half believe there are "demonic principalities and powers" that should be confronted with "campaigns of spiritual warfare and prayer to displace high-level demons."

NAR's theocratic quest to conquer the "mountain" of government is also rolling ahead. Undaunted by the debacle of January 6th and unfazed by its many false prophecies, NAR mounted another massive mobilization in 2024 that helped put Trump back in the White House, vindicating—with some creative interpretation—the original prophecies. Trump has delivered bigly on the Cyrus anointing, with Supreme Court appointments and an extreme policy agenda that is reshaping America for right-wing Christians. NAR's influence over Republican politics is now undeniable. As of this writing, at last twenty of my congressional colleagues were flying Dutch Sheets's beloved "Ar
flag in front of their offices in the Capitol. And Speaker Mike Jo
second in line to the presidency, is so bonded to NAR that he partnered with them to create a flagship annual event, the "National Gathering for Prayer and Repentance" where dozens of members of Congress join NAR *Ekklesia* at the Museum of the Bible for a live-streamed spiritual warfare program against abortion, LGBTQ rights, and secular culture.

NAR stands out as the dominant religious faction in the restive MAGA Christian nationalist movement. But our other two Christian supremacist subcultures are also surging. Rad Trads are riding high with powerful allies entrenched in the highest places, and integralist memes pulsing through online circles thanks to influencers like Nick Fuentes. Meanwhile, Doug Wilson and the Theo Bros, with their symbolic new kirk near the Capitol, are raising and accelerating their theocratic ambition as they leverage the power of billionaire tech allies and Pete Hegseth flexing Christendom on the national stage.

Unraveling the theology that drives these ascendant religious power players is important. But so is understanding the Christian nationalist playbook and how the movement is using it to dismantle the wall of church-state separation and impose Christian dominion. That is our next stop.

CHAPTER 4

FOUNDING FICTION

IF YOU DIDN'T KNOW BETTER, PRESIDENT DONALD Trump's executive order on May 1, 2025, creating the Commission on Religious Liberty might have seemed unobjectionable, even noble. Draped in gauzy platitudes about "restoring the Founders' vision" and "honoring America's sacred heritage," the order appeared to simply establish a commission to examine the state of religious liberty and offer policy recommendations to protect religious freedom. With a patriotic flourish, Trump set the deadline for the commission's final report for July 4, 2026: the 250th anniversary of the Declaration of Independence.

But looking closer, it's clear this was no ordinary commission and that Trump's promise to restore "citizens' pride in our foundational history" masked a deeper agenda. The order reeled off a list of "emerging threats" that echoed longstanding legal arguments from Christian nationalist groups. This threat list included claims that government policies were infringing on freedom of conscience, restricting access to religious education, and attempting to "remove religion entirely from public life." The order went on to disparage vaccine mandates, restrictions on government religious displays, and limits on prayer and religious instruction in public schools.

The mask slipped at the Rose Garden signing ceremony. Trump mused aloud about church-state separation—"I don't know, is that a good thing or a bad thing?"—before announcing his pick to chair the commission: Texas Lieutenant Governor Dan Patrick. A former sportscaster turned right-wing radio host, Patrick built his political brand on weaponized Christian grievance. He helped pass one of the nation's harshest abortion bans and championed a Texas law (quickly blocked by a federal court) that would have forced public schools to display the Ten Commandments in every classroom. As if that wasn't disqualifying enough, Patrick once declared that America was "founded not on the words of our founders, but on the words of God—because He wrote the Constitution."

Then came the commission's venue announcement. Instead of meeting in the customary setting of a federal building, they would convene at the Museum of the Bible, a 430,000-square-foot shrine to Christian nationalism four blocks from the Capitol. Bankrolled by the billionaire evangelical Green family, owners of Hobby Lobby, the museum offers a triumphalist spin on scripture's role in American history and functions as a right-wing religious annex to the federal government.

We begin this chapter by zooming in on Trump's Commission on Religious Liberty, not because it is a serious inquiry into religious freedom, but because it provides a case study into the strategies and tactics Christian nationalists are using to gain power and justify their antidemocratic aims. We'll delve into their relentless revisionist history about America's founding and founders, especially Thomas Jefferson, and their central narrative: that our country was founded as a "Christian nation" and must stay that way. We'll explore their mythology of recasting Christians as a persecuted minority and their claim that church-state separation is a secular scheme to drive Christians out of public life. These claims aren't just false, as we'll show; they're cynically deployed to erode real religious freedom and rebrand Christian cultural and political dominance as religious liberty. That's why it's important to set the record straight on America's secular foundations and understand the true story of religious liberty, as envisioned by the founders.

Our journey starts at the Museum of the Bible on June 16, 2025, the opening salvo in a year-long Christian nationalist PR blitz that would culminate with America's sestercentennial celebration. The commission's thinly veiled agenda was to give the story of America's founding a religious makeover and replace the actual Thomas Jefferson—the deist who famously cut the miracles out of his Bible and warned against clerical meddling in politics—with a proto-evangelical mascot for their "Christian nation" mythology. The purpose behind this historical revisionism is to dismantle Jefferson's "wall of separation" between church and state once and for all.

AHEAD OF THE FIRST HEARING, progressive faith leaders put Trump and his commission on notice that they saw through the charade. The national multifaith coalition Faith in Action issued a scathing statement denouncing the commission as a "theocratic power grab" that "accelerates the collapse of our democracy." The Interfaith Alliance, a national religious freedom and social justice coalition, urged the commission to examine real threats to religious liberty, including "how the Trump administration is attacking faith communities that refuse to bend the knee." And the watchdog group Americans United for Separation of Church and State blasted Trump for designing the commission to favor conservative Christians "who want to use government power to impose their religion on others."

On June 16, Chairman Patrick gaveled the commission to order and wasted no time proving the critics right. After asking Commissioner Robert Barron, a Catholic bishop, to lead an opening (sectarian Christian) prayer, Patrick began by congratulating himself for giving Trump the idea for the commission. He recalled a post-election conversation where he outlined the ideal roster for Trump: "We want faith leaders. We want scholars. We want historians. We want people who have been to the Supreme Court and been involved in a number of cases on religious liberty." From that ideal, Patrick proceeded to introduce a commission that looked like a casting call for Celebrity Christian Nationalist Apprentice. Among them: the second-place runner up in the 2009 Miss USA pageant, back when Trump owned the franchise; TV shrink Dr. Phil McGraw; and an assortment of Christian nationalist academics, media personalities, and televangelists—in total, twelve conservative Christians and one orthodox Jew.

Patrick then launched into the heart of the agenda: "the Founders' intent" behind the First Amendment's religious protections. A great modern-day example of the old-fashioned religious liberty the founders cherished, Patrick argued, was his Texas law to require posting of the Ten Commandments in every public school classroom. The chairman seemed blissfully unaware that his Texas scripture-posting mandate contravenes the First Amendment in ways that are almost too obvious to parody. After all, nothing says religious freedom like Commandment #1: "You shall have no other gods before Me."

After Patrick was Carrie Prejean Boller, the former beauty queen turned culture warrior. During Trump's 2009 pageant she was asked her position on gay marriage and gave a faith-based answer opposing it. Boller blames that response, which many considered homophobic, for her runner-up finish. It may have cost her the crown, but it catapulted her to right-wing media stardom. Now, she was back on stage, picking up right where she left off, minus the tiara. Boller launched into a remix of American history, cherry-picking religious quotes from the founders and waxing nostalgic about the golden age of Christian textbooks in public schools. She reverently quoted a theocratic gem from an eighteenth-century Supreme Court justice, who wrote: "It is the duty as well as the privilege and interest of our Christian nation to select and prefer Christians for their rulers." Boller then lamented that ever since liberal courts started restricting prayer and Bible readings in schools, "morality has dropped across America," triggering spikes in suicide, divorce, and mental health crises.

Next up: Dr. Phil. Because who better to discern the founders' intent about religious liberty than an unlicensed TV therapist who once juiced his ratings by counseling a woman who claimed to be pregnant with the baby Jesus. His testimony, like his broadcasts, opened with folksy plain talk: the founders often mentioned God. *True*. And they put "In God We Trust" on our currency. *False*. That motto was stamped onto our coins in 1864 and our paper currency in 1957, in both cases long after the founders were in the ground. Dr. Phil closed with this whopper: "Our founders didn't view religion as a threat to liberty. They saw it as Liberty's guardian. They didn't create a secular state."

Chairman Patrick took Dr. Phil's fabrication and, Texas-style, made it even bigger. The founders, he claimed, created "a government built on the Bible." As proof, he cited the sacred harmony between scripture and the Declaration of Independence: "The Declaration of Independence is consistent with the Bible, and the Bible is consistent with the Declaration of Independence."

At this point, one must pause and ask: Has the lieutenant governor actually read either document? Because you can admire both, but you can't credibly claim they're consistent, much less doctrinal twins. The declaration is a product of Enlightenment rationalism, steeped in natural rights philosophy and political rebellion. The Bible is a collection of ancient religious texts featuring tribal law codes, moral parables, and prophetic visions. Chairman Patrick's blunder deserves more than ridicule. It's a teachable moment, a case study in Christian nationalist revisionism.

So, let's dissect his claim that the Declaration of Independence proves our founders created "a government built on the Bible." To do so, we must start with an inconvenient truth: The Declaration of Independence—stirring breakup letter with the crown that it was—carried no binding authority. It didn't establish a country, enact a constitution, or create a government. In that sense, it's not a founding document of the United States as we know it.

Don't take my word for it. Just look at how the document's two references to "united States" both conspicuously avoid capitalizing "united." The signatories call themselves "These United Colonies" and declare that they "are, and of Right ought to be Free and Independent States." Plural, as in multiple independent states, which were not yet committed to being a single nation. I can't imagine a packed stadium of American sports fans chanting "U-C-A! U-C-A!" But that's how it might have ended if the hard work of nation-building that took us from United Colonies to the United States hadn't happened years later. It wasn't until ratification of the Articles of Confederation in 1781 that the moniker "United States of America" was officially endorsed, and our federal government didn't exist until the Constitution, which came eleven years after the declaration.

The declaration was important for other reasons. It formally severed ties with England, rallied the colonies, and made a moral and legal case that justified our rebellion to the world—especially potential allies like France, whose support was essential to winning a revolution that was already well underway.

It was also our founders' first platform for burnishing radical new political ideals that defied the "divine right of kings," the prevailing European doctrine under which monarchs were deemed to derive power from God and stand above earthly law. By contrast, the declaration was a secular thunderclap proclaiming consent of the governed, inherent equality, and inalienable rights to life and liberty. The specifics would be worked up later in the Constitution and legislation, but from the beginning the American experiment was anchored in the revolutionary premise that power flows from the people, not from a throne.

This directly contravenes the Bible. The biblical command is clear: Obey kings and governing authorities, because they are ordained by God. It appears over and over, including in Romans 13:1–2, 1 Peter 2:13–14, Titus 3:1, and Hebrews 13:17.

This wasn't lost on clergy of the time. Robert Boucher, a loyalist Anglican minister, put it plainly: "The uniform doctrine of the Scriptures [is] that it is under the deputation and authority of God alone that kings reign . . . far from deriving their authority from any supposed consent or suffrage of men, they receive their commission from Heaven." He nailed the biblical position: Scripture abhors rebellion and demands obedience. There is no way to reconcile this position with the declaration's rejection of King George III, who wore both the crown of England and the mitre of the Church of England.

For all the exhaustive arguments Jefferson mustered in the declaration, he never once cites scripture, because there was no scripture to support rebellion against a king. As constitutional attorney Andrew Seidel succinctly put it, "The bible undercut the American cause." Which is precisely why our founders used other arguments, including Enlightenment philosophy, natural rights theory, and appeals to reason and justice to support their cause.

So no, the declaration wasn't remotely biblical. It defied the theological scaffolding of the time, not echoed it. But what about the fact that the Declaration of Independence contains not one but four quasi-religious references to a higher power? Specifically:

1. "the Laws of Nature and of *Nature's God*"
2. "endowed by their *Creator*"
3. "appealing to the *Supreme Judge of the world* for the rectitude of our intentions"
4. "reliance on the protection of *divine Providence*"

Christian nationalists routinely cite these phrases as proof that Jefferson and his compatriots intended to center the American experiment in Judeo-Christian religion. But as Seidel meticulously documents in *The Founding Myth,* that assertion is specious.

Only one of the four phrases, "the Laws of Nature and of Nature's God," appeared in Jefferson's original draft, and even that phrase is religion-adjacent at best. Jefferson, like Franklin and many other founders, was a rationalist. The rationalist search for truth prioritized observations of nature and the exercise of reason ("natural religion") over the "revealed religion" of scripture. Jefferson also embraced the Enlightenment concept of natural law, a secular political theory asserting that basic rights are inherent and do not derive from kings or clergy. As a deist, Jefferson accepted the idea of a higher power who *designed* the universe but rejected any supernatural meddling thereafter. So, the phrase "Nature's God" was vintage Jeffersonian rationalism—and not remotely biblical.

The other three references were added later, likely at the suggestion of others, according to historians. Jefferson could accept them because they didn't compromise his core philosophical arguments. They were rhetorical flourishes, not theological declarations. "Their Creator," a phrase likely suggested by Adams or Franklin, was a throwaway—inoffensive to deists, vague enough for believers, and politically useful in appealing to religious colonists. "The Supreme Judge of the world" was nonsectarian and served as another moral appeal to pious colonists, not a doctrinal claim. "Divine Providence," added by the Continental Congress, was a Rorschach phrase—meaning good fortune to skeptics or divine guidance to believers. Jefferson and his colleagues were savvy politicians and purposeful drafters. These additions were strategic, not theological. As Seidel concludes, they were "the coonskin cap of the Declaration," a symbolic flourish, like the frontier costume Franklin donned in Paris to charm the French court and win support for the revolution.

If Jefferson had intended the declaration to be a religious document, readers would know it, and he would've said so. In fact, he said the opposite. In his later reflections, he confirms that his only thoughts about religion at the time were aimed at challenging faith-based orthodoxy. Just days before his death in 1826, Jefferson wrote a letter describing the declaration's legacy as: "arousing men to burst the chains, under which monkish ignorance and superstition had persuaded them to bind themselves." In the same letter, he mocked the notion that God's grace causes any human to be "born with saddles on their backs."

But if the declaration isn't biblical, or even generically religious in any meaningful way, then what about the Constitution, the actual founding document? Unfortunately for Christian nationalists, that's an even harder sell.

The heavy lifting of nation-building fell to the Constitutional Convention of 1787, and to James Madison, the man tasked with drafting the charter that would define our republic and establish its legal architecture. Madison was even less accommodating than Jefferson when it came to religion. He assiduously avoided any mention of God, Jesus, Christianity, or even a vague nod to a higher power. His opening line—the soaring "We the People" preamble—lays a secular, and dare I say godless, foundation for the American experiment.

The only reference to religion in the entire main body of the Constitution is buried in Article VI. And even that is prohibitory. With unusually specific language, Article VI draws an unmistakable line between church and state: "No religious test shall ever be required as a qualification to any office or public trust under the United States." That's not a wink to Christianity. It's a wall.

If it were up to Madison, that lone Article VI clause would have been the Constitution's final word on religion. But others demanded a clearer enumeration of individual liberties, and ratification hung in the balance. Jefferson, ever the strategist, urged Madison to include a Bill of Rights to unify the fledgling republic around shared principles. Madison relented. And so, religious liberty—alongside free speech, freedom of assembly, a free press, and the right to petition the government—was enshrined in the First Amendment.

But Madison's conception of religious liberty bears no resemblance to the Christian nationalism on display at Trump's Religious Liberty Commission. Madison was emphatic that religion and government must remain separate. That's why he grounded the First Amendment's religion clauses in the Virginia Statute for Religious Freedom, a law Jefferson had drafted the year after the declaration. That statute was a legal bombshell: the first enacted law in the newly independent colonies to guarantee church-state separation. It was also a radical departure from colonial norms, where most colonies had official state churches that were endorsed and subsidized by the government. Jefferson's statute disestablished the Church of England in Virginia and declared that no person should be compelled to support any religious worship or ministry, and that civil rights must never hinge on religious belief. He described its protections as extending to "the Jew and the Gentile, the Christian and Mahometan, the Hindoo, and Infidel of every denomination."

Yes, Religious Liberty Commissioners, even the infidels.

If Trump's commission was genuinely interested in the founders' intent behind the First Amendment, this would have been the obvious place to start—not with specious assertions, but with Jefferson's Virginia Statute for Religious Freedom, the intellectual and legal cornerstone of the First Amendment. Or, if they truly wanted to excavate the foundation of religious liberty in America, they would go back to the Puritan dissenter Roger Williams. More than a century before the constitutional debates in Philadelphia, he planted the radical seed of tolerance for all religious views and the concept that civil authorities must not enforce religious doctrine. Williams was exiled from Massachusetts in 1635 for preaching these principles, which the Puritan theocracy rebuked as "Satan's policy." Forced to flee, he founded the colony of Rhode Island as a haven for religious liberty where Baptists, Quakers, Jews, and dissenters of every kind were welcome as equals. By royal charter, Rhode Island became the first government in the Western world to legally enshrine freedom of conscience and church-state separation.

That was the radical model of religious liberty that Jefferson, Madison, and the other founders ultimately embraced. For Jefferson, his Virginia statute declaring universal religious liberty was so central to his legacy that he had it etched on his gravestone, alongside the Declaration of Independence and the founding of the University of Virginia. Notably absent: his presidency, which perhaps he felt would dilute from the greater achievements.

Madison's derivative product, the First Amendment, distills Jefferson's vision into a concise, two-part framework: "Congress shall make no law respecting an establishment of religion, or prohibiting the free exercise thereof." The framers thus enshrined both freedom *of* religion and freedom *from* religion, reflecting their deep wariness of religious entanglements in government. Jefferson famously described this as a "wall of separation" between church and state in his 1802 letter to the Danbury Baptist Association. Madison, though he never used that metaphor, went further. He insisted the Constitution requires "perfect separation" between church and state—a phrase that, in Madison's hands, meant no public chaplaincies, no national days of prayer, no religious proclamations, and no moral policing masquerading as governance.

Clearly, neither the declaration nor the Constitution lend credence to the "Christian nation" founding myth. America's origin story is extraordinary in many ways, but we need to accept the truth: The founding was not biblical, not by a long shot. Which is fine. Plenty of wonderful things are unbiblical—women's rights, mixed fabrics, and NFL games on Sunday, to name a few. It takes nothing away from America's greatness.

But what about Jefferson himself? Jefferson poses a major dilemma for Christian nationalists. They can't dismiss him; any serious inquiry into "Founders' intent" runs straight through him. But they're also unwilling to acknowledge that he was a profound skeptic of organized religion and a fierce opponent of religious influence over government. So, they swap out the real Jefferson for a counterfeit. They cherry-pick quotes, strip away context, ignore mountains of contrary evidence and, when that's not enough, just make stuff up.

No one has mastered this better than right-wing Christianity's reigning mythmaker-in-chief: David Barton. When Christian nationalists like Chairman Patrick wax poetic about America's religious founding or Jefferson's piety, they're often parroting Barton, a self-styled historian and major player in Republican politics. Patrick calls him "one of the leading experts on America's Christian heritage." Yet Barton's sole credential is a bachelor's degree in religious education from Oral Roberts University. For the past three decades, Barton has relentlessly promoted a fantastical Christian nationalist version of history, becoming the embodiment of the old maxim: To sell one big lie, you have to tell a thousand little ones. He curates "Christian nation" mythology through a firehose of books, videos, podcasts, and media appearances that canonize the Founding Fathers and dismiss church-state separation as a liberal canard.

Of all Barton's lies, perhaps none is greater and more influential than the way he has recast Jefferson as a misunderstood Christian visionary. His flagship book, *The Jefferson Lies,* was so thoroughly debunked by scholars across the political and religious spectrum that its Christian publisher pulled it from shelves in 2012, sheepishly explaining they had "lost confidence in the book's details." The fallout was brutal. Multiple historians and Christian academics meticulously reviewed Barton's work and eviscerated it; there's even a multivolume history series dedicated entirely to documenting and refuting Barton's lies.

Yet Barton still hawks the discredited book and a trove of other counterfeit history on his website. He's greeted like a conquering hero at right-wing Christian gatherings, revered by prominent Christian nationalists like Senator Ted Cruz and former Arkansas governor Mike Huckabee, who once said that "I almost wish there would be . . . a simultaneous telecast, and all Americans would be forced—forced at gunpoint no less—to listen to every David Barton message. And I think our country would be better for it." Barton's reputational Teflon and the surprising stickiness of his fake history owe much to his friends in high places. And none is friendlier—or higher—than Speaker Mike Johnson.

Johnson calls Barton not just a dear friend, but "a profound influence on me, and my work, and my life and everything I do." That "profound influence" was on full display on January 3, 2025, when Speaker Johnson gaveled in the 119th Congress and delivered a nationally televised speech featuring a poignant Christian prayer he claimed was written by Jefferson, recited daily in the White House, and "every day thereafter until his death." The prayer ended with the familiar evangelical flourish: "All of which we ask through Jesus Christ our Lord, Amen." Johnson vouched for its authenticity, calling it "quite familiar to historians and probably many of us."

There was just one problem: It was a lie. The fabricated prayer is lifted straight from Barton's *Jefferson Lies* and has long since been debunked by the Jefferson Foundation at Monticello, among others. According to historians, Jefferson never wrote it, never prayed it, and never invoked Jesus Christ in any such fashion. The actual Jefferson was an enemy of theocracy. Throughout his career, he was denounced as an "infidel" and a "heathen" by the Mike Johnsons and David Bartons of his time. He would have seen straight through today's parade of Christian nationalist myths, curated to bulldoze the "wall of separation" between church and state that he so purposefully built. He would have recognized Trump's Religious Liberty Commission for what it is: a sham.

I was the first member of Congress to publicly rebuke Johnson for parroting Barton's lies. But like his mentor Barton, Speaker Johnson never apologized, retracted, or flinched. And that's the point. When the Speaker of the House, members of Trump's Commission on Religious Liberty, and other officials traffic in Christian nationalist lies, they're not just echoing Barton's mythology: They're operationalizing it. These aren't abstract distortions of history; they're the scaffolding for a theocratic agenda with real-world consequences.

With Barton revving up his fake history machine, Johnson holding the third-highest office in the nation, and Trump's Commission on Religious Liberty lending a veneer of legitimacy and a national spotlight, Christian nationalists have never been more poised to drive their "Christian nation" narrative deep into the heart of our national discourse. This is a big moment for them—a project they've been building for decades.

Which raises a deeper question: Why is this Christian nation myth so central to their efforts? On its face, it looks like a strategic dead end. The idea that America was founded as a Christian nation is easily debunked. And the narrative is out of step with a country that's growing more diverse and less religious by the year. In a functioning democracy, it shouldn't be a winning formula. So why do they keep pushing it—relentlessly and obsessively?

First, because it subtly erodes the imperative of church-state separation. By normalizing the idea that America is and always has been a Christian nation, it reframes religious favoritism in civic life as not only acceptable, but also historically valid and patriotic. It paves the way for habituation to more faith-based symbols, language, and policies embedded in government. Over time, these myths have the potential to blur the boundary between religion and governance to the point that church-state separation becomes meaningless.

And there's another strategy at work. The extreme theocrats who push "Christian nation" narratives are not trying to persuade a majority—they're trying to outflank it. They know Christian nationalism is broadly unpopular, but they don't need mass appeal. Fewer than 40 percent of eligible voters show up in most elections, and Democratic turnout is notoriously unreliable. What they need is unity, intensity, turnout, discipline, and strategic control. The Christian nation narrative helps with that because it hits like a sermon at sunrise for key demographic subgroups.

The Public Religion Research Institute's 2024 survey of twenty-two thousand Americans found strong support for Christian nationalist messaging among Republicans, regular churchgoers, white Christians, and consumers of right-wing media. Sociologist Sam Perry explains that for this cohort, the power of Christian nationalism is that it isn't just rhetoric. It's sacred code that signals belonging. In the face of rapid diversification, it fortifies white Christian group identity, but more than that it sacralizes it by wrapping the group's sense of cultural loss, racial resentment, and entitlement in divine legitimacy. In Perry's words, it infuses their conception of national identity with "transcendence and ultimate value."

The power of Christian nation mythmaking goes further than electoral strategy. The data shows that these ideas are a gateway to fanaticism and violence. Among self-identified Christian nationalists, two-thirds believe God anointed Trump to win in 2024, and one-third agree that "true American patriots may have to resort to violence to save the country."

Elizabeth Neumann, a former senior official in Trump's Department of Homeland Security, describes Christian nationalist myths as the scaffolding for a high-stakes covenant narrative. In this view, America is a vessel of divine purpose, chosen by and bound to God through obedience. The covenant is imagined as fragile and conditional. If our sacred agreement with God is broken by national sins like secularism or liberal culture, the entire nation risks divine punishment. Neumann saw this belief system as a ladder of religious and ideological escalation leading step by step to January 6th:

> They see it in cataclysmic terms: This is the moment, and God's going to judge us. They view the last 50 years of moral decline as us breaking our covenant, and that because of that, God's going to remove His blessing. When you paint it in existential terms like that, a lot of people feel justified to carry out acts of violence in the name of their faith.

Like many who sounded the alarm on Christian nationalist beliefs, Neumann's warnings were not heeded. She resigned several months before the insurrection over the administration's failure to confront right-wing extremism.

As Neumann points out, this mythology is a potent weapon that can be—and was—used to justify Christian nationalists' attempts to conquer our government. If enough believers are convinced that America was founded as a Christian nation, chosen by God to fulfill His plans for humanity, and if enough believers become afraid that our secular democracy is breaking the covenant and triggering God's wrath, then democracy becomes expendable.

As corrosive as the "Christian nation" myth is to religious freedom, as dangerous as it is as a gateway to extremism and violence, it doesn't work alone. With church-state separation squarely embedded in the Constitution, reinforced by decades of legal precedent, and embraced as a core value by most Americans, Christian nationalists know that airbrushed history alone won't make it go away. They need to flip the script. That's where their "naked public square" myth comes in.

The "naked public square" theory posits that Christians are being excluded from public life and marginalized to the point where they may be required to conceal their faith, if not abandon it. The argument derives from Rev. Richard John Neuhaus's 1984 book *The Naked Public Square: Religion and Democracy in America*. A Lutheran pastor who later became a Catholic priest, Neuhaus was an unofficial faith advisor to President George W. Bush and a sharp critic of secular liberalism. In his prolific writing, he railed against two decades of Supreme Court decisions that enforced the First Amendment's prohibition against any government "establishment of religion." Neuhaus argued that the court got it wrong. In his telling, the founders didn't really want to separate church and state; they were just politely declining to establish an official state church. Neuhaus contended that court rulings that enforced strict separation had left our civic world "naked" of religious speech, much to our detriment. He insisted religion in government is not only fair game but also essential for a healthy nation, especially to ensure fair treatment of Christians who want to inject their moral convictions into public life.

The "naked public square" theory, especially as deployed by today's Christian nationalists, reframes religious pluralism as persecution and church-state separation as tyranny. Yet it has always been a straw man. Throughout the 1980s when this myth took root through the present day, Christians have dominated every corner of American public life, including all three branches of government, education, and American culture writ large. Their moral and ethical views were never barred and never discouraged. American public life remains saturated with Christian symbols, traditions, and speech.

So, what triggered this Christian persecution complex? Beginning in the 1960s, courts enforced the Establishment Clause by placing modest limits on the ability of Christians to impose religious practices on others and required that public laws have a nonreligious purpose. That's it. No gag orders. No faith bans. But facts have been no match for myth. In a rapidly diversifying and secularizing nation, the "naked public square" captures a feeling of lost privilege that resonates deeply with Christian nationalists. Today, this myth has grown to cartoonish proportions.

To hear today's Christian nationalists tell it, believers are being barred from public life and forced to worship in secrecy. No public prayer. No "Merry Christmas." No mentioning Jesus at a school board meeting. In this gripping fantasy, Christians wander around clutching their Bibles like contraband, while secular elites and Jews patrol the perimeter with copies of *The Origin of Species* and NPR tote bags. In this imaginary America, the First Amendment has been turned into a muzzle, the public square has been hermetically sealed off from anything Christian, and the faithful are exiled in their own land.

Unsurprisingly, this vision of America made several appearances at the Religious Liberty Commission's inaugural hearing. Commissioner Ryan Anderson described the secularization of public life as "a disaster" that denies "robust religious liberty." He ridiculed the (nonexistent) requirement that Christians only "worship in the privacy of your chapel or your home," and insisted that true religious liberty means the freedom to "bring your religious values into the public square for discussions of public justice and the common good." Which, of course, he does all the time. It is literally his full-time job.

Commissioner Barron, the Catholic bishop, used the "naked public square" trope to reimagine Jefferson's wall as more of a theocratic gateway: "The thing about the separation of church and state, that wall was not intended to inhibit the churches. The wall was to protect them. That's what Jefferson meant." Then he exposed the endgame of the "naked public square" mythology. Christians, Barron argued, should no longer "stay in our little, you know, self-imposed ghettos," but instead "invade that space." Yes, *invade*. Not participate. Not share. *Invade*.

While commissioner Eric Metaxas wasn't at the hearing, his writings also reveal the veiled theocratic ambition behind the "naked public square" myth. He turns it into a legal argument that church-state separation itself is unconstitutional—an illegal establishment of "secular religion" that suppresses Christian "truth." Metaxas casts court decisions restricting compulsory school prayer and protecting abortion rights as acts of religious persecution, stretching the "naked public square" myth to a revealing endpoint: It's not about defending religious expression in public life; it's about using religious liberty as a pretext to impose Christian "truth" society-wide.

Once you recognize this Christian nationalist myth, you'll start noticing how central it is to their antidemocratic vision for America. At the commission's first hearing, Notre Dame law professor Gerald Bradley pinpointed the moment our Godly republic opened its secular trench coat and streaked into naked tyranny: the Supreme Court's school prayer case in 1962. "To put it bluntly," Bradley advised, "I think it's time to kick in the rotten door that's barring religion from the public square." Bradley urged revival of two "vibrant traditions": (1) government prayer for the exclusive purpose of religion—not ceremonial solemnity but actual worship, like Pete Hegseth's new Pentagon prayer services; and (2) government support for religion without a secular purpose—in other words, outright state sponsorship and funding for churches purely for the sake of religion. Similarly, Mark Rienzi, CEO of a conservative religious legal organization, urged the commission to "reclothe the public square" by having government actively promote religion. "Having a religious and virtuous citizenry is good for everybody," Rienzi declared—without specifying which religion, or whose virtue, but I think we can guess.

The absurdity of the commission's first hearing—with bishops calling for Christian invasion, activists who tout Christianity full-time in the public square claiming their faith is being muzzled, and law professors demanding state-sponsored church services—shouldn't blind us to the dangerous implications it reveals. These commissioners and their Christian nationalist allies aren't just peddling fake history; they're promoting myths that fuel extremism and violence, and advancing a vision where sharing the public square on equal terms is rejected as tyranny and oppression to Christians, and "religious liberty" is simply a euphemism for Christian dominion.

Beyond these obvious dangers, Christian nationalist mythmaking also sets a trap for the rest of us. Some of these myths contain kernels of truth. America does have a deep history of religious devotion that coexists uneasily with the scars of religious extremism. And we have long struggled to define and enforce precise boundaries between church and state. In our zeal to counter Christian nationalist overreach, we should not conjure a secular utopia that never existed. Nor should we airbrush away the religiosity of our history; that would be a different kind of myth.

Legally and constitutionally, Christian nationalists are wrong: The United States was not founded as a Christian nation. But culturally and functionally? That's more complicated. For Jefferson, Madison, and other founders, theocracy wasn't just a threat, it was a lived reality. Especially at the local and state levels, Christianity was woven into the fabric of public life through laws, public rituals and ceremonies, and education. The Bible was cited in political discourse far more than Enlightenment thinkers, and even founders who were deists or skeptics (like Jefferson, Madison, and Franklin) operated in a world where Christian morality was idiomatic.

Our nation's lineage includes the brutal theocracies of colonial New England, where Baptists were whipped, Quakers mutilated, and heretics executed under Puritan rule of the Massachusetts Bay Colony. It also includes early New York, where the Dutch Reformed Church monopolized public worship. At the time of the Revolution, most colonies had an official church legally chartered and subsidized by the government—a status that, outside of Rhode Island, Virginia, and a few other states, persisted well into the nineteenth century. Although the overt theocratic regimes of the seventeenth century faded under pressure from religious dissent, growing pluralism, and the influence of Enlightenment ideals, traces of theocracy persisted in our nation's legal bloodstream.

One of the clearest examples is our nation's blasphemy laws. English common law, the default framework in the colonies, treated blasphemy as a criminal offense. Denying the existence of God or hurling "contumelious reproaches on our Saviour Christ" was a jailable offense. The rationale: "Christianity is part of the laws of the land." That wasn't metaphor—it was jurisprudence. After the Revolution, the new states didn't rush to secularize. Most retained their colonial blasphemy statutes or drafted fresh ones. Even into the early twentieth century, blasphemy laws were still nearly universal across the states. The last notable prosecution for blasphemy was upheld by Maine's Supreme Court in *State v. Mockus* (1921). In the 1920s and

1930s, however, the judicial tide began to turn as state and federal courts interpreted First Amendment protections more expansively. Blasphemy laws slowly began to be struck down, culminating in the landmark 1952 Supreme Court decision *Burstyn v. Wilson*. In that case, the state of New York had tried to censor a film that mocked Catholic doctrine. The Court ruled that such censorship violated both the Establishment Clause and freedom of speech. After *Burstyn*, most states quietly stopped enforcing their blasphemy laws. But in many states, they remained on the books. As recently as 2010, the state of Pennsylvania tried to enforce its colonial-era blasphemy law when a filmmaker was denied a state business license for trying to name his company "I Choose Hell Productions." This prompted a lawsuit and federal court ruling that the law violated both freedom of expression and the Establishment Clause. Blatantly unconstitutional blasphemy laws still litter the books in at least four states, including Massachusetts, Michigan, Oklahoma, and South Carolina.

Other theocratic vestiges have persisted in much the same way. Chief among them: state-imposed religious tests for public office. These tests were active constitutional provisions in at least eight states well into the twentieth century. In 1961, a Supreme Court decision should have definitively ended this practice. In *Torcaso v. Watkins*, the court unanimously struck down Maryland's requirement that public officials profess belief in God, declaring it a violation of both Article VI and the First Amendment. But some states didn't get the message. As late as 1997, South Carolina was still enforcing its religious test clause, which reads: "No person who denies the existence of a Supreme Being shall hold any office under this Constitution." That is, until Herb Silverman, a mathematician and outspoken atheist, was denied a notary public license for theological noncompliance. Silverman litigated all the way to the South Carolina Supreme Court to finally get the law overturned—thirty-six years after the Supreme Court had ruled unambiguously that such religious tests are unconstitutional. Despite all the court rulings, seven states still have unconstitutional religious test requirements in their constitutions: Arkansas, Mississippi, North Carolina, Pennsylvania, Tennessee, and Texas.

This gradual evolution underscores how theocracy in America

didn't vanish with the Puritans. For much of our nation's history, the First Amendment's promise of religious freedom was often honored more in theory than in practice. Only through the sustained efforts of religious dissenters, skeptics, and civil libertarians did the country inch closer to constitutional secularism. Most of that progress was hard-won, met at every turn by fierce resistance as theocracy morphed, adapted, and dug in legally and culturally wherever it could.

Madison's notion of "perfect separation" has always been aspirational, if not unrealistic, and Jefferson's "wall of separation" has never been absolute or impermeable. Our imperfect separation of church and state has always been negotiated, and occasionally trampled. Understanding America's theocratic past is essential if we're to effectively refute the "Christian nation" mythology and defend a future of true religious liberty.

Secularists should especially take care in navigating the false choice inherent in the "naked public square" trope. Church-state separation requires nothing more or less than government neutrality on matters of faith. That means a public square that is neither a religious sanctuary nor a spiritual void, but rather a shared civic commons. Explaining that is easy. The harder part is pushing back against Christian nationalist mythology without inadvertently feeding the "naked public square" myth. Christian nationalist thought leaders are quick to seize on any rhetoric they can frame as antireligious, spinning it into a false narrative of persecution.

The best church-state separation advocates understand this. Rachel Laser, president of Americans United for Separation of Church and State—probably the country's leading church-state separation watchdog—makes it a point to welcome religious voices in public discourse, as long as religion is not imposed on people through government. The distinction is vital.

It also helps that many of the strongest advocates for church-state separation are themselves people of faith. For example, Holly Hollman, general counsel for the Baptist Joint Committee for Religious Liberty, explains that "the First Amendment has never required a public square devoid of religious influences or banned the government's acknowledgment of religion in the lives of its citizens." Religious leaders, she argues, not only have the right but a moral duty to speak out on policy issues, so long as they respect constitutional boundaries like everyone else. "The Constitution is not a reason to be silent," she insists. "In fact, the opposite is true; our democracy depends on a well-informed and engaged citizenry." For Hollman, religious liberty is a sacred trust, grounded in both theology and democracy, and best preserved by keeping government out of the pulpit and religion out of the law.

So let's be clear: Separation of church and state does not mean a "naked public square." Faith will always have a place in the values and voices of public life in America. Politicians, celebrities, and athletes will proclaim how their faith shapes and inspires them. People will wish each other Merry Christmas, privately and publicly. Children will pray in public schools if they want to (especially before pop math quizzes). And all of it will be fine, as long as our government remains a neutral referee. But Christian nationalists like those on Trump's sham commission don't want neutrality; they insist on dominion. We've unpacked the false narratives that are central to their playbook, and seen their strategies on glaring display at the Commission on Religious Liberty. But refuting their myths is the easy part. The harder work is awakening America from our sleepwalk to theocracy, because that requires a reckoning with something far more entrenched than fake history. It requires naming and challenging Christian privilege—the next chapter in saving democracy.

CHAPTER 5

CHRISTIAN PRIVILEGE

FOR A FEW FLEETING DAYS AFTER JANUARY 6TH, TRUMP'S spell over the Republican Party was broken. You could see it in the eyes of those who had enabled him: if not genuine contrition, at least regret. A reckoning was at hand. And then it wasn't.

Watching congressional Republicans' moral courage curdle into cowardly retreat was one of the most pathetic spectacles I've ever witnessed. Some offered sheepish semi-rebukes, hoping to buy some time while they waited to see if the tyrant had finally fallen. Senate GOP Leader Mitch McConnell delivered a scathing floor speech declaring Trump "practically and morally responsible" for the insurrection—but that speech came just minutes after he voted to acquit in Trump's impeachment trial. House Republican Leader Kevin McCarthy briefly blamed Trump for the coup. But nothing says "I meant what I said" like jetting off to Mar-a-Lago two weeks later for a grinning photo op. And then there was Senator Lindsey Graham delivering a Cirque du Soleil-level contortion act: opening with a dramatic "count me out," then folding himself neatly into the familiar Trump-as-victim pose ("he was told things that just weren't true"), before sticking the dismount by slinking back to the golf course with Trump as if nothing had happened.

Which made my colleague Rep. Liz Cheney (R-WY) such a refreshing exception. Before Trump's hostile takeover of the GOP, Cheney was on the rise. She was right-wing royalty, the daughter of a vice president with unassailable conservative credentials, including hawkish foreign policy just like her dad. Elected by her peers to chair the House Republican Conference, Cheney had quickly become the third-highest ranking Republican in the House. No one had more to gain from toeing the party line in early 2021 than she did.

But unlike so many others after January 6th, she unapologetically broke ranks with Trump. On January 13, 2021, she was one of only ten House Republicans to vote to impeach Trump for inciting the insurrection. And it cost her. She narrowly survived a February attempt to strip her of her leadership post, and under pressure from Trump, Kevin McCarthy—once a defender—was caught on a hot mic saying, "I've had it with her." Cheney's response was defiant: "I will not sit back and watch in silence" as the Republican Party is led "down a path that abandons the rule of law and joins the former president's crusade to undermine our democracy." Cheney wanted to draw a line, in hopes of stirring others in her party to rediscover their conscience. Knowing the long odds and the risk, she did it anyway.

Meanwhile, McCarthy faced mounting pressure to support a bipartisan commission to investigate the insurrection. He initially endorsed the idea and even dispatched a trusted ally, Rep. John Katko of New York, the ranking Republican on the Homeland Security Committee, to negotiate with Democratic Chairman Bennie Thompson. On May 14, 2021, Katko and Thompson announced they had struck a bipartisan deal to create an investigative commission.

But just four days later, Trump denounced the deal as a "Democrat trap," prompting McCarthy to reverse his stance within hours. The following day, Senator Mitch McConnell also aligned with Trump. Katko was blindsided, and the chances of passing bipartisan legislation to establish a commission were effectively quashed. The message was unmistakable: Loyalty to Trump would continue to be the GOP's guiding principle. That left Speaker Nancy Pelosi no other option but to move forward with her contingency plan: a House Select Committee, which she could establish without the approval of McCarthy or McConnell.

With McCarthy now re-tethered to Trump, the response from House Republicans was predictable: Virtually all of them denounced the Select Committee except for two, Rep. Cheney and Rep. Adam Kinzinger, both of whom Pelosi appointed to the committee. McCarthy branded them "Pelosi Republicans." The Republican National Committee censured them. Within a little over a year, both would be out of politics. Cheney was ousted by a Trump-backed challenger, and Kinzinger read the writing on the wall and opted not to run again.

Over an eighteen-month period starting in the summer of 2021, the Select Committee conducted an exhaustive investigation cataloging not only the events of January 6th but also tracing the full arc of the conspiracy to overturn the 2020 presidential election with forensic precision. At the outset, Thompson appointed Cheney vice chair, an acknowledgment that her leadership would anchor the committee's claims to bipartisan credibility. Committee members and staff interviewed more than a thousand witnesses, subpoenaed records, combed through over a million documents, and pieced together a timeline that revealed not just the chaos, but the planning and coordination.

The committee's ten public hearings were tightly scripted, visually immersive, and relentlessly focused on Trump. Using video montages, live testimony, and damning excerpts from depositions, the committee laid bare the mechanics of the attempted coup. On December 19, 2022, the committee took the unprecedented step of referring a former president—Donald J. Trump—to the Department of Justice for criminal prosecution on recommended charges of obstructing an official proceeding, conspiracy to defraud the United States, conspiracy to make false statements, and incitement of insurrection. Three days later, the committee released its final, meticulously sourced 845-page report.

Throughout the investigation and the public rollout of the final report, Liz Cheney led with poise and grit. She stood tall. She told the truth. Just not all of it.

This chapter reveals one of the most wrongheaded and consequential political cover-ups in recent history: the deliberate erasure of Christian nationalism from the January 6th committee report. Scrubbing Christian nationalism from the final report wasn't just a lapse in candor and courage; it was a major security blunder that left our country more vulnerable to what has now become America's most dangerous political movement. Cheney's stubborn demand, and the committee's acquiescence to it, provides a potent case study in the power and peril of Christian privilege. America's default deference to all things Christian clouds our judgment, obscures the truth, and especially in this moment of rising Christian nationalist extremism, makes us less safe.

EVIDENCE OF CHRISTIAN NATIONALISM turned up throughout the Select Committee's investigation. At the very first hearing on July 27, 2021, Capitol Police Officer Daniel Hodges described the chilling religious fervor of the rioters who attacked him: "The terrorists perceived themselves to be Christians," Hodges testified. "I saw the Christian flag directly to my front. Another read 'Jesus Is My Savior, Trump Is My President.' Another, 'Jesus Is King.'" Officer Hodges was just the start. The public record teemed with evidence that Christian nationalist extremists, including faith leaders tied to NAR, played a central role in the insurrection.

And it wasn't just witnesses and committee investigators unearthing this connection. Social media was flooded with images and analysis from journalists, academics, and concerned citizens using the hashtag #CapitolSiegeReligion. Among them was Peter Manseau, historian of religion and curator at the Smithsonian's National Museum of American History. Just days after the riot, he posted: "I'm convinced [religion] is the story of what happened. . . . Not everyone wore a Guns & God hoodie or carried a Jesus flag, but they all shared the psychological safety net such symbols provided."

As the Select Committee's investigation gathered steam, the Smithsonian—partnering with the University of Alabama's Department of Religious Studies—launched a sweeping online exhibit titled "Uncivil Religion" to mark the one-year anniversary of January 6th. The exhibit compiled hundreds of photos, videos, and other evidence to show that religion was anything but incidental; they described it as "a thread that weaves through the entirety" of the insurrection.

This vast digital archive was shared with the committee, as were many other testimonies about the unmistakable role of Christian nationalism. The Freedom From Religion Foundation submitted six pages of testimony, accompanied by fifty pages of meticulously annotated appendices drawn heavily from the Uncivil Religion exhibit. Their message was blunt and urgent:

> This committee must investigate the role Christian Nationalism played in fomenting and justifying this attack. The committee cannot ignore Christian Nationalism or treat it with timorous indifference simply because there are religious aspects to this identity. Of course, government officials must be careful to not trespass on true religious freedom. But we must be just as careful not to go too far in the other direction. We must not ignore genuine threats for fear of the false cries of persecution. An unwillingness to investigate and discuss Christian Nationalism as a driver of this attack, for whatever reason, only increases the likelihood of a repeat attack.

Christian faith groups echoed the warning. On June 2, 2022, a coalition called Christians Against Christian Nationalism, including denominational leaders from several faith traditions, submitted pointed testimony asking the committee to thoroughly investigate the role that Christian nationalism played in the attack. The faith coalition emphasized that confronting Christian nationalism is not "anti-Christian," nor does it mean "banishing religion or religious people from the public square." Attached to their letter was a comprehensive report detailing the right-wing Christian networks involved in the insurrection and the religious events and rallies leading up to it.

Yet none of this information made it into the Select Committee's final 845-page report. Amazingly, the report conspicuously avoids discussion of anything involving religion or Christianity, including the glaring throughline of Christian nationalism.

What did make it into the report? There were specific sections for white nationalists, Proud Boys, Oath Keepers, QAnon, Three Percenters, and Trump's merry prankster Roger Stone, but nothing about their Christian nationalist beliefs and entanglements with Christian nationalist networks. And not a single mention of NAR. Nothing about Dutch Sheets and his team of fourteen apostles and prophets who went to the White House on December 29 for an "amazing" and "very strategic" two-hour meeting with high-level officials. Nothing about how they bunked at The Willard, the same hotel where Trump's insurrection brain trust—including Giuliani, Bannon, Stone, and Eastman—had set up war rooms. Nothing about the three dozen NAR-affiliated faith leaders documented at or near the Capitol on January 6th.

Search the report for "Christian nationalist" and you'll find one lonely reference: a passing mention on page 521 of Nick Fuentes and his "Groyper" movement, noting their promotion of "white supremacist and Christian nationalist beliefs." But that passing reference failed to mention that Fuentes is a Rad Trad and his hostility to democracy is rooted in Catholic integralism.

In other places, the report detours around the subject of religion even when the evidence screams for inclusion. Take Michael Sparks, the first rioter to breach the Capitol. The report notes cryptically that he had "expressed a desire to kill people." But the source it cites—*The Washington Post*—reveals something far more specific: Sparks's social media posts in the weeks leading up to the riot were a volatile cocktail of Trump, Jesus, prophecy, and Christian nationalism:

> Nov. 8: damning liberals like Joe Biden as "strait evil who only think of the present and who *don't acknowledge eternity*";
> Dec. 3: praising Trump: "*God has put you where you are*";
> Dec. 16: "We're getting ready to live through *something of biblical proportions* be *prayed up* and be ready to defend your country and your family and the United States of America."

The committee staff clearly read the article, but someone chose to ignore the theology. It's as if the drafters of the report were under a specific order not to say *anything* about religion, Christianity, or Christian nationalism.

Because they were.

How that happened is an untold story that played out entirely behind the scenes. It began in the fall of 2022, as the Select Committee raced to finish its comprehensive report before year's end. That deadline, originally self-imposed, suddenly became existential. Republicans had won enough seats in the November midterms to flip control of the House. When the new majority was sworn in on January 3, 2023, Kevin McCarthy would likely become Speaker and the committee would be terminated. Everything the committee had built was at risk of being buried or erased unless the report was finalized and released before time ran out.

As the deadline loomed, committee staff split into color-coded drafting teams, each assigned a major topic. The Gold Team tackled Trump. Green followed the money trail behind the insurrection. Blue focused on law enforcement and the intelligence community. And the Purple Team was tasked with right-wing radicalism and extremist groups, including Christian nationalism.

The Purple Team followed the leads that witnesses, faith groups, and religious liberty advocates had given them. They tracked the role of right-wing Christian extremists, the radicalization pipelines, the network of faith leaders embedded in the insurrection, and the profusion of religion at the Capitol that day. According to multiple committee members I spoke with, the Purple Team's internal report contained extensive documentation and analysis of these dynamics. Chairman Bennie Thompson told me, "We asked the Purple Team to look into the role of religion in what happened, and they came back with a report that shows those people, right-wing Christian extremists, actually had a lot to do with it."

Then came the veto.

Liz Cheney made it clear: That part of the Purple Team's work would not see daylight. Everyone understood her value: Her imprimatur gave the final report bipartisan credibility. That's why she had been named vice chair. And she knew it.

Every Democrat admired Cheney's grit and courage in standing up to Trump, and many praised her for it. Publicly, the committee projected seamless unity. Privately, however, Cheney's abrasive leadership style caused friction. Some described her approach charitably as "hands-on"—a constant push to keep the team on track, meet deadlines, and maintain focus on Trump. Others were less flattering, calling her imperious and more concerned about positioning herself for a 2024 presidential run than telling the full story of January 6th.

What everyone understood, however, was that anything Cheney vetoed was out.

Cheney's objection to the Purple Team's write-up on Christian extremism was strategic and absolute. According to members of the committee, she thought it would distract from the central narrative of Trump's personal culpability. Any criticism of right-wing Christians, she warned, would be weaponized by Fox News and conservative media to discredit the entire report and alienate millions of ordinary Christians. Kinzinger, with characteristic bluntness, summed up her argument: It would be like "lighting a cigarette in a bomb factory."

But not everyone agreed. Reps. Jamie Raskin and Pete Aguilar supported the Purple Team's report. Chairman Thompson argued for including it. Committee staff fought hard to keep it in. Even if it didn't center on Trump, they insisted, it was essential to understanding the forces that animated January 6th and to present a complete and accurate record to help prevent something like this from ever happening again. Kinzinger wanted it in, too. Perhaps more than anyone else on the committee, he grasped the prophetic fervor that drove the siege. As a lifelong evangelical, he recognized the theology pulsing through the crowd. "It was just dripping thick," he said. Christian nationalism, in his words, wasn't merely "a big part" of the insurrection: "I think it was *all* of it. Right? I think it was *all* of it."

But Cheney would not budge. According to Chairman Thompson, "We tried. We left it out there to debate for a good while, but there just wasn't going to be consensus and so it was one of the few issues we decided not to address—it was left on the cutting room floor." Facing a looming deadline and with no real alternative, the committee relented. There would be no religion in the January 6th committee report. That part of the insurrection was buried, not because it lacked relevance, but because it was the proverbial cigarette in the bomb factory: just too damn explosive.

"It probably should have been in there," Kinzinger said, adding with some amusement that "we were rushing at the very end. I'm surprised there weren't a shitload of typos in that thing because it was a panic to put together." Aguilar was circumspect: "It wasn't worth compromising the bipartisan nature" of the report. And, as both Aguilar and Kinzinger acknowledge, Cheney made some valid points about how it would be perceived.

"Think about how Fox News works," Kinzinger told me. "You could put out this thick compelling book on January 6th and say it was Trump's fault, and then there's this tiny couple pages about Christian nationalism in there, and Fox News—the people we actually would like to turn the most (which we didn't, but if you could)—they would focus on that thing. And then that becomes the report: They say it's attacking Christians." He pointed to Barack Obama's 2008 remark about economic despair causing some Americans to "cling to guns or religion," a line instantly weaponized against him, even by Hillary Clinton. "Obama wasn't attacking religion," Kinzinger noted, but the backlash was swift and enduring. "The second you put the word Christian in there," suddenly you're on defense.

Even with the risks, if it had been up to Kinzinger, those findings would have made the final cut, accompanied by a careful distinction between the violent Christian zealots that fueled the Capitol mob and the millions of decent, devout Americans who are not radicalized. He thinks it could have been framed "from a perspective of compassion—here's how these people got there, this is why they've been misled to believe things and have so much passion." Kinzinger knows sometimes you just have to do the right thing and absorb the blowback. "I always say it like, I'm still a Christian. I've spent probably a quarter of my time now attacking Christian nationalism. And there are so many people that think I am now attacking Christianity, when in reality, I actually think I'm defending the *real* Christianity."

I wasn't surprised that Cheney prioritized goodwill with conservative Christians over telling the full story of January 6th. Back in January 2019, as the 116th Congress was finalizing committee rules under the new Democratic majority, I supported scrapping a dusty relic from the Natural Resources Committee: a rule requiring all witnesses to swear a religious oath affirming belief in God before testifying. It was a clear constitutional violation. But Cheney and future Speaker Mike Johnson responded with a full-blown sanctimony parade on right-wing media, accusing me of "trying to remove God." Cheney delivered the snark-de-gras, telling Fox News: "We'll be praying for him."

It was a revealing window into her worldview, in which Christian faith can be used as a cudgel against political adversaries and an instrument of performative piety on Fox News. Cheney reportedly had presidential ambitions at the time the report was being drafted. She was fine with the Purple Team's discussion of other extremist groups and individuals—she was prepared to incur their wrath. But she did not want to be branded "anti-Christian" on Fox News. Beyond that raw political calculation, it's possible that her cultural affinity for conservative Christianity blinded her to the key role it played in the insurrection. Or perhaps, as Chairman Thompson assessed, it was just her "basic conservatism." Whatever the reason, Cheney was immovable. The decision was made.

None of this played out in public. The only glimpse of internal friction at the committee came in a *Washington Post* story, where fifteen staffers aired their frustration with Cheney's heavy-handed control and her insistence that the final report remain narrowly focused on Trump. They believed vital findings were being excluded, findings that could have helped the American people understand the full scope of the threat, including "important findings unrelated to Trump." When anonymous staffers criticized Cheney's editorial control, her response—via spokesperson Jeremy Adler—brushed off the Christian nationalism issue with a defensive barb about "liberal biases" and "sociological issues outside the scope of the Select Committee's work." Casting the kerfuffle as a secular smear campaign, Adler defended Cheney's refusal to endorse any "narrative" suggesting that "every American who believes God has blessed America is a white supremacist."

To their credit, Kinzinger and Raskin spoke out publicly about their concerns throughout the investigation. Raskin repeatedly cited the role of "white Christian nationalism" in the insurrection during public appearances. Kinzinger went further, calling out Christian nationalists in his own party as the "American Taliban." When the final report failed to mention Christian nationalism at all, he voiced his disappointment publicly. "Had there not been some of these errant prophecies, this idea that God has ordained it to be Trump, I'm not sure January 6 would have happened like it did."

Kinzinger would later tell me, "I do think this is an area where we missed it. And now I feel like I'm kind of personally on my own playing catch up with trying to make people aware of how powerful this stuff really is." The Smithsonian's Peter Manseau echoed that lament, suggesting the final report's "scant attention" to "the religious dimensions of the attack . . . may prove a disservice to history."

Mainstream Christian leaders called the omission a "missed opportunity" to educate people of faith about the danger of Christian nationalism. Scholars Dr. Bradley Onishi and Dr. Matthew Taylor went further, calling it a dangerous mistake "rooted in politics and the privileged status of the Christian majority in the US." Instead of being held accountable or disempowered for their role in January 6th, they argued, violent religious extremists like NAR were allowed to emerge stronger, "advertising themselves as a ready-made force for the next leader willing to activate them."

If Christian privilege caused the Select Committee to pull punches and look the other way, what other institutional failures are we missing? Were security mistakes on January 6th compounded by the default setting to give Christian extremists—even those with known violent elements—a pass?

In the aftermath of January 6th, Buzzfeed News filed a Freedom of Information Act lawsuit to unearth details about the permits Capitol Police had approved for demonstrations that day. Buzzfeed's litigation revealed that five of the six permits for the Capitol complex—including one right outside my office—went to groups that evoked God and religion in their names or mission statements. Three of them were directly tied to NAR, which had been openly stoking violent incitement for months. These red-flag permit applications had been rubber-stamped by Capitol Police like they were for a garden club. At the perfunctory security briefing for our Democratic Caucus on the morning of January 6th, we weren't even told about them.

SOCIAL SCIENTISTS WHO STUDY Christian privilege describe it as a kind of culture reflex that manifests in several ways: a default resistance to criticizing anything "Christian"; a tendency to conflate structural favoritism with earned merit; and a cultural taboo so strong that even naming Christian privilege is treated as sacrilege. According to experts, Christian privilege operates across societal, institutional, and interpersonal domains, where Christian dominance dictates norms, shapes policy, and influences education and culture in subtle ways that masquerade as neutrality or tradition. But outside of academia, there's little awareness about the extent of Christian privilege and how it stifles honest critique.

Americans are very good at diagnosing dangerous extremism so long as it comes from "the other." If a Muslim man commits violence, authorities raid first and ask questions later. What mosque radicalized him? Is he part of a movement? We mobilize vast security and intelligence resources to dissect the threat, trace its roots, and prevent its recurrence. But when violent extremists come clutching a cross, we look away. Those who do investigate are instantly shamed as "anti-Christian."

This is how Christian privilege works. To avoid threatening the status quo, we minimize or ignore real threats, and the institutions tasked with protecting us are rendered less vigilant, less objective, and at times pressured into outright paralysis. The Select Committee's erasure of Christian nationalism was a textbook example of that kind of malignant privilege.

And it isn't an isolated failure—it is part of a long line of megachurch-sized fumbles that left Americans less safe. Christian privilege allowed the most notorious Soviet spy in FBI history, for example, to evade scrutiny while selling America's most sensitive national security secrets. Special Agent Robert Hanssen was a devout Catholic who flexed his faith to fit in with senior FBI colleagues. Over a two-decade period starting in 1979, Hanssen sold over six thousand classified documents revealing US nuclear strategy, advanced weapons systems, counterintelligence protocols, and the identities of Soviet informants, some of whom were executed. Hanssen displayed obvious red flags: unexplained wealth, suspicious computer activity, obsession with surveillance, requests for roles with access to sensitive data, and erratic behavior. He even confessed some of his crimes to a priest. But his betrayal went undetected at the FBI largely because his obsessive religiosity was mistaken for moral rectitude—proof, in the eyes of his peers, that he was beyond reproach. It wasn't until a Russian intelligence officer sold the FBI a secret dossier in 2000 that Hanssen was finally identified and caught.

Few Americans have ever heard of Hanssen, and fewer still know the role religion and Christian privilege played in his story. Like the erasure of Christian nationalism from the Select Committee's report, it has been quietly omitted from the public reckoning. But if Hanssen had been Muslim, Congress would still be holding hearings, the FBI would still be wiretapping the mosque that "radicalized" him, and cable news would still be dissecting his religious rationalizations with forensic zeal. But he was a good Catholic, and that's different.

As Hanssen's story illustrates, our federal law enforcement has long had a blind spot for traitors or extremists who seem "just like them": white, Christian, affluent, and not otherwise marked as "other." Nevertheless, in the 1990s the FBI did take the threat of Christian-influenced right-wing militias seriously. As Taylor recalls, "The joke was, by the end of the '90s, half the people at a Klan meeting were undercover FBI agents or informants." After 9/11, however, the FBI pivoted almost entirely to the War on Terror. Domestic counterterrorism resources were focused almost exclusively on Muslims—monitoring mosques, charities, and immigrant communities. In Taylor's view, this shift "caused agencies to lose their muscle memory for tracking Christian and far-right threats." By the time of the first Trump administration, warnings about Christian nationalist extremism from experts like Elizabeth Neumann were brushed aside. Under the second Trump administration, tracking right-wing domestic terror threats simply stopped.

Simple math reveals the absurdity of prioritizing extremist threats from Muslims over their Christian counterparts. Taylor estimates that violent radicalization, the kind that could spur terrorist acts or hate crime, affects about 1 percent of both the Islamic and Christian faiths in this country. Which means there is a potential pool of 2.1 million radicalized Christians in our nation—who are unmonitored—versus 40,000 potentially radicalized Muslims, where nearly all federal resources are concentrated. The math isn't just lopsided; it's a case study in how Christian privilege is distorting our national security priorities.

Obviously, most Christians are not extremists. Many are appalled by the desecration of their faith. But the same can be said of Muslims. When we refuse to name the threat of Christian nationalist extremism, we don't just protect the feelings of the faithful; we protect our illusions, at a terrible cost.

Terrorism is defined as using or threatening violence to instill fear or coerce governments or societies in pursuit of political, religious, or ideological goals. The religious rioters on January 6th and those who radicalized and mobilized them are Christian terrorists. But the media, most of my congressional colleagues, and, I imagine, most Americans would bristle at that term. Why? If the attackers had worn hijabs it would be easy. The Select Committee's report would have dissected their every religious connection with surgical precision. Politicians would have demanded every imam in America denounce the attack in triplicate. Cable news would still be asking what role Islam played. But because the attackers carried Bibles instead of Qur'ans, we called it complicated, a distraction, anything but what it was.

There is real urgency in overcoming this taboo. Across America, many conservative churches and ministries are so saturated with political grievance and raw partisanship that they function more like MAGA political temples than houses of worship. And some of them blur the lines between faith, politics, and armed rebellion.

Pastor Ken Peters, for example, oversees a half-dozen self-styled "Patriot Churches" where Trump is exalted alongside God and Jesus. Peters portrays himself and other right-wing pastors as modern heirs to the so-called Black Robe Regiment, a wholly invented Christian nationalist myth that imagines colonial pastors commanding militias in the American Revolution. His preaching invokes apocalyptic themes and urges congregants to arm themselves in preparation for violent spiritual battle. Meanwhile in Pennsylvania, Pastor Sean Moon of Rod of Iron Ministries sports a gold AR-15 and wears a crown made of bullet casings. His sermons demonize Democrats and depict Jesus as an assault weapons booster. But the main functions of this unusual church, which the Southern Poverty Law Center describes as an antigovernment gun cult, seem to be offering survivalist classes that teach Christians marksmanship and self-defense, and staging partisan political rallies that platform Republican candidates alongside MAGA power players like Steve Bannon, Mike Flynn, and Sebastian Gorka.

Here lies another hidden cost of Christian privilege: American taxpayers subsidize this charade of partisan extremism and violence with tax-exempt status. We would never allow a mosque to operate this way. But it's easier for institutions and officials to look the other way and pretend these are legitimate "churches" than incur the wrath of powerful Christians by enforcing the legal requirement that houses of worship, if they want to be exempt from taxation, must refrain from partisan politics.

NO HONEST RECKONING with Christian privilege would be complete without turning the lens inward toward my own political party. Before doing so, however, I need to be clear: Democrats have some problems with Christian privilege, but it's fundamentally unlike what we see in the GOP, a party co-opted by and fused with Christian nationalism. The ranks of senior Republicans include extremists who seem just as eager to jettison democracy as Dutch Sheets, Doug Wilson, or Nick Fuentes. I don't know a single Democrat who dreams of replacing secular democracy with a "biblically sanctioned government" as Speaker Mike Johnson does. And there's no trace of Seven Mountains dominion theology among Democrats, in my experience. Every Democrat I know supports some kind of meaningful separation between church and state.

Another key distinction is religious diversity. Republicans in Congress are a Christian monolith: 100 percent of senators and 98 percent of House members are Christian. The GOP's only claim to religious diversity is uneasily tolerating a few conservative Jews, such as Florida's Rep. Randy Fine, who fits in by spewing anti-Muslim vitriol, including demanding that all "mainstream Muslims" be deported and labeling Muslim members of Congress as "terrorists." Democrats are far more reflective of America's actual religious mosaic. Our House Democratic caucus includes not only devout Christians and Jews, but also Muslims,

Hindus, a Buddhist, and a smattering of agnostics and infidels like me. Most of my Democratic colleagues practice their faith without proselytizing, legislate without sermonizing, and honor the spiritual autonomy of others, all of which I admire.

A good example is House Democratic Leader (and future Speaker) Hakeem Jeffries, a devout Christian who's attended Cornerstone Baptist Church in Brooklyn his entire life. At a Democratic Caucus meeting in the spring of 2024, he delivered a soaring speech urging support for military aid to Ukraine. He drew a historic parallel to Hitler's aggression in the late 1930s, and quoted FDR's famous "Four Freedoms" address in which Roosevelt declared we fight "so each man can worship God the way they want." At that point, Jeffries paused and added with sincerity: "Or in Jared's case, the right to *not* worship God." Laughter rippled through the room, including from several closeted nonbelievers who later joked, "If he only knew how many of us there are." I've had many similar, good-natured exchanges with former Speaker Nancy Pelosi, a devout Catholic who often waxed poetic about saints, angels, and papal blessings—and then, usually looking at me, would note her respect for the other faith perspectives in our caucus. Even when the acknowledgment of nonbelievers is an afterthought, I appreciate the gestures of respect and inclusion that I regularly see from my colleagues.

At a 2024 fundraising dinner for the Democratic Congressional Campaign Committee, Pelosi and Jeffries were asked by one of the guests how Democrats planned to win over voters of faith. They each gave anodyne answers. Then Pelosi surprised me by asking me to stand and offer my thoughts. I told the group I thought Democrats should stand for religious freedom, but not any one religion, and that the growing nonreligious community deserves equal respect. I added that rooting policy in facts and reason should be a core value, and that defending secular government, as the founders did, isn't anti-faith; it's pro-democracy. More than a few attendees thanked me afterward for putting it in those terms and I felt, as I often do, grateful to be in a political party that respects diversity and pluralism.

But Christian privilege still rears its righteous head among Democrats. Sometimes it's a colleague whose faith blinds them to attacks on church-state separation. Sometimes it's the quiet complicity with "theocracy lite": the failure to see how Christian nationalism threatens democracy and fundamental rights. I've been dismayed to see fellow Democrats sign on to a letter promoting a bigoted right-wing pastor's Capitol Bible study (only to learn how toxic the pastor is and sheepishly withdraw). Others have lent legitimacy by co-hosting the Congressional Prayer Breakfast even as Speaker Johnson turned it into a Christian nationalist spectacle. And four of my Democratic colleagues continue to enjoy discounted rent and amenities provided by the scandal-plagued right-wing Christian group known as "The Family." These things frustrate me not because my colleagues are Christian, but because they sometimes forget that pluralism and church-state separation aren't just talking points.

My greatest recurring frustration with fellow Democrats is how some still operate from a 1980s playbook on religion and politics, seemingly unaware that the terrain has shifted beneath our feet. Republicans have spent decades constructing their own version of Christianity, turning it into a defining feature of the modern GOP, and weaponizing it to advance an increasingly anti-democracy agenda. Yet too many Democrats are unwilling to see that, or they cling to the notion that the only way to win elections is to project more Christian religiosity, authentic or not, in hopes of competing with the GOP for voters of faith. Some Democratic colleagues seem almost embarrassed that our party doesn't preach Christian faith as a central political plank. They appear oblivious to the fact that polls show voters don't want sermons and religiosity from politicians.

A prime example of this disconnect came at our Democratic Issues Conference (our annual caucus retreat) in the spring of 2025. A panel of top pollsters and political consultants was presenting the latest data, focus group insights, and messaging analysis to help congressional Democrats understand what went wrong in the 2024 election and how to recalibrate our message. One of the panelists was John Anzelone, a veteran pollster who'd worked for Hillary Clinton in 2016 and Biden in 2020. Democrats pay people like Anzelone for empirical, data-driven advice. And after the sting of the 2024 presidential loss, we needed it.

But as the panel wrapped up, Anzelone tossed out a final thought: "One more thing—I just need to say that Democrats tend to vilify

One of several large wooden crosses erected near the east steps of the Capitol on January 6, 2021, with evangelical worshippers joining in prayer before the violent insurrection erupted. *(Getty Images)*

Two evangelical Christians blowing shofars on the east side of the Capitol the morning of January 6, 2021, signaling that the "Jericho March" promoted by the New Apostolic Reformation and its allies was getting underway. Note the Hebrew prayer shawl worn by the woman on the left, a telltale sign of Christian Zionism. *(Lloyd Wolf)*

Christian nationalist symbols on the west side of the Capitol, where barricades were overrun and the building was breached. Note the "Appeal to Heaven" flag behind the banner proclaiming "Jesus Is My Savior, Trump Is My President." *(Lloyd Wolf)*

Followers of white nationalist and Rad Trad integralist Nick Fuentes revel in the mayhem as the Capitol is breached. The green "Kek" flag is one of the alt-right memes promoted by Fuentes's "Groyper" movement. Fuentes himself stood nearby, shouting encouragement to the rioters with a bullhorn. *(Evelyn Hockstein)*

Evangelical pastors pray over Trump in the Oval Office on March 18, 2025, led by televangelists Robert Jeffress and Paula White standing just to Trump's left. White boasted during Trump's first presidency of surrounding him with prominent evangelicals "to make sure that door and that access continues for people of faith." In the second Trump presidency, White leads a newly created White House Faith Office and serves on Trump's Commission on Religious Liberty. *(White House Press Office)*

Apostle Lance Walnau of the New Apostolic Reformation helped catapult Trump to victory in 2016 by promoting the prophecy that God had annointed Trump as the modern-day King Cyrus to save his chosen people. Walnau promoted it relentlessly, including writing the book *God's Chaos Candidate* and selling special gold coins depicting Trump and Cyrus. *(John Fea)*

Days after becoming Speaker of the House in the fall of 2024, Mike Johnson welcomed prominent Christian nationalist leaders to the Capitol for a private tour and prayer moment in Statuary Hall. To the left is Kelly Shackelford, president of the First Liberty Institute where Johnson formerly worked as an attorney, and David Barton, whom Johnson cites as a "profound influence" in everything he does. Shackleford was appointed to Trump's Commission on Religious Liberty in January of 2025.

With help from Speaker Johnson, David Barton leads special Capitol tours for hundreds of pastors and ministry leaders twice a year, including VIP access to Statuary Hall and meetings with top GOP leaders from the House and Senate.

people of faith." No data. No examples. Just a vague indictment hanging in the air. I found Anzelone afterward in the lobby and asked what he meant by claiming Democrats "vilify people of faith." Did he have any data, or even a single example, to back that up? No, he admitted. It was just his *sense* as a person of faith that a lot of Democrats *feel* that way. Exasperated, I pressed him on what nonreligious "nones" like me, the largest and fastest-growing religious group in America, should *feel* about such a baseless assumption delivered as expert advice to the entire House Democratic caucus? He cut me off: "I think we're done here."

This interaction underscored that Democrats are not immune to Christian privilege—embodied, in this case, by Anzelone's temerity in telling a roomful of Democratic members of Congress that we "vilify people of faith," knowing full well he couldn't cite a single example. I suspect Anzalone is nostalgic for the era of Christian political hegemony, when both parties tacitly endorsed his faith as a semiofficial national religion. And I suspect he's unsettled by the way Republicans now weaponize that nostalgia to paint Democrats as hostile to Christians.

But Democrats can't allow nostalgia and a perception of lost status—elements of Christian privilege—to cloud our judgment. Nor should Democrats avoid talking about religion out of deference to Christian privilege, as I see all too often from colleagues who feel afraid to speak candidly, reluctant to even name the scourge of Christian nationalism, even when it attacks them, for fear of offending people of faith, or worse, being branded anti-Christian.

America, Democrats included, is overdue for a candid national reckoning with Christian privilege. For most of the last two and a half centuries, Christianity presided comfortably as the religious and cultural default. The secular guardrails of our Constitution were invoked rarely, and unevenly, for most of our history. That legacy has left us with a reflex so deeply engrained that even today, even with all the damage it inflicts, our Christian privilege distorts our politics and leads us to coddle, ignore, and subsidize violent religious extremism.

We've already encountered various facets of Christian privilege: in the security fumbles leading up to January 6th; in the swaggering arrogance of Pete Hegseth's Pentagon prayer service and the Catholic League's attack-dog tactics when the FBI dared to scrutinize Rad

Trad extremism; in the brash revisionism of Trump's Commission on Religious Liberty; and in the zombie theocracy that lingered in states long after the First Amendment was ratified. Christian privilege enabled Robert Hanssen's espionage and abetted Liz Cheney's erasure of Christian nationalism from the Select Committee's report. It will surface again in the chapters ahead, most starkly when we examine the influence of prophetic Christian beliefs (Christian Zionism) on American foreign policy.

Saving democracy from Christian nationalism requires us to recognize that Christian privilege is all around us, not just in our institutions but sometimes in our own assumptions and judgments. We must dare to break taboo and give Christian extremism the same serious scrutiny we apply to other virulent threats. When it causes harm, we must name it and defend others who do so. We cannot allow extremists to shut down debate by simply branding their critics "anti-Christian." We must be willing to bear the discomfort of their false accusations, because we know that calling out violence, hatred, and privilege is not an attack on faith. It is protecting true religious freedom for all faith perspectives.

Right now, that precious freedom is more imperiled than most Americans realize. We'll peel back another layer of the threat in the next chapter by going inside the Capitol and illuminating how the Christian nationalist movement is building momentum through a shadow theocracy operating behind the scenes at the highest levels of government.

CHAPTER 6

THE SHADOW THEOCRACY

IF YOU VISIT THE UNITED STATES CAPITOL, I RECOMMEND starting with the free tour offered by the Capitol Visitor Center. It's a great way to take in the building's history and grandeur: the ornate halls, the rotunda's frescoes, statues, and paintings of historic figures. Friendly tour guides explain the machinery of government, including how Congress works with the other branches to sustain our constitutional order and protect our rights.

But on any given day, there's another story unfolding in the Capitol that the official tour doesn't cover. Once you know what to look for, you see elements of it everywhere, coursing through the marble corridors, hustling in and out of offices and conference rooms. The Capitol complex teems with Christian nationalist power players, faith leaders, religious networks, advocacy groups, and a steady wave of religious programs converging with a common purpose: to embed right-wing Christian influence in government and manifest biblical dogma into policy.

This chapter takes you inside Washington to expose what I call the shadow theocracy: the diffuse matrix of Christian nationalist operatives working to thread their religion into the institutions and daily workings of government in order to establish dominion, just as their theology commands. It's not a single coherent structure with titles and org charts, nor is it an outright theocracy—not yet. But these theocratic crusaders are deeply entrenched at the highest levels, pushing America ever closer to official Christian rule. These days, you can't swing a shofar without hitting some aspect of it: prayer meetings, Bible studies, pastoral briefings, staff trainings, and more, happening across the Capitol every day in open defiance of the Constitution's wall of separation between church and state. In fact, it now stares back at me when I open my office door.

In early 2025, as I arrived at my office on the third floor of the Rayburn building, I noticed a new flag across the hallway in front of Republican Congressman David Rouzer's office. I don't think of David as a religious firebrand. He's a mild-mannered business conservative from North Carolina who's friendly and pleasant to work with. Which is why the flag surprised me. I immediately recognized the stark white background with a simple green pine tree and the words "An Appeal to Heaven." That flag is more than a decorative flourish: It has become the battle standard of Christian nationalism.

For the past decade, the "Appeal to Heaven" flag has been aggressively promoted by NAR apostle Dutch Sheets. Sheets and his allies tout it as both a symbol of America's Christian founding and an emblem of the theocratic ambition central to NAR's Seven Mountains Mandate. Dozens of rioters carried it on January 6th when they stormed the Capitol.

I pointed out Rouzer's flag to one of my staffers and quipped that we're "sleepwalking to Gilead." The reference, only half joking, was to the dystopic theocracy depicted in Margaret Atwood's 1985 novel, *The Handmaid's Tale*. Atwood's story of fearful and distracted Americans drifting into the grip of religious tyranny before realizing what hit them has chilling resonance for me because, as Atwood has acknowledged in interviews, she didn't conjure Gilead from thin air. She reverse-engineered it from America's real theocratic impulses, our fundamentalist Christian backlash against feminism, civil rights, and modernity, and our ho-hum ambivalence to the dangers of Christian extremism.

One of Rouzer's aides walked past, visibly annoyed. "Don't you know that flag was flown by George Washington?" she snapped, unaware that I had done my homework. "Actually, that's not true," I called after her as she slipped into Rouzer's office. "And it's the flag of Christian nationalism now," I added as the door closed behind her.

Had the irritated aide given me a chance, I could have explained the flag's real history. Starting with this truth: There's zero evidence it ever flew in Washington's presence. Colonial America's military was a motley patchwork of regiments with no unified iconography. Dozens of quirky regimental and regional flags fluttered across the Revolutionary landscape. One of them was the "Appeal to Heaven" flag, which was commissioned by Washington in 1775, likely without ever even seeing it, for a squadron of six naval vessels in Massachusetts. From that tenuous connection, right-wing Christians have built a myth that Washington himself flew this flag and that this obscure emblem was our nation's true founding credo. This is more proof, they contend, that we were founded as a Christian nation.

Not only does this torture the historic record, it also misunderstands the phrase "appeal to heaven" itself. It wasn't a call for biblical governance. It was lifted straight out of John Locke's *Second Treatise of Government*, a cornerstone of Enlightenment political theory that, like the Declaration of Independence, rejects the biblical "divine right of kings" doctrine under which Europe's theocratic monarchies claimed authority.

Following the Revolutionary era, the flag vanished from public memory for two centuries. That is, until 2015, when Sheets resurrected and repurposed it as a symbol of Christian dominion. Sheets published a book about it and relentlessly incorporated it into sermons, prophecies, and kitschy merchandise until the flag became both a sacred icon of Christian nationalism and a cash cow. Today, you can buy "the first flag of our nation" for $45 on his website, along with "Appeal to Heaven" mugs, T-shirts, and other merch.

I'm not sure if Rouzer or his staff know the Dutch Sheets backstory, if they share NAR's Gilead-like ambitions, or if they care about the fake history tied to this flag. Judging by the frosty reception, they don't want to talk to me about any of it.

But there's no mystery to why "Appeal to Heaven" flags are sprouting up all over Washington these days: Extreme Christian nationalism is pulsing into the mainstream of Republican political identity to the point that even mild-mannered conservatives like Rouzer feel compelled to fly the colors. This flag hangs on the wall of Christ Church

DC, the new Beltway embassy for Pastor Doug Wilson and his Theo Bros. Supreme Court Justice Samuel Alito flew it at his beach house in 2024 until public scrutiny forced its removal and a sheepish attempt to blame it on his wife. I've seen it flying in front of a house a few doors down from my residence near the Capitol. At last count, twenty of my Republican colleagues were flaunting it in front of their Capitol offices—a choreographed tribute that shows how Christian nationalism is on the march in Congress.

The first of my colleagues to hoist the "Appeal to Heaven" flag, however, was Rep. Mike Johnson of Louisiana. Johnson is the member of Congress most devoted to transforming theocratic ambition into the real thing, which he euphemistically calls "biblically sanctioned government." In normal times, a member with his extreme record could never be Speaker of the House. But in the fall of 2023, Johnson breezed into the Speakership with no serious public scrutiny or debate, and Christian nationalism took another giant step into the mainstream. He is now the third-highest ranking elected official in the United States, just two heartbeats away from being president. Johnson not only embodies the Christian nationalist movement's surging momentum; he is leveraging the power of his Speakership to advance the movement's cause in unprecedented ways. For all these reasons, he merits closer examination.

Before becoming Speaker, Johnson was a backup player. To the extent he was known at all, it was for being a deeply ideological, party-line loyalist (dubbed "MAGA Mike" by some). In the weeks leading up to the insurrection, he distinguished himself as the primary legal strategist behind congressional Republicans' failed efforts to overturn the 2020 election results. That role helped him win the support of his colleagues for vice chair of the House GOP conference in 2021.

Johnson's big moment came unexpectedly two years later, when a disgruntled faction inside the GOP's so-called Freedom Caucus, of which Johnson was a member, deposed Speaker Kevin McCarthy. This plunged the House into an unprecedented twenty-two-day leadership vacuum with Republicans unable to rally the votes to either reinstate McCarthy or elevate a successor. During this period of chaos, Johnson says, God began speaking to him about a coming "Red Sea moment."

According to Johnson: "The Lord began to wake me up, through this three-week process, in the middle of the night to speak to me." He initially believed God was preparing to choose a new Moses, and that he—given his junior status—would play the role of Aaron, Moses's brother and key assistant. But when candidate after candidate failed to secure the gavel, Johnson says God gave him a new instruction: "Step forward." As Moses.

Minutes after winning a narrow party-line vote, Johnson stepped up to the dais to give his first speech as Speaker of the House. I knew Johnson was a hardcore evangelical and a Christian nationalist, but I held out hope that the awesome responsibility of being Speaker would temper his extremism. Instead, Johnson's speech leaned hard into the David Barton school of fake history. The Declaration of Independence, he proclaimed, reveals the deeply religious DNA of America's founding, and Thomas Jefferson's use of the word "Creator" proves with "almost theological lucidity" that the United States was "founded upon a creed." Not a good start.

Afterward, Johnson was asked by reporters about the "Appeal to Heaven" flag flying outside his office. He deflected: "It's George Washington's flag. It goes back to the founders' era. I've always flown that flag." But with a little forensic digging, you can trace Johnson's connection to this flag straight to Dutch Sheets. Johnson has very close ties to NAR, including one of Sheets' protégés in Louisiana, the NAR apostle Timothy Carscadden. In 2015, Johnson held his ceremonial swearing-in to the state legislature in Carscadden's Shreveport church. The pastor posted about it on Facebook where his profile picture is—you guessed it—the "Appeal to Heaven" flag. Johnson's attempt to downplay the flag's meaning and hide his entanglements with NAR were another bad sign.

And then it got worse, as Johnson sent a confounding message in one of his first interviews. In response to Fox News host Sean Hannity's softball question about his worldview, Johnson said: "Well, go pick up a Bible off your shelf and read it. That's my worldview." What the heck did *that* mean? That the Bible *informs* his worldview? Or that this ancient religious text—which prescribes death by stoning for anyone who "blasphemes the name of the Lord" (Leviticus 24:10–16), and dictates patriarchy under which women must "submit to your husbands as to the Lord" (Ephesians 5:22–24)—actually *is* his worldview?

Hoping to clarify some of this, Rep. Jamie Raskin and I, on behalf of the Congressional Freethought Caucus, wrote to Johnson a few days later. We congratulated him and cordially invited him to meet with our group to discuss religious freedom and the constitutional separation of church and state. It was a long shot, but we hoped to establish a constructive dialogue at the outset of his tenure and to give him a chance to clarify, or perhaps even reconsider, some of his more controversial views.

When Johnson ignored our request, the Freethought Caucus had no choice but to comb through his record and draw our own conclusions about what his "worldview" portended now that he held the Speaker's gavel. We released a meticulously researched, eleven-page white paper showing that the new Speaker of the House was the most radical religious zealot to hold that powerful office in modern history. But the mainstream media and political establishment treated it as background noise—another signal flare ignored.

The details of Johnson's breathtaking Christian extremism could fill the rest of this chapter and several more, but a few highlights give you the basic picture. Johnson rejects church-state separation outright and has long advocated what he calls "biblically sanctioned government" where the Bible is the "owner's manual" for how everything operates.

He's more subtle than Christian nationalist jackhammers such as my GOP colleague Rep. Lauren Boebert of Colorado, who blurts the quiet part out loud. "I'm tired of this separation of church and state junk," she says. "The church is supposed to direct the government." Johnson holds the same blatantly unconstitutional view, but he cloaks it in lawyerly sleight-of-hand and the reassuring cadence of a Sunday School teacher. He calmly dismisses "so-called church-state separation" as a misunderstanding of the founders' intent. For Johnson, the Establishment Clause is just a paltry restriction on chartering a national church. And the only reason the founders did that, he claims, was to protect *churches* from the government.

Johnson's emasculation of the First Amendment's Establishment Clause is extreme even by the standards of recent GOP leaders who pushed the boundaries of religion in government. Presidents Reagan,

Bush Sr., and Bush Jr. all at least paid lip service to church-state separation. Going back further, Republican presidents like Richard Nixon and Theodore Roosevelt staunchly defended it, and President Ulysses S. Grant passionately aligned himself with Jefferson and Madison in defending secular governance: "Leave the matter of religion to the family altar, the church, and the private schools, supported entirely by private contributions. Keep the church and state forever separate."

Johnson's vision of "biblically sanctioned government" leans heavily on enshrining Old Testament morality codes into law and policy. He is particularly opposed to women's control of their bodies. He has fought against access to contraception and in vitro fertilization (IVF), tried to ban the "holocaust" of abortion nationwide, and advocates prison and hard labor for abortion providers.

The "sin" of gay sex is nothing short of an obsession for Johnson, for reasons I lack the clinical training to diagnose. He supports criminal penalties for consensual gay sex among adults, champions the pseudoscience of conversion therapy, and wants to ban same-sex marriage because, he contends, allowing it creates a slippery slope to pedophilia, bestiality, and eventually civilizational collapse. He authored a federal version of Florida's "Don't Say Gay" law that prevents teachers and students from talking about sexual orientation and gender identity in school. He also advocates legal carve-outs for Christians to discriminate against LGBTQ people and wants to criminalize gender-affirming care.

There's also the issue of marriage. Like many fundamentalist Christians, Johnson opposes modern "no-fault" divorce laws, which allow marriages to be terminated for any reason by mutual consent and have been enacted in all fifty states. He doesn't just preach against it: In Louisiana, Johnson spearheaded legislation to legally enshrine "covenant marriage." For those who choose this religiously inflected marriage contract, it's much harder to get out of a bad marriage. Spouses must justify divorce by proving fault based on narrow, often painful criteria like adultery, abuse, or abandonment. Johnson calls it honoring the biblical marriage covenant; domestic violence experts call it empowering abusive spouses to obstruct their victims' paths to safety.

If you're hearing echoes of medieval Christian tyranny, there's a reason for that. Johnson spent eight formative years as a litigator and national spokesperson for a designated hate group called the Alliance Defending Freedom (ADF). The mission of ADF, and I swear, these are their actual words, is to "recover the robust Christendomic theology of the 3rd, 4th, and 5th centuries." For history buffs, the golden era Johnson's longtime employer strives to recreate was also known as the Dark Ages. Back then, the church didn't just advise the state, it *was* the state. Religious liberty meant you had choices: Convert or die. And the church/state often sponsored fun outdoor events like stoning, heretic hunts, and the warm glow of bonfires for books. That's the old-time religion ADF pines for.

Johnson's moralizing may be medieval, but he welcomes modern surveillance technology to enforce it. The Speaker is a longtime booster of "Covenant Eyes," a tracking app that can monitor every click and scroll on your phone and alert your "accountability partner" anytime you wander into sinful parts of the internet, or even glance at something porn-adjacent, like "a picture of women talking." Using Covenant Eyes, Johnson's phone is linked to his teenage son's phone, so that each receive a steady stream of screenshots from the other's device. Just normal everyday algorithmic chastity enforced by the digital panopticon. Johnson is not sleepwalking; he's running to Gilead. But for anyone who thinks that is hyperbole, I'll concede this point: Gilead *wishes* it had tech like Covenant Eyes.

Johnson has systematically leveraged the power of his Speakership to collapse the boundary between *his* religion and *our* government. Central to that effort is Johnson's strategic elevation of Christian nationalist power players, none more influential than David Barton.

Barton does a lot more for the Christian nationalist movement than churn out "Christian nation" mythology. He's a crusader for mandatory Christian prayer, Bible classes, and postings of the Ten Commandments in public schools. He urges school boards to unilaterally impose these unconstitutional measures in hopes of provoking the golden-ticket court case—the perfect legal challenge that allows the Supreme Court to scrap church-state separation once and for all. He's been a GOP luminary for years, but his access, influence, and power have swelled now that Johnson holds the Speaker's gavel.

Barton gloats about advising the Speaker on staffing decisions and raves that his closeness to Johnson puts new "tools at our disposal." Barton has seized the moment to expand his Christian nationalist indoctrination tours that are now all but co-branded as a de facto extension of the Speaker's office. Twice a year, hundreds of right-wing pastors join Barton in the Capitol for facetime with Speaker Johnson, prayers and political briefings with top congressional Republicans, and VIP access to Statuary Hall where they don wireless headsets to hear Barton regale them with revisionism about the deep religious heritage of America's secular citadel.

His grip on virtually everything the Speaker does is evident not only in the Bartonesque distortions of history woven into Johnson's speeches, but also in the strategic chiseling at church-state separation that began from the outset of his Speakership. One of his first strikes carried unmistakable symbolism: relocating the fledgling Congressional Prayer Breakfast from a backwater meeting room in the Capitol Visitor Center to the main stage of Statuary Hall.

The Congressional Prayer Breakfast is a recent spinoff of its scandal-plagued predecessor, the National Prayer Breakfast. It emerged in 2023 as a supposed clean break from the long-running gathering at the Washington Hilton Hotel hosted by the mysterious Fellowship Foundation, aka "The Family." What began decades ago as a solemn gathering of presidents and members of Congress to pray for the nation devolved over the years into a multiday bazaar of corporate glad-handing, influence peddling, and even espionage. The 2017 Prayer Breakfast featured a cameo by Maria Butina, a Kremlin operative later convicted for using the event as a backchannel to influence US officials. Two years later, the Netflix documentary *The Family* pulled back the curtain, exposing how the Fellowship Foundation's secretive network operates as a hub of covert right-wing Christian influence.

The 2023 rebooted version of the prayer breakfast, according to co-chairs Senators Chris Coons (D-DE) and James Lankford (R-OK), would be low-key, bipartisan, and under congressional control—a firewall against scandal. But this reform came with baggage. Several board members had deep ties to The Family, which had recently been exposed for helping Uganda's dictator enact an anti-homosexuality law that carried the death penalty. And now, Speaker Johnson was ditching the "low-key" promise by moving the event into the spotlight of Statuary Hall.

And so it came to pass that on February 1, 2024, an all-Christian lineup of speakers staged a nationally televised sectarian church service endorsed by Congress. To my dismay, some Democratic colleagues signed on as co-hosts, and President Biden agreed to attend. The message to millions of American Jews, Muslims, Hindus, Buddhists, Sikhs, and secular citizens was unmistakable: This government belongs to Jesus. The House co-chair, Rep. Tracy Mann (R-KS), practically said as much in his prayer: "Gathering in the spirit of Jesus and calling on the Lord in prayer is transformative for this body and is part of our heritage as Americans."

I attended the service wearing a "Entering Gilead" lapel button in protest. I also spoke out publicly, likening it to the wave of religiosity injected into American government during the Cold War to showcase moral superiority over the "godless" Soviet Union. In rapid succession, those changes included the National Day of Prayer (1952), the National Prayer Breakfast (1953), adding the phrase "under God" to the pledge (1954), building a prayer chapel near the Speaker's office (1955), replacing "E Pluribus Unum" with "In God We Trust" as the national motto (1956), and printing our new Godly motto on paper currency (1957).

But I might as well have been talking to the statues in Statuary Hall. The media covered the event as if there was nothing out of the ordinary, focusing on the president's remarks, the bipartisan lineup of speakers, and the musical performance by Andrea Bocelli. Only one journalist bothered to write about my concerns. Most of my congressional colleagues treated it with a shrug.

But Johnson wasn't satisfied with repurposing Statuary Hall for a nationally televised Christian church service; he also wanted to upstage it. The prayer breakfast was far too restrained and bipartisan for the movement-driven Christian nationalists Johnson runs with—people like Tony Perkins, leader of the SPLC-designated hate group Family Research Council; and NAR apostle Jim Garlow, the "profound influence" on Johnson who collaborated with the future Speaker on weekly prayer network calls to mobilize right-wing Christians in the lead-up to January 6th.

Johnson, Perkins, and Garlow had come up with an idea for something bolder to showcase unapologetic MAGA Christian power and unflinchingly denounce evils like abortion, homosexuality, and deviations from biblical gender norms: a revival-style "National Gathering of Prayer and Repentance." They had rolled it out in 2023, but now that Johnson held the Speaker's gavel, the 2024 version could be marketed as conceived and consecrated by the Speaker of the House, elevating it into the GOP's flagship annual religious event. And just to drive the point home, they would schedule it one day before the prayer breakfast.

And lo, a great multitude—including two dozen GOP lawmakers from the House and Senate—did gather at the Museum of the Bible on January 31, 2024, for the Speaker's huge, live-streamed prayer and repentance spectacle. It was headlined by NAR apostle Alma Rivera, whose résumé includes praying over the January 6th rioters during the insurrection. Johnson and his colleagues lent official gravitas by joining Rivera, Garlow, Dutch Sheets, and other prophets onstage for an emotional altar call, begging divine forgiveness for America being such a terrible, sinful, liberal nation. A new Speaker-sanctioned tradition was born.

Johnson also broke new ground as the first Speaker to commandeer the tiny prayer chapel near his office for piety performances with the media. The chapel is a closet-sized room that most members of Congress have never even seen. But soon after becoming Speaker, Johnson squeezed television crews inside and vowed to Fox News' Kayleigh McEnany, "This will be my discipline, to come in here and seek the Lord's guidance for what we do each day."

It's a good thing former Speaker Sam Rayburn wasn't there to see it. Back in the early 1950s when Congress debated installing the little chapel, Rayburn, a Baptist Democrat from Texas, pleaded for modesty and restraint: "I do trust that there will not be a show made of this thing. . . . I trust that never will any motion pictures be taken of members in this room who want to be alone with their God." Republican Richard Poff of Virginia went further, warning that the chapel must never become a stage "through which demagogues and hypocrites can parade their religion." Fast forward seventy years and Johnson was doing exactly that.

He repeated the stunt in May of 2025. Right after the House voted to pass Trump's "One Big Beautiful Bill," Johnson brought the Associated Press into the little chapel and boasted, "Been here a lot this week, right there on my knees. Just praying. . . . That's what the founders did." In a single sound bite, he God-washed a partisan bill that gutted the social safety net to pay for billionaire tax giveaways, retrofitted our rationalist founders into zealots, and crowned himself heir to that fake tradition. It was too much for his fellow Baptist, Rev. Brian Kaylor, who torched the Speaker in an article in *Religion News*: "When Jesus said to go pray in a closet, he didn't mean you should then show it off to Fox News or The Associated Press."

Speaker Mike Johnson is a glaring embodiment of America's tilt toward theocracy. In a functioning democracy with secular guardrails, a congressman with his radical beliefs, unchecked theocratic ambitions, and extreme record would never have breezed into the Speakership. His relentless chiseling at church-state separation would be coming from the fringe of the House Freedom Caucus, not the Speaker's dais. And it would be met with outrage, not shrugs. But our democracy is unwell, our secular guardrails are buckling, and Speaker Johnson is just the most prominent public face of the problem. Behind the scenes in Washington, there is an entire Christian nationalist ecosystem that makes the phenomenon of Speaker Mike Johnson possible.

UNTIL I GOT TO CONGRESS, I had no idea that a constellation of Christian nationalist power brokers and advocacy groups cloaked as "ministries" operates inside the Capitol with a stamp of approval from Congress. This ministry-industrial complex strategically blends prayer, ideological grooming of lawmakers and staff, and political lobbying into a seamless enterprise—recruiting members of Congress to Bible studies and other religious gatherings and then fundraising outside the Beltway by touting their access and proximity to power. Few Americans know that any of this exists, let alone its sweeping reach and quasi-official status. But Republican members of Congress know it intimately.

In 2018, Rep. Barry Loudermilk (R-GA) couldn't resist bragging to the Faith & Freedom Coalition: "How many of you know that we have a church service every Wednesday night right here in the Capitol building?" The crowd nodded like congregants at a revival. He continued: "We have dozens of Bible studies that happen throughout the week. We have ministers that do nothing but walk the halls of the office buildings and drop in and pray with members."

He wasn't exaggerating. Many of these pastors are Capitol regulars, lurking like the lobbyists they essentially are in places like the Rayburn tunnel escalator, where they intercept members in route to votes and hand out pocket-sized invitations to the next Bible study. It's a well-oiled operation. Curiously, they never hand me a card and avoid eye contact—I think they know who I am.

Standing tallest in the ministry-industrial complex is Pastor Ralph Drollinger's Capitol Ministries. At 7'2", Drollinger once towered over opponents on UCLA's championship basketball team. Today, he plays a different kind of inside game, one that pushes his extreme Christian theology into policy by "teaching" political leaders what God wants them to do with their authority. Like Speaker Johnson, Drollinger is a shadow theocracy power player who merits closer attention. Drollinger's twice weekly congressional Bible studies, one in the House, another in the Senate, draw dozens of top GOP lawmakers and staffers. His weekly White House Cabinet Bible Study has been just as popular under the Trump administration. Few figures wield such influence while carrying such a long public trail of bigotry, extremism, and controversy.

Over the course of his long career blurring the line between preaching and lobbying, he's managed to offend nearly everyone who doesn't share his extreme conservative theology—and some who do. I remember meeting Drollinger in Sacramento back in 2008, when I was serving in the California Assembly. Back then, Capitol Ministries was mostly a California operation and Drollinger went through the motions of engaging Democrats. I knew nothing about him beyond his basketball résumé, which is probably why I took his request for a meeting in my office. He assumed I was a Christian (an assumption I didn't rush to correct at that point in my career), and he launched into a pitch about biblical literalism as the necessary moral framework for public policy. I pushed back politely, but firmly. Not long after, Drollinger published a blistering screed in the *Capitol Morning Report* titled "A Chaplain's Worst Nightmare." He railed against a dozen unnamed legislators he'd recently met with, one of whom was Jewish, and another of whom I'm fairly certain was yours truly, declaring that God was "disgusted" with us for "rejecting the Jesus of Scripture."

By 2009, Drollinger's bigotry and ego were burning bridges in every direction. He had infuriated female legislators by declaring that mothers who held jobs outside the home were violating "God's revealed design." He had called homosexuality "an abomination." He had chastised legislators who skipped his prayer sessions for their lack of piety. His fundamentalist ministry had always been an awkward fit in the progressive enclave of Sacramento, but he kept picking public fights with no regard for the fallout. His California operation finally imploded in mass resignations, and the evangelical megachurch affiliated with Capitol Ministries cut ties over his conduct, declaring him "not biblically qualified." Drollinger became a pariah.

But he was resilient. After the California fiasco, he pivoted and expanded Capitol Ministries into other state capitols and, by 2010, into Washington, DC, where he found fertile ground among Republican members of Congress. Within a few years, Drollinger's congressional Bible study had attracted more than sixty sponsors from both the House and Senate. The Sacramento setback had opened a door to something bigger and bolder.

In 2016, Drollinger went all-in for Donald Trump. He claims to have sent Trump copies of his Bible studies during the campaign and that he received friendly notes in return. Drollinger saw Trump as a kindred spirit, someone who shared his authoritarian view that government must "bear the sword" and act as "an avenger of wrath" against evildoers. His bet on Trump paid off when several of his congressional Bible study devotees found their way into cabinet appointments, including Senator Jeff Sessions (attorney general), Rep. Mike Pompeo (CIA director, later secretary of state), and Tom Rice (secretary of health and human services). This allowed Drollinger to add a weekly Bible study for White House officials.

Drollinger's fingerprints began appearing all over public policy. Attorney General Sessions justified Trump's harsh new family separation tactics at the border by citing the Bible's book of Romans, just like Drollinger taught in his Bible study on immigration. Within a few months of each other in 2018, the Departments of Justice and Health and Human Services—two agencies led by his Bible students—issued new guidelines giving religious individuals and organizations leeway to resist government "lifestyle" regulations, echoing Drollinger's hard-line teachings against homosexuality. And Drollinger, who preaches against environmentalism as a sin against God's dominion mandate, surely rejoiced when EPA Administrator Scott Pruitt, fresh off rolling back twenty-two environmental regulations in his first year, told the Christian Broadcasting Network how "wonderful" it was to attend his weekly Bible studies.

In an interview with Christian media, Drollinger boasted about the influence his "ministry" was having on policy, noting that Attorney General Sessions, in particular, will "go out the same day I teach him something and he'll do it on camera. And I just think, man, these guys are faithful, available, and teachable."

Drollinger's influence was peaking in the spring of 2020 with multiple cabinet officials in his weekly Bible studies and policy triumphs continuing to unfold. But his hubris caught up with him again. He published a blog post declaring that COVID-19 was God's punishment for America's "national sin" of homosexuality. It was standard fare for Drollinger, but with the pandemic ravaging communities and roiling the presidential election, the timing was disastrous. National backlash ensued: Public health experts and LGBTQ advocacy groups condemned the statement as dangerous and grotesque; the media pounced, casting Drollinger as a "shadow diplomat" and the "Trump Cabinet's Bible teacher;" and the White House scrambled to contain the fallout. Trump's deputy press secretary disowned the suddenly radioactive Drollinger, denounced his bigoted screed as "disgusting," and claimed with a straight face that Trump knew nothing about the pastor or his Bible study.

Just like that, Drollinger went from spiritual consigliere to political liability. The White House Bible studies quietly disappeared, and a few months later Joe Biden became president.

But Drollinger never really left. He just decamped back to Capitol Hill where congressional Republicans were happy to keep attending his weekly sessions. And when Trump returned to the White House in 2025, so did Drollinger. Capitol Ministries is now stronger than ever, with weekly Bible studies for White House officials, alongside its House and Senate sessions, which are now officially sponsored by Speaker Mike Johnson and Senate President John Thune. Capital Ministries claims to have expanded these "discipleship Bible study" offerings to forty-three state legislatures, local government leaders in nine states, and multiple foreign countries.

Now that Drollinger has elbowed his way back into the Christian nationalist winner's circle, he is once again weaving religious extremism straight into public policy. If you wonder what our nation's top cabinet officials, legislators, and staff are learning each week from their Bible coach, you can find the lessons on Capitol Ministries' website and see for yourself how Drollinger mixes and matches Bible verses to reveal God's conspicuously right-wing political agenda. Beyond fierce opposition to abortion and homosexuality, you'll find the free-market gospel of Wall Street, the pull-yourself-up austerity of slashing welfare programs, and disdain for the "false religion" of environmentalism. Many Christians will be surprised by God's hard line on immigration and righteous exuberance for the death penalty. But my personal favorite Bible study lesson is: "Should You Argue from the Bible in a Secular Capitol?" Drollinger not only teaches hell yes, he also offers this pro tip for proselytizing to those in power: "When challenged with 'Well, I don't view the Bible as authoritative,' answer with, 'Oh yes, you do; it is just that you are suppressing its authority.'" Praise be!

The political punch of Drollinger's teaching is undeniable. Participants like my former colleague Rep. Michele Bachmann don't even realize they're being spun. Bachman raves how these biblical lessons coincidentally "tend to intersect with the decisions we are making every day in Washington, D.C." She went further: "I can tell you from personal experience that members of the House, members of the Senate, members of the cabinet, are transformed by this word," and those "transformed lives," she claimed, are leading to "a transformed nation."

Drollinger's Capitol Ministries may have the most notoriety, but it's only one of dozens of nodes in the Capitol's sprawling ministry-industrial complex. Most follow the same basic blueprint: using Bible studies, prayer meetings, and other "discipling" activities with members of Congress and staff as a pipeline to power. For example, Jim Garlow's *Well Versed Ministries* convenes lawmakers in "micro-congregations" to instruct them on "biblical principles of governance." Prophetic pastors like Sean Feucht drop in for worship services and religious programming for lawmakers and staff. And Tony Perkins's Family Research Council deploys its "Watchmen on the Wall" pastors network to the Capitol for culture war lobbying under the cloak of prayer events, religious summits, and pastoral briefings.

Other groups use grassroots political mobilization in churches to recruit Christians to swarm to the Capitol for large advocacy blitzes. For example, Awake America Ministries, based in Clinton, Maryland, brings delegations consisting of hundreds of pastors and worshippers from across the country to the Capitol for a whirlwind of receptions, prayer sessions, and meet-and-greets with GOP lawmakers.

And some, like the Faith and Law ministry, stand out for their sophistication and strategic discipline. Faith and Law doesn't bother with splashy prayer breakfasts or revival-style blitzes. With quiet precision, it targets congressional staffers who write legislation now, and who might become members of Congress themselves. It offers free meals (always a draw on the Hill), monthly reading groups, "Friday Forums," and a twice-yearly, twelve-week mentorship program designed to steep Christian staffers in scripture and strategy. There's also an annual invitation-only conference for select staffers, and quarterly breakfasts that bring members of Congress and their spouses together with faith leaders for a dose of spiritual alignment. Speaker Johnson and Senate Chaplain Barry Black sit on the advisory board, lending institutional gravitas to the operation.

Lest we forget, The Fellowship Foundation, aka The Family, still haunts the Capitol despite the damning Netflix exposé and a trail of scandals. The Family's flagship outpost, a large house on C Street two blocks from the Capitol, remains fully operational—offering discounted housing, catered meals, cleaning services, and special events that fuse religion and policy for the eight to ten bipartisan members of Congress who bunk there. The house still hums with political influence, but The Family has always insisted it's just "Jesus and nothing more."

Beyond Capitol Hill, the shadow theocracy is reshaping the executive branch from inside the Oval Office thanks in large part to one of the most powerful Christian nationalists in Washington and a lead sponsor of Drollinger's White House Cabinet Bible Study: Russell Vought. As Trump's director of the Office of Management and Budget, Vought has outsized influence over all aspects of federal policy, especially budgets, agency mandates, and personnel decisions. He is the quiet mastermind of Trump's authoritarian redesign of America.

After serving in Trump's first administration, Vought spent the Biden years hatching plans for the unrestrained vengeance tour that would become Trump's second presidency. Much of his "post-constitutional" philosophy was laid out in Project 2025, the authoritarian policy roadmap he helped write for the Heritage Foundation. To correct the problem of America being "too secular," Vought vowed Christian nationalist priorities would be "plugged right in" to a second Trump term. Among his Project 2025 recommendations: criminalizing pornography, adopting biblical definitions of gender, marriage, and family, codifying the Christian sabbath as a federally enforced day of rest, and generally imbuing government "with biblical principles."

One of Vought's signature new initiatives for Trump is an Orwellian expansion of the shadow theocracy: the Anti-Christian Bias Task Force, created by executive order in February of 2025. Premised on the fallacy that Christians in the federal workforce are being systematically harassed, the task force launched sweeping ongoing reviews to identify and purge policies, practices, or conduct offensive to Christian sensibilities. In practice, it works like a conservative Christian culture cop embedded in federal agency HR departments, rooting out and dismantling anything the task force deems unwelcoming of Christians—including protections for LGBTQ+ people, programs involving diversity, equity, and inclusion, and reproductive health initiatives. Meanwhile, the task force has given a green light to Christian proselytizing with new workplace guidelines. The result is a federal workplace increasingly governed by right-wing religious dogma as official personnel policy.

Shadow theocracy has long thrived in America's military institutions, as well. Indeed, it is so entrenched that the Military Religious Freedom Foundation (MRFF) has spent the past two decades confronting coercive proselytizing, sectarian favoritism, and marginalization of non-Christians. Led by former Air Force officer Mikey Weinstein, MRFF defends cadets, midshipmen, reservists, active-duty personnel, and veterans against the stubborn culture of coercion and harassment of non-Christians.

One of MRFF's recent battles: a towering painting of Jesus Christ looming over midshipmen in the Elliot M. See hearing room at the US Merchant Marine Academy. The painting started out as a noncontroversial symbol of faith in the Academy chapel, but after a new chapel was built in the 1960s, the room was repurposed for disciplinary hearings, and the huge depiction of Jesus gazing down at midshipmen took on a troubling new meaning. A prominent academy alumnus described for me how he and other non-Christians felt facing the crucible of honor code tribunals under the towering Christian mural: "Do we even belong in this institution, or are we just being tolerated in a Christian house of discipline?"

In 2023, the discomfort finally compelled twenty-two midshipmen to file a complaint through MRFF asking that the painting be relocated to the chapel. The Biden administration agreed and started the process, but in 2025 it became culture war fodder for Trump's secretary of transportation, Sean Duffy. Sensationalizing the painting relocation as an attack on Christianity, Duffy took to social media vowing to "bring Jesus up from the basement." He even gave a commencement speech at the academy where he invited the audience to applaud for Jesus Christ.

At a committee hearing that summer, I pressed Duffy on how he squared his position with the First Amendment and what message it sent to non-Christians. His reply could have been cribbed from a Christian nationalist bumper sticker: "In this country, we have freedom *of* religion, not freedom *from* religion." That same sense of impunity drives other policy choices. Duffy has transformed transportation infrastructure funding into a conservative Christian reward system by prioritizing grant awards for communities with the highest marriage and birth rates.

Like so many Christian nationalists flexing power in the shadow theocracy these days, Duffy operates on the belief that church-state separation means nothing: that government can shove Christianity down people's throats, and no one can stop it. The reason for their bravado is chillingly straightforward: They do these things because they can.

But they also do it because we let them, and the price of that social license is coming due. America is at a crossroads where our theocratic past is clawing its way back to power with a vengeance. What is the endgame for Christian nationalists and their shadow theocracy? Could some violent sequence of events, some combination of real and fake emergencies, lead to "temporary" suspensions of constitutional safeguards? Could a manufactured crisis like the 1933 Reichstag fire ruse in Germany be manipulated into authoritarian takeover? You'd have to be truly sleepwalking not to see all the elements of that in our country right now.

But as far into our government as the shadow theocracy reaches, as much impunity with which it flexes power, the wall of separation between church and state hasn't officially or legally fallen. Whether it holds may depend on our ability to protect religious freedom without allowing the agenda of an extreme religious minority to cause massive harm—to prevent one group's conception of liberty from becoming everyone else's oppression. To understand what's at stake in that challenge for America, it helps to pay a short visit to Israel.

CHAPTER 7

CHRISTIAN ZIONISM

ON AUGUST 14, 2025, SPEAKER OF THE HOUSE MIKE JOHNson stood atop a dusty hilltop with a sweeping view of the rugged lands surrounding Ariel, one of Israel's largest settlements in the occupied West Bank. He was already making history as the highest-ranking US official to ever visit a disputed Israeli settlement. But it was the speech he was about to deliver that would truly reverberate far beyond the red-roofed homes of Ariel and into the heart of American politics.

Flanked by local settler mayors, Israeli officials, Trump's ambassador to Israel Mike Huckabee, and a delegation of four Republican congressman, Johnson had come to this controversial community built on land captured from Jordan in the 1967 war to reject international law and defy decades of carefully balanced US foreign policy. For Johnson and his delegation, and more importantly for roughly forty million evangelicals back in America known as Christian Zionists, it was past time to put legal, diplomatic, and national security considerations aside and heed the ancient words of the Bible.

Johnson spoke with biblical precision and unmistakable political intent. He renounced the terms "West Bank" and "occupied territories" long embedded in international diplomacy and US foreign policy. Instead, he invoked "Judea and Samaria," the names favored by Christian Zionists and right-wing Israelis. Then, in a sermon to both audiences, he pronounced Israel the winner by divine right in the decades-long dispute over this land. "Scripture teaches us that the mountains of Judea and Samaria were promised to the Jewish people, and they belong to them by right . . . Every corner of this land is important to us. It is an integral part of our faith . . . Every mayor here should know exactly where we stand regarding this issue—and we stand with you."

Thirty-five miles south of Ariel lies Israel's capital city of Jerusalem, a place where faith and territory have collided virtually nonstop for the past three thousand years. In this city, three great religions converge in uneasy, sometimes bloody proximity, each staking sacred claim to the same few acres of stone and dust inside the ancient walls of Old Jerusalem, each believing it to be a portal to Heaven for different reasons.

For Jews, the Temple Mount is sacralized in rabbinic tradition as the *Even ha-Shetiyah*, the Foundation Stone from which the universe sprang forth from God's command. It's said to be where Adam was molded from clay, where Noah offered his post-Flood sacrifice, and where Jacob dreamed of a ladder to Heaven. These and other sacred myths and legends inspired Jews to build their First and Second Temples on this site. After centuries of destruction, exile, and political upheaval, the Temple Mount, including the Western Wall, the last remaining piece of the Second Temple, remains the holiest site in Judaism.

For Muslims, the Temple Mount is *Haram al-Sharif*, the Noble Sanctuary, revered as a celestial departure gate. According to Islamic tradition, the Prophet Muhammad arrived here during the *Isra* and *Mi'raj*, his miraculous Night Journey. From that very spot, now enshrined within the Dome of the Rock, Muslims believe Muhammad was miraculously lifted skyward, ascending through the seven heavens to receive divine instruction and stand in the presence of God. This moment cements the Temple Mount as the third holiest site in Islam.

For Christians, the Temple Mount is the dramatic New Testament setting for some of Jesus's most confrontational and prophetic moments: where he overturned the money changers' tables; taught, scolded, and sparred with imperial and priestly authorities; and declared a new covenant marking a shift from temple-based rituals to a more personal, spiritual path to God. Christians revere the Temple Mount mostly for what it foreshadowed—the hinge between old covenant and new—and as the prelude to the Passion, the stage before the cross. But even more sacred are the places immediately surrounding it: Calvary, where Jesus was crucified, and the Church of the Holy Sepulcher, believed to be the site of his resurrection. Pilgrims come from around the world to feel the sacred history of this place.

Three competing claims to divine real estate, each rooted in different mythologies, covenants, and directives from the same God, all involving one rocky hilltop and a few thousand years of holy drama. Everything about Israel is complicated and always has been. But in American politics, Israel's web of ancient myths and territorial claims is further tangled by the collision of high-stakes foreign policy decisions, partisan hardball, and the weaponization of faith as campaign fodder.

Israel is the epicenter of apocalyptic fantasies for millions of Christian Zionists—the folks Speaker Johnson was courting with his "biblical birthright" remarks in the settlement of Ariel. This faction of evangelical Protestants believes the modern state of Israel is fulfilling biblical prophecy and that the United States must support Israel unconditionally to hasten the Second Coming of Jesus Christ. Christian Zionists are not just a major force in Republican politics; they also are central to the rise of extreme Christian nationalism. Indeed, their formidable influence is bending American institutions toward religious goals to such a degree that major foreign policy decisions are routinely justified by nothing more than the Bible.

In the pages ahead, I trace how the explosive theology of Christian Zionism burst into the mainstream, and how it distorts our foreign policy and undermines democracy. Along the way, we'll examine the profound tradeoffs, wrapped in fervent declarations of support, these beliefs present for Israel and the Jewish people. Christian Zionists ultimately want something very different than Judaism and self-determination for the Holy Land. Which leaves Israel caught in a bind: navigating the absolutism of its most ardent religious allies in America while contending with the rising power of its own religious extremists whose beliefs threaten not only Israel's commitment to democracy but the very viability of the Israeli state. Before delving further into the American part of that paradox, I need to tell you about the *shiksa* in the shadows.

There's a woman I know in Israel, an ultra-Orthodox Haredi

matriarch living in a community so insular it's cut off not just from gentile society, but from most other Jews. Her world runs on an extreme interpretation of strict religious rules known as *halakha*: arranged marriages, gender segregation, and total devotion to Torah law. Between her twelve children, dozens of grandchildren, and a growing number of great-grandchildren, she has 124 living descendants and counting. All of them are devout Haredim.

She belongs to Agudat Yisrael, a Haredi political party so religiously extreme that it rejects the legitimacy of the Israeli state and its military. Their belief is simple and absolute: that Jewish sovereignty over the Holy Land can only be restored by the Messiah, not by secular politicians or military force. And yet, until recently, Agudat Yisrael was part of Prime Minister Benjamin Netanyahu's governing coalition, sacrificing ideological purity for political leverage to protect Haredi interests.

But unbeknownst to her Haredi community, this woman is a convert—what some hardliners would derogatorily call a *shiksa* (non-Jewish woman) notwithstanding her conversion. I know because she's my older sister. Blood may bind us, and I respect her right to choose a life of religious absolutism, but there are aspects of my sister's story that underscore the importance of having strong secular guardrails to prevent unchecked religious extremism from spiraling into terrible harm.

To protect her secret, I'll call her Mirriam, though she was born Theresa. My sister abandoned Christianity in high school, drifted spiritually, and found Judaism through a college boyfriend. By the time she took me to Shabbat services at a Kansas City synagogue when I was seven, she was already deep in religious devotion, whispering explanations about the rabbi, the cantor, the Hebrew prayers. She was one of the few swaying in prayer, "shuckling," as if her soul had found its rhythm.

After college, she broke up with the boyfriend but doubled down on Judaism, moving to Israel for graduate school. The Yom Kippur War broke out just after she arrived. I remember watching the nightly news, terrified until Israel's swift victory reassured me that my big sister was safe. After she married an Israeli man, my sister buried her Christian background, took a new Hebrew name, and completed the rigors of converting from mainstream Judaism to an ultra-Orthodox sect—the only way to be accepted in the Haradim enclave she longed to join. As she and her husband began having children and raising their Haredi family, her origin story remained a deep secret.

We corresponded sporadically over the years. During my sophomore year of college, when I was wrestling with the collapse of my own faith, she sent long letters full of theological fire. In one, my *shiksa* sister ridiculed Christians and mocked Reform and Conservative Jews for their openness to intermarriage and assimilation, without a hint of irony. "Judeo-Christian is a word invented by Christians to validate themselves—like a cheap imitation trying to borrow the good name of the original. Judaism is not dead. It is vibrant and beautiful and totally relevant to the modern man. I must exclude here the weakened forms which are called reform (their temples are like churches without crosses) and the conservative . . . I feel sorry for them . . . intermarriage and assimilation are desecrating their ranks." I still marvel at the intensity of her belief and the uniformity of her family's religious identity. Some married into other Haredi subgroups, but all her descendants remain devout. I suppose it's a testament to the power of group identity, reinforced in this case by a gatekeeper of Jewish purity who is herself a convert.

In 2014, I invited Mirriam to lunch at the King David Hotel in Jerusalem with two of my colleagues, Reps. Steny Hoyer and Henry Waxman. We were there on a congressional delegation trip and my colleagues were curious to hear from someone inside the Haredi world. After politely listening to her praise Haredi tradition and defend gender segregation at the Western Wall, they asked Mirriam about the Iron Dome missile defense system we'd just visited at the border with Gaza. She was unimpressed, asking rhetorically: "Isn't it a miracle that God causes so many missiles to miss their targets and fall harmlessly into fields?" We pointed out that the "miracle" was a joint US-Israeli military project costing billions of dollars, and that some missiles do still get through and kill people. We had just met with the families of victims. Waxman, stunned, asked: "If God is all you need to protect the Jewish people, what about the Holocaust?"

Her reply: "But who really won?"

"What?" Waxman asked.

"They're with God now, rewarded for their righteousness," she said. "But not the Nazis. So who really won?"

I think about that exchange as a glimpse into what would happen if extreme religious zealots were allowed to steer public policy. If my sister's worldview and that of her Agudat Yisrael party ever commands a political majority, Israel's enemies would cheer the dismantling of its military and the broader societal unraveling that would ensue from a majority that rejects pluralism, imposes religious absolutism, and dismantles the institutions of government. It's not a remote hypothetical. With ultra-Orthodox families multiplying at a 4 percent annual rate—the fastest growth of any population in the developed world—the Haredim, which now comprises 14 percent of the country's population, are on pace to force these issues within the lifetimes of my Israeli nieces and nephews.

For Israel to survive and maintain its legally enshrined commitment to religious freedom and democracy, something has to give. The orthodox Judaism embodied and fiercely guarded by the Haredim is a foundational part of Israel's identity, rooted in a post-Holocaust commitment to preserve religious continuity and honor the spiritual legacy of European Jewry. But the Haredim's rapid growth, special privileges (military exemptions, state funding, and autonomy for religious institutions), and rejection of the state's legitimacy sit uneasily alongside Israel's other national interests. To prevent its own demise, Israel must find a balance between respecting the Haredim's right to hold extreme religious views while preventing fanaticism from metastasizing into something harmful and untenable for everyone else.

In the United States, a parallel kind of reckoning is taking shape with our own bloc of ascendant religious extremists, Christian Zionists. Though out of sync with most American Christians, Christian Zionists have undeniable clout inside the Republican Party. Especially under Donald Trump, whose largest and most loyal base of political support is white evangelicals. Because most of them are Christian Zionists, this movement is a dominant force shaping Republican positions on Israel. Which means that right now, a significant slice of US foreign policy comes straight out of their strained interpretations of the Bible.

A hybrid of theology and politics, Christian Zionism—also called dispensationalism—traces its religious scaffolding to nineteenth-century evangelical theologians John Nelson Darby and Cyrus Scofield, who taught that the Jewish return to the Holy Land was a necessary precursor to Christ's return. But it wasn't until the Cold War that this framework detonated into mainstream American consciousness, thanks to evangelical author Hal Lindsey. His 1970 blockbuster, *The Late Great Planet Earth*, the decade's #1 bestselling "nonfiction" book, proclaimed Israel's 1948 founding as "the most important prophetic sign" of the end-times. *The Late Great Planet Earth* dragged dispensational prophecy out of the abstract and into churches all over America.

The impact of *The Late Great Planet Earth* was undeniable: Sales stayed strong well into the 1980s because of Lindsey's unique formula. The book tapped into America's existential dread over nuclear destruction, pattern-matched modern events with end-times Bible verses, and put it all into a spooky, fast-paced page-turner. I read it wide-eyed as a teenager, and I can vouch that in that era of peak Cold War anxiety—when every neighborhood had a fallout shelter and schools marched kids through "duck and cover" drills to prepare for a Soviet missile attack—anyone who believed the Bible and picked up *The Late Great Planet Earth* got chills.

On its face, Lindsey's vivid, almost cinematic vision of Israel as the epicenter of the end-times seemed meticulously validated by both Old and New Testament. He strung together Bible verses, sometimes with creative leaps and interpretive flair, to suggest a looming cataclysm he claimed to have decoded. The book argued that modern headlines about Israel had been foretold if you knew where to look in the Bible, evidence that Christ's return was near. Some of the key verses included Isaiah 11:12 (a prophecy about gathering "the scattered people of Judah from the four quarters of the earth," seemingly fulfilled in 1948 by the modern state of Israel), Ezekiel 38–39 (a prophecy about Gog invading from the northern land of Magog that was decoded as a coming Soviet-led invasion of Israel), and Matthew 24 (whose references to desolation, famine, false prophets, and war Lindsey correlated with current events to predict that Christ would return around the year 1988).

Of course, Lindsey's predictions were a total whiff. They now reside in the dustbin of great prophetic flops, including radio evangelist Harold Camping's breathlessly promoted rapture date of May 21, 2011, followed by the full doomsday of October 21, 2011; televangelist Jerry

Fallwell Sr.'s warning that Y2K would trigger Armageddon; and Rev. Pat Robertson's apocalypse countdowns that came and went like bad weather forecasts.

Even though it was total bunk, *The Late Great Planet Earth* has an enduring legacy. Lindsey's basic formula—pairing Bible verses with headlines and casting Israel as the centerpiece of an unfolding cosmic drama—is now embedded in the evangelical mainstream. Today, roughly eight in ten US evangelicals embrace the core tenets of Christian Zionism. With his bestselling book, Lindsey elevated this worldview into a core belief for an entire religious subculture.

Perhaps an even bigger accelerant of Christian Zionism's rise was a series of Christian novels called *Left Behind*. I was no longer interested in prophetic pulp fiction by the time these books came out, but a lot of other people were. Between 1995 and 2007, these novels sold more than sixty million copies, taking Lindsey's formula of biblical codebreaking and applying it to page-turner plots about airline pilots, globe-trotting journalists, and Antichrist intrigue. By weaving doomsday eschatology into mass-market suspense, *Left Behind* made Christian Zionism thrilling and accessible to millions.

It's no accident that Christians United for Israel (CUFI)—now the nation's largest Christian Zionist advocacy group, with over ten million members—was launched in 2006, as the *Left Behind* wave was cresting. In the same period, Friends of Zion, an American evangelical group headquartered in Jerusalem, sprang up, claiming thirty million members worldwide devoted to spreading "true Christian love to the Jewish people." The powerful prophetic network of NAR, which is deeply steeped in Christian Zionism, began hitting its stride at about the same time.

There are now an estimated thirty to fifty million Christian Zionists in the United States —more than double the roughly fifteen million Jews worldwide. For scale, the America Israel Public Affairs Committee (AIPAC), the largest pro-Israel advocacy operation in the US, has a roster of five million members, half the size of CUFI.

That's not to suggest that AIPAC has lost its mojo. It remains a bipartisan lobbying juggernaut. But under Trump, the ascendant power in the GOP is white evangelical Christians, most of whom are

Christian Zionists. The math says it all: thirty to fifty million mostly Trump-voting Christian Zionists concentrated in red states, compared to America's roughly seven million Jews mostly concentrated in blue states, two-thirds of whom voted against Trump. Trump knows who fills the pews, packs the rallies, and delivers the votes for him and his fellow Republicans.

For now, AIPAC and Christian Zionists seem fully aligned. Both demand unwavering support for Israel and treat it as a litmus test for the candidates they support. They collaborate on marquee issues like securing US military aid to Israel, opposing Iran's nuclear ambitions, and fighting the Boycott, Divestment, and Sanctions movement. It's a formidable strategic alliance: AIPAC brings policy expertise, deep pockets, and high-level bipartisan access; CUFI mobilizes a vast grassroots army of white evangelicals to pressure Republicans from the ground up.

But this uneasy coalition of America's two most militantly pro-Israel groups is a chariot pulled by two very different horses. One is chasing prophecy, the other chasing policy. They're currently galloping in the same general direction, but their destinations couldn't be more different.

The destination for Christian Zionists is all about religion. They see Israel as the main stage for God's end-times drama. Geopolitical conflict, suffering, and global cataclysm are welcomed as necessary preludes to Jesus Christ's triumphant reign. They believe that this kind of global catastrophe is part of God's plan for His son to vanquish evil in a prophetic arc that will culminate in global Christian hegemony.

There's a lot of fine print in Christian Zionists' contract of convenience with Israel. Sometime between now and Jesus's return, Christian Zionists believe that all Jews must abandon Judaism and convert, or else face judgment which may include an eternity in hell. This theology does not consider Jews autonomous people with a right to self-determination; they're fetishized as divine instruments for Christians in a story that ends with their submission to Christianity. This expectation of mass Jewish conversion is not a new or fringe belief; it's been a theological throughline for American Protestants stretching back to the Puritans.

AIPAC, meanwhile, steers clear of all that. Their interests are in influence, stability, and strategic leverage, not religion. The organization has spent decades cultivating the broadest possible base of support for Israel by framing the US–Israel relationship in pragmatic, secular terms. They portray Israel as a strategic, democratic partner of the United States. AIPAC's messaging emphasizes that the US–Israel relationship "saves lives and advances American interests and values, helps protect our troops, strengthens our economy, and addresses 21st-century challenges." Search the AIPAC website and you'll find almost no mention of religion aside from the nod to Israel's legal protections for religious freedom in the "shared values" part of their disciplined message. You won't find Bible verses, messianic language, or apocalyptic narratives. AIPAC is too savvy to wade into those waters, which alienate not only most Jews, but also many non-evangelical Christians whose support for Israel isn't rooted in end-times prophecy.

AIPAC is bipartisan, albeit with an increasingly rightward tilt. In recent years, controversial Israeli policies—including settlement expansion, settler violence and systemic oppression of Palestinians, the humanitarian catastrophe in Gaza, and Netanyahu's Trumpian efforts to weaken democracy and the rule of law—have driven a wedge between many Democrats (myself included) and AIPAC. The group's donor base and political spending have shifted toward Republicans, but it still supports many Democrats and maintains bipartisanship as a strategic priority.

Not so with CUFI and its allies. They want nothing to do with Democrats. Their support for Israel is framed in explicitly biblical terms that are repellant to most in my party. For example, CUFI founder John Hagee recently defended his blanket support for Israel, notwithstanding global outrage over the brutal war in Gaza, with a theological flourish: "Jesus said, 'You will be my witnesses in Jerusalem and in all Judea and Samaria.'" Televangelist Franklin Graham, one of America's most prominent evangelicals, echoed the sentiment: "Most evangelical Christians believe the Bible and, of course, we believe Genesis. We believe God gave the land to Abraham, Isaac and Jacob—and that every inch of that land belongs to the Jews." The unspoken caveat, of course, is that the land will ultimately belong to Christians.

CUFI's fierce ally NAR preaches support for Israel with cosmic drama that makes *Left Behind* and *The Late Great Planet Earth* feel sleepy. Apostle Lou Engle, known for rallying hundreds of thousands of young evangelicals in stadiums through his movement The Call, infuses his sermons with the biblical centrality of Israel. He leads "Esther fasts": multiday prayer and fasting campaigns modeled on Queen Esther's biblical plea for divine intervention. Just as Esther called for a three-day fast before confronting Haman, the royal advisor who plotted genocide against the Jews, Engle urges Christians to confront modern-day "Hamans" who threaten America and Israel, and to prepare for the apocalyptic battles ahead.

NAR apostle Dutch Sheets takes it even further. He has mapped demonic territories across the Middle East—essentially all Muslim countries—and launches spiritual warfare campaigns against them as enemies of Israel. In a June 2025 devotional, Sheets claimed divine revelation about the ancient "prince of Persia," a spiritual adversary cryptically identified as a demonic principality in the Bible. "Demons don't die," he wrote. "The 'prince of Persia' is still alive. . . . This evil principality over Persia/Iran influences nations and individuals to oppose Israel today, just as it did in Daniel's time." In this worldview, war in the Middle East is a supernatural battle between God's angelic forces and entrenched demonic powers, with Israel at the epicenter.

Other NAR apostles, including Chuck Pierce and Cindy Jacobs, lead pilgrimages to Israel where they perform prophetic rituals like releasing "apostolic authority" over Jerusalem, blowing shofars at the Western Wall, holding prayer vigils on Mount Zion, and conducting spiritual warfare to break demonic "strongholds." These aren't sightseeing tours; NAR's traveling prayer warriors are staking spiritual claim to future Christian territory.

For many Christian Zionists, the duty to support Israel is not just about waging cosmic battle against demons or hastening the end-times: It's a spiritual investment that promises wealth, health, and other real-world rewards. The fusion of Christian Zionism with the so-called prosperity gospel, especially popular among charismatic evangelicals, interprets Genesis 12:3 ("I will bless those who bless you") as a divine transaction in which an alliance with Israel guarantees tangible benefits. Some, like Pastor Wes Hall of International House of Prayer Kansas

City, aka IHOPKC, believe that supporting Israel is God's "strategy" for unleashing supernatural power across churches, cities, and nations.

Which brings us back to the fine print of Christian Zionism: Supporting Israel isn't altruistic, and it's not just about prosperity. It's a theological playbook that calls for Jewish "salvation" and "spiritual awakening"—code for mass conversion—as prerequisites for Christian dominion. When Dutch Sheets calls for mass intercession to "break the back" of evil spirits in the Middle East and "free millions to see the light of the gospel," he's not just talking about converting Muslims in Iran. He's invoking a theology that sees Jewish conversion as essential to the Second Coming.

Listen closely, and you'll notice what's missing: any vision for Israel as a long-term Jewish and democratic state. In dominionist theology, Jews are not partners in a shared future. They're prophetic instruments, destined to become Christians under King Jesus. NAR's prayer movements, prophetic decrees, and spiritual warfare aren't just religious exercises; they're tactical campaigns to "awaken" Israel—code for Christian conversion. Religion scholar Holly Pivec, who has written extensively on NAR, lays it bare: "They're doing a classic bait-and-switch."

Christian Zionists are so hyped with biblical zeal that they reflexively support Israel's most extreme and contentious actions, rushing in where even AIPAC fears to tread. AIPAC, for all its hawkishness, has at least gestured toward openness to a two-state solution; CUFI rejects a Palestinian state outright. AIPAC avoids talking about the radioactive politics of West Bank settlement expansion; CUFI praises the settlements and, like Speaker Johnson, frames the territory as Israel's divine inheritance of "Judea and Samaria." On these and other flashpoints, CUFI casts support for Israel as a religious duty. Every policy, every military action, every inch of contested land becomes part of a cosmic drama. They frame territorial compromise as biblically forbidden. And because they believe America's own covenant with God is intertwined with Israel's, they view the US–Israel relationship as an existential imperative: *America* will face God's wrath if we fail to ensure Israel's obedience to biblical prophecy.

In June of 2025, Senator Ted Cruz echoed this familiar theological script in an interview with Tucker Carlson, citing Genesis to justify his blanket support for the Israeli government: "Those who bless Israel will be blessed, and those who curse Israel will be cursed." I rarely credit Carlson for anything, but on this occasion, he was right to push back. He asked Senator Cruz how a verse written three thousand years before the founding of the modern state of Israel, and clearly referring to the descendants of Abraham, could be used to justify unconditional allegiance to a contemporary government. Cruz doubled down, insisting his support was based "first and foremost" on the Bible. He sidestepped the theological flaw and leaned into the bumper-sticker logic that now dominates much of the GOP: *The Bible says it. I believe it. That settles it.*

With regards to Israel, this biblical intransigence has become standard operating procedure among senior Trump officials and Republican leaders in Congress. For example, when Rep. Elise Stefanik was going through her Senate confirmation hearing to become Trump's ambassador to the United Nations (a nomination later withdrawn), she aligned herself with Christian Zionists and hard-line Israeli figures like Finance Minister Bezalel Smotrich and National Security Minister Itamar Ben-Gvir. Stefanik testified that Israel has a "biblical right to the entire West Bank." Trump's ambassador to Israel, Mike Huckabee, has gone even further. He insisted there's "no such thing as a West Bank" and claimed that Israel holds the biblical "title deed" to all the land "from the river to the sea" and beyond. In his 2024 book, Trump's former ambassador David Friedman, a close ally of CUFI and longtime advocate of settlement expansion, proposed repurposing $1 billion in US aid to Palestinians to fund Israeli annexation of the West Bank. Knowing who he needed to persuade, Friedman justified his proposal "based first and foremost on biblical prophecies and values," adding that the annexation movement "hearkens back to basic Judeo-Christian values of kindness, human dignity, humility and prosperity."

CUFI's influence in Congress is surging. In the spring of 2025, House Republicans launched a "Judea and Samaria Caucus" and introduced legislation that proposes amending all official US government documents to reflect the biblical terms of "Judea and Samaria" instead of "West Bank," mirroring the language of Israeli settlers and CUFI talking points. A few months later, Speaker Johnson was in the settlement of Ariel echoing the same Christian Zionist themes.

With this kind of maximalist support and deep influence within the GOP, it's no surprise that Prime Minister Benjamin Netanyahu—who surely chuckles privately about the likelihood of the Second Coming and mass Jewish conversion—showers Christian Zionists with praise, calling them some of Israel's "greatest friends." But their dual agenda has sparked fierce debate in both Israel and the American Jewish community. Prominent rabbis have accused Christian Zionists of reducing Jews to props and likened their proselytizing and obsession with mass Jewish conversion to missionary tactics with an endgame of spiritual erasure.

For now, the alliance between Israel/AIPAC and Christian Zionists holds. The optics of unity serve both camps well, even as the theological fault lines beneath them grow increasingly irreconcilable. AIPAC walks a precarious tightrope, trying to preserve some semblance of bipartisanship and broad-based advocacy while reaping short-term gains from the GOP's current Christian Zionist alignment. But the ground beneath this alliance is starting to shift.

Most Americans, including many who support Israel, are appalled by Christian Zionists' extremism—from the glorification of end-times calamity and the fantasy of mass Jewish conversion, to cheerleading Israel's most brutal actions in Gaza and the West Bank, indifference to democratic norms, and blindness to Palestinian suffering. CUFI and its allies aren't about to temper their fanaticism, so the disconnect with mainstream Americans, including most Christians, will only widen. Even among evangelicals, cracks are showing. Surveys show that younger evangelicals are far less inclined to embrace unconditional support for Israel than their parents' generation—with most younger evangelicals expressing discomfort with the basic theological tenets of Christian Zionism.

Meanwhile, there's an emerging schism over Israel within the MAGA Christian nationalist coalition. As fervently as right-wing evangelicals are devoted to Israel, the other ascendant religious factions of MAGA Christian nationalism are not. Both Rad Trad Catholics and the Reconstructionist Theo Bros reject the theology of Christian Zionism, and anti-Semitic currents have long coursed through both of these religious subcultures. Their disdain for Christian Zionism has begun to surface in public controversies, including Nick Fuentes's Holocaust denial, Tucker Carlson's sharp attacks on Israel, and even in Congress. Rep. Marjorie Taylor Greene—an avowed Christian nationalist who in 2022 was lavished with praise and prophetically anointed by none other than NAR apostle Dutch Sheets—has blasted the Gaza war and criticized Israel. What once looked like unified and unconditional devotion to Israel among right-wing Christians is fracturing into rival camps. One faction of the GOP is still clinging to the Christian Zionist script and trying to manage its renegade younger generation; another is increasingly ambivalent about Israel and hostile to Christian Zionism.

For these reasons, the marriage of convenience between AIPAC and Christian Zionists is headed for trouble. Israel and its allies will have to confront the theological Trojan horse they've welcomed inside the gates of Jerusalem. Just as Americans, including a growing number of Republicans, are starting to reckon with the tremendous power and influence Christian Zionists have amassed, to the point that major elements of US foreign policy are being based on nothing more than dubious interpretations of the Bible.

If the tide is starting to turn against Christian Zionism, I wish I could say it was because Americans were rising up against the dangerous reality of Bible-as-policy theocratic governance. But it probably owes just as much to the broad unpopularity of Israel's Gaza war, and within Republican circles, to old-fashioned isolationism and its close cousin anti-Semitism. Or simply the fact that after several decades of growth, Christian Zionism is waning. Whatever the motivation, at least some Republicans are questioning the wisdom of letting an ancient Bible verse steer foreign policy in a modern nation with enough nuclear firepower to incinerate the planet.

Our examination of Christian Zionism, including the parallel reckonings in both the United States and Israel, underscores the importance of secular guardrails against the danger of religious extremism. The complexity of Israel—and its centrality in the religious beliefs of many American Christians—has always been shaped by powerful myths. We can appreciate that, and respect those who choose to sanctify and live by those myths, but allowing fundamentalist zealots to embed their end-times prophecies into real-world national security decisions is madness. A long overdue debate about the alarming influence of Christian Zionism may finally be breaking into the open. But with other points of attack by the Christian nationalist movement—where there is more religious unity within the MAGA coalition and less pressure from the outside—it's harder to discern a serious pushback. Christian nationalists' war on secular education, science, and rational inquiry is a high-stakes example, and the subject of our next chapter.

CHAPTER 8

THE DUMBING OF AMERICA

"Fix reason firmly in her seat, and call to her tribunal every fact, every opinion. Question with boldness even the existence of a god; because, if there be one, he must more approve the homage of reason, than that of blindfolded fear."

—THOMAS JEFFERSON, LETTER TO PETER CARR (AUGUST 10, 1787)

QUOTING ADOLF HITLER IS AN UNCONVENTIONAL WAY to start your congressional career, but that's how it began for newly sworn-in Rep. Mary Miller (R-IL). On January 5, 2021, she took the stage to address a group of right-wing protestors rallying near the Capitol building. The demonstration was hosted by Moms for America, a Christian nationalist group focused on championing biblical values and parental control in education. Fresh off a 73 percent win in the first campaign of her life, Rep. Miller opened with standard-issue right-wing tropes about wokeness and transgenderism in public schools. The speech was on track to be entirely forgettable until she invoked Der Führer: "Hitler was right, whoever has the youth has the future."

Moms for America applauded. The internet exploded. The World Jewish Congress condemned her. A bipartisan chorus of politicians issued blistering rebukes. But the rally rolled on, and by the next day, Miller's homage to Hitler had been eclipsed by wall-to-wall coverage of the insurrection. Miller later issued a tepid apology, but the mask had slipped, and not for the last time.

Fast forward to June 2025: A Sikh cleric from New Jersey, Giani Surinder Singh, delivered a peaceful, ecumenical guest invocation in the House chamber wearing a yellow turban. Singh's prayer was a plea for peace, humility, and service, but the sight of a turban-wearing non-Christian—whom she ignorantly assumed to be a Muslim—leading a prayer in Congress triggered Miller into full-blown moral panic. "It's deeply troubling that a Muslim was allowed to lead prayer in the House of Representatives this morning," she tweeted. "This should never have been allowed to happen. America was founded as a Christian nation, and I believe our government should reflect that truth, not drift further from it. May God have mercy!" Miller's tweet drew another chorus of bipartisan shaming, enough to humiliate most people into a public apology. But not Miller. She edited the tweet to identify Singh as a Sikh, but never apologized. This, after all, was the same person who celebrated the Supreme Court's overturning of *Roe v. Wade* as a "victory for white life."

Miller's hardcore biblical worldview extends to climate science as well. When asked by a Christian media host whether promoting solar panels was "against God's design for nature and how he created this world we live in," Miller agreed. "The whole climate change is a sham. First of all, God controls the climate, because he controls the sun, and the sun controls the weather, primarily." Give her credit for not quoting Hitler again, but this was bad.

Miller belongs to a nondenominational Protestant Christian church rooted in the "Restorationist" movement, a conservative subculture of noncharismatic evangelicals. That places her theologically closer to CREC and the Theo Bros, with their emphasis on biblical literalism, than to NAR. From that point in the right-wing Christian spectrum, the "homeschooling mom" of seven channels her extreme beliefs—including disdain for public education, strict Bible-based governance, science skepticism, culture war maximalism, and rejection of religious pluralism—into one of the most hyper-partisan voting records in Congress.

Yet her extremism hasn't hurt her electorally. She won reelection in 2022 with 71 percent and cruised to a 99 percent victory in an uncontested 2024 race. In her district, where white evangelicalism dominates and church attendance far exceeds the national average, she's a rock star. And she's not an outlier on the national stage. *The New York Times* recently published a university study that flagged Miller specifically for rhetoric that "would have been unacceptable a generation ago, unthinkable, possibly disqualifying," but today it is a run-of-the-mill example of how conspiracism, religious absolutism, and anti-intellectualism have ascended into the mainstream of the Republican Party. Miller sits comfortably within a large bloc of kindred lawmakers, including the thirty-one members of the House Freedom Caucus, numerous Trump administration officials, and many national luminaries in the MAGA Republican Party, all of whom push the same agenda that substitutes biblical decree for critical thought.

Previous chapters have traced how we arrived at this unsettling moment as well as what the rise of militant right-wing Christian extremism into the mainstream of Republican politics portends for democracy and our constitutional order. But there's even more at stake here. The religious agenda driving the Christian nationalist movement strikes at the very foundations of knowledge and the institutions that safeguard our health, security, prosperity, and collective future. Rep. Miller may personify the assault, but it permeates the highest levels of government, especially since Trump's return to the White House.

The high cost of this war on knowledge, reason, and science—the dumbing of America—is the focus of this chapter. At its core, this crusade challenges the capacity of modern society to do what the Enlightenment supposedly guaranteed and what our founders like Thomas Jefferson fought for: *to think for ourselves*. Today's battle to relitigate the Enlightenment carries staggering consequences. Because the eighteenth-century fight for knowledge and liberty is now a fight that could determine whether humanity survives existential threats of our own making.

Jefferson's towering legacy, of course, is not without its shadows. His ownership of hundreds of slaves, and his failure to extend the high-minded principles of justice and equality to all people, remain indelible stains on his greatness. In recent years historians and institutions such as the Monticello Foundation have confronted these moral contradictions and woven them into a more complete portrait of Jefferson. Exhibitions like *Slavery at Jefferson's Monticello: Paradox of Liberty*, developed in partnership with the Smithsonian, have helped ensure that his foundational contributions are not celebrated without reckoning with the human cost of his blind spots. It is important to acknowledge these unflattering truths about Jefferson—not to excuse the injustice, but to resist the temptation to see only the parts we like, as Christian nationalists do when they cherry-pick his quotes and retrofit him with false religiosity. Jefferson's full complexity is part of the legacy we've inherited.

Reason, critical inquiry, and knowledge were among Jefferson's most cherished values. It wasn't just Enlightenment swagger: He considered them essential bulwarks against religious tyranny. He used his writing and platform to warn against theocratic rule masquerading as governance—it was his lifelong crusade. That's why he challenged Americans to resist the seduction of certainty, to defend reason when it's least convenient, even to "question with boldness" the existence of any god—trusting that truth, if it's real, can withstand scrutiny.

Convinced that democracy could survive only with a well-educated citizenry, Jefferson labored more than any other founder to embed secular public education into the fabric of America. He began by proposing a system of free public education for primary grades in Virginia in the 1780s and continued pushing it for decades. He then sketched the blueprints for what would grow into our national system of free, universal, and secular public schools, which were designed to ensure that every citizen, regardless of wealth, "would be qualified to understand their rights, to maintain them, and to exercise with intelligence their parts in self-government." In letters to his friend and former rival John Adams, he gushed about this vision, stressing that it would elevate "the mass of the people to the high ground of moral respectability necessary to their own safety and to orderly government, and would [complete] the great object of qualifying them to secure the veritable *aristoi* for the trusts of government, to the exclusion of the pseudalists."

Jefferson also helped lay the groundwork for America's world-class higher education system. Our 112 land-grant colleges and universities—spanning every state, the District of Columbia, and five territories—trace some of their DNA to Jefferson's work on the Land Ordinance of 1785, which created a framework for westward expansion that set aside dedicated space for state universities. Jefferson's Northwest Ordinance of 1787 helped embed education as a core value of governance by declaring: "Knowledge, being necessary to good government and the happiness of mankind, schools and the means of education shall forever be encouraged." Perhaps Jefferson's proudest achievement was founding the University of Virginia: America's first public university conceived as a secular temple to reason, with no chapel or clergy. Its founding was a testament to the radical proposition that citizens should think for themselves.

Throughout his life, Jefferson clashed with religious absolutists who opposed secular public education and any scientific advance that threatened their biblical precepts. Take Benjamin Franklin's lightning rod, for example, which was designed to save lives by providing a conductive path for a bolt of lightning and thus protecting buildings like churches. Yet many clerics denounced lightning rods as heretical, claiming they interfered with God's will. Their preferred method of storm protection: climbing into the tops of steeples to sprinkle holy water and ring bells—a ritual that got many of them killed. In Jefferson's era, the same faith-based superstition fueled opposition to smallpox inoculation. Inoculation was considered such an affront to God's will that Puritan Minister Cotton Mather's brave campaign to promote the life-saving treatment was met with mob violence, threats of hanging, and the bombing of his house.

Jefferson rebuked this kind of superstition by swearing "eternal hostility against every form of tyranny over the mind of man." He likened religious science denial to witchcraft, saying that "the priests of the different religious sects . . . dread the advance of science as witches do the approach of day-light, and scowl on it as the fatal harbinger announcing the subversion of the duperies on which they live." He mocked blind faith as a shipwreck of "delirium" and "gullibility." And he declared that "in every country and in every age, the priest has been hostile to liberty." He was such a fierce champion of reason that he famously took a razor to the New Testament, carving out the miracles and mysticism to create his own "Jefferson Bible." In an 1814 letter to John Adams, he explained his editorial surgery, which preserved Christ's important teachings and removed the passages he considered gratuitous and "inferior": "It is as easy to separate those parts, as to pick out diamonds from dunghills."

Jefferson's confrontations with theocrats of his era came at a steep price. Federalist clergy branded him an "infidel" and "atheist," and their attacks nearly cost him the presidency in 1800. Tim Dwight, the Puritan minister and president of Yale, thundered in a sermon that Jefferson's election would bring Bible burnings, sacraments paraded on donkeys, and children mocking God in the streets. In the face of pushback, Jefferson argued for the value of science as both a practical and moral imperative. In a letter thanking Harvard's president for an honorary degree, Jefferson reflected that his generation had spent its prime securing liberty as "the great parent of science and of virtue," and warned that America's continued freedom depended on future generations defending those ideals.

Thankfully, future generations did just that. Two centuries of progress were built on the intellectual scaffolding Jefferson erected, culminating in the United States' emergence in the twentieth century as the world's undisputed superpower in science, medicine, research, and higher education. America built that global leadership, and maintains it to this day, not because of divine favor or biblical covenant, but because we engineered it through decades of bold public investment and visionary policies. That's how we built the labs, funded the moon shots, and harnessed the power of knowledge like no nation in history has ever done. We did this by founding and investing in agencies like the National Institutes of Health (NIH), National Science Foundation (NSF), Department of Education, National Aeronautics and Space Administration (NASA), Defense Advanced Research Projects

Agency (DARPA), and National Oceanic and Atmospheric Administration (NOAA), all of which contributed to America becoming the world's epicenter of science and innovation.

Our core scientific engine is the NIH, the world's largest public funder of biomedical research. In 2022 alone, it poured $48 billion into the pursuit of medical progress, backing over three hundred thousand scientists across more than 2,500 institutions. Its fingerprints are everywhere in modern medicine: from the 52 percent reduction in premature heart attacks thanks to the Framingham Heart Study, to breakthrough cancer treatments and genetic therapies born of the Human Genome Project, to the pandemic-busting vaccines of Operation Warp Speed, to GLP-1 drugs, and countless other medical miracles quietly underwritten by NIH.

Close behind is the NSF, the nation's powerhouse for basic research. Each year, it fuels discovery across 2,000 institutions and fifty thousand researchers, seeding innovation with the earliest, riskiest grants that private industry won't touch. NSF has catalyzed revolutions ranging from the modern internet and artificial intelligence, to CRISPR gene editing and brain mapping. Its impact extends into nuclear fusion, to materials science, and climate modeling, and includes investments in the scientific infrastructure and education that sustains America's scientific edge.

The other essential science and research component that makes America the envy of the world is our colleges and universities. Partnering with federal agencies on cutting-edge research, they've become global magnets for talent and hubs of innovation. The unique resources and synergies forged by decades of American policies and investments are the reason so many of them are ranked among the world's best higher education institutions, why we consistently boast a disproportionate share of the world's most-cited research papers, and why our scientists have earned over 420 Nobel Prizes—more than any other nation.

None of this would have happened in a small-minded nation that feared challenging narrow biblical worldviews. Every bit of this progress was built on the Enlightenment scaffolding of secular education, reason, and critical inquiry, and generations of forward-looking leadership that amplified and expanded that vision.

Yet today, America's engines of progress are being assailed by the Christian nationalist movement as if they are mortal threats. Evidence-based learning is dismissed as elitist noise. Climate science is rejected as a hoax. And public health protections are recast as a supposed globalist scheme to erode national sovereignty, shutter churches, and reorder society. Conspiracy theories are embraced with near-religious fervor. And unlike the first Trump presidency, when these attacks were largely background grievances contained at the grassroots level, the second Trump presidency has elevated them to a governing creed and is now waging war on education and science with a Luddite fury, oblivious to how it is damaging current and future generations.

What could explain this seemingly irrational crusade? And why is this seemingly happening all at once? Unraveling that paradox starts with recognizing the convergence of two forces: a long-running campaign driven by hardcore religious beliefs that has been brewing for years in statehouses and school boards; and a newer surge at the national level, powered not only by a grassroots religious agenda, but even more so by the dark logic of Trump's drive for absolute power. Before examining these two lines of attack, however, we should consider what set all this in motion long ago.

For almost two hundred years following the Protestant Reformation of 1517, Europe was engulfed in bloody intermittent wars between Catholics and Protestants. The religious wars ended thanks to the seventeenth- and eighteenth-century intellectual movement known as the Enlightenment, which elevated reason and individual rights over religious dogma and laid the foundation for secular governance and tolerance. The gradual shift of authority from church to state reduced conflict over which sect should hold sway over government, thus easing conditions that fueled sectarian wars.

The American experiment was a crucible for the Enlightenment, carrying it forward by embedding religious freedom and secular governance into our constitutional order. Most of Europe, and to varying degrees most of the Christian world, followed this general course. But nowhere has it worked better than in the United States. For two and a half centuries, our Enlightenment framework has not only helped blunt the impulse for Christians to kill each other over sectarian differences; the elevation of knowledge, critical inquiry, and science has also unleashed extraordinary advances and social progress—in medicine, industry, democracy, and human rights—transforming modern life and expanding the horizons of human possibility.

Despite all this success, however, fundamentalist elements of American Christianity never bought in. They rejected the Enlightenment's elevation of rationality and science over the Bible, and they resented the vesting of civic authority in secular institutions rather than the church. Since the founding era, these Christians have been fighting skirmishes against Enlightenment values, especially the advancement of science. Secular education has always been a key battleground.

These fights were epitomized by the Scopes "Monkey Trial" of 1925, in which high school teacher John Scopes was prosecuted under Tennessee's Butler Act, a law that made it illegal to teach human evolution in public schools and required instruction to uphold the biblical account of creation. The fundamentalists won that battle. Scopes was convicted, and the law remained on the books for decades. But they ultimately lost the war, as the science of evolution overtook creationism, and America's courts, states, and school boards gradually yielded to the scientific consensus.

By the 1980s, the fight had shifted. The "New Religious Right" movement profiled in Chapter 1, spearheaded by Rev. Jerry Falwell Sr. and his Moral Majority, marked a pivot from reactive fights to a more systemic campaign to reshape society. Right-wing Christians had long resented public schools for exposing children to ideas like evolution, sex education, and racial equality that clashed with their conception of traditional Christian values. In the 1960s, that resentment deepened at the university level, amid campus protests against Vietnam, civil rights activism, and the rise of feminism.

As Professor Capps observed, the New Religious Right was the birth of a culture war, and the movement's attacks on universities represented an unprecedented challenge to the societal standing of academia. Capps warned that the higher education establishment had been arrogant and complacent in failing to grasp the seriousness of

Falwell's movement and the chilling vulnerability it exposed: the real possibility that the uneasy truce between Christianity and the rationalist humanism, science, and free thought of the Enlightenment could be broken.

Falwell's movement collapsed in the early 1990s, but the anti-Enlightenment project it embodied persisted. One of the most enduring strands—the crusade against the evils of secular education—built strength and momentum over the next two decades. James Dobson, who rose alongside Falwell and Rev. Pat Robertson as a major figure in the New Religious Right, became one of the movement's most impactful survivors. Dobson's Focus on the Family group grew into a $100 million radio, television, and advocacy empire during the 1990s with relentless attacks on the "godless and immoral" curriculum of public schools. Homeschooling and "parental rights" became core pillars of conservative Christian activism, aided by strategic legislative and legal initiatives from groups like Alliance Defending Freedom and the Home School Legal Defense Association.

By the 2010s, these initiatives had matured into a sophisticated ecosystem—legal, political, educational, and media—that was ready to drive aggressive wedges into the secular scaffolding of the Enlightenment. One of the most audacious was a Trojan horse operation dubbed Project Blitz which attacked secular governance by cleverly weaving Christian themes and doctrines into public institutions. It was formally launched in 2017 by David Barton, the fake historian we met in previous chapters, as a coalition led by his Wallbuilders advocacy group in partnership with the Congressional Prayer Caucus Foundation and the Christian National Legal Foundation. Their strategy, revealed in chilling detail when the Project Blitz Playbook was leaked in 2018, activates the nation's thirty state-level legislative prayer caucuses to "frame the narrative" by passing low-friction, "Tier 1" bills such as "In God we Trust" specialty license plates, Bible "literature" classes, and resolutions honoring Christian heritage. What begins as seemingly innocuous interventions metastasizes into writing Christian doctrine into laws, public school curriculum, and more. The next phase escalates to more intrusive second- and third-tier measures that create sweeping religious carve-outs in education, health care, and civil rights protections; restrict reproductive choice; and undermine LGBTQ rights—with all of it framed as protecting "religious liberty."

Project Blitz is designed to soften the ground for other theocratic assaults by habituating the public to Christian authority through familiarity and routine. When students see the Ten Commandments and "In God we Trust" on every classroom wall, when the Bible is their textbook for literature and history, when Christian symbols and themes are ubiquitous in public spaces, the line between church and state becomes meaningless.

The formula seems to be working. In less than a decade, dozens of first-tier Project Blitz bills have been enacted into law, including twenty states that now offer "In God we Trust" specialty license plates. Second- and third-tier bills are passing, too: Over a dozen states have enacted Project Blitz-inspired legislation on issues ranging from Bible mandates in classrooms to anti-LGBTQ policies. Barton fundraised for Texas's law to mandate Ten Commandment displays in all public school classrooms, before it was blocked by a federal court for violating the First Amendment. Louisiana and Arkansas passed similar bills, with similar court rulings stopping them, for now.

Meanwhile, Republican-led states like Florida and Texas have waged an aggressive crusade to impose conservative political control over nearly every aspect of public education from K-12 schools to universities. Florida's censorious "Parental Rights in Education" law, known colloquially as "Don't Say Gay," empowers parents with mechanisms to override educators by challenging, blocking, or removing instructional content, even when it is evidence-based and aligned with state standards. Florida has also extended its ban on classroom discussion of sexual orientation and gender identity through the 12th grade, chilling inclusive education and threatening teachers with penalties for violating vague standards. The state's sweeping voucher expansion makes every K-12 student eligible for an $8,000 voucher that can be used for tuition at private religious schools, many of which teach creationism and reject scientific curricula. The 2022 "Stop WOKE Act" further tightened ideological control over classrooms, and in 2023, Florida approved curriculum from unaccredited PragerU, which is widely criticized as a "propaganda factory" that distorts science and rewrites history.

Texas has done many of the same things. After tightening political control over curriculum, policing library books, and launching a sweeping voucher program, state officials worked with homeschooling and anti-abortion groups to pass a "Parents' Bill of Rights" constitutional amendment in November of 2025. Parental primacy in all decisions regarding children's "upbringing" is now the law in the Lone Star State.

Both states have targeted higher education with a vengeance. Florida launched a barrage of heavy-handed laws and executive actions to impose conservative governance over the state's universities, chill student activism, and rein in academic freedom including restrictions on what faculty can teach and pursue in their research. Texas empowered politically appointed boards to rewrite general-education requirements, eliminate degree programs, and override faculty governance, while creating a statewide ombudsman to investigate complaints and enforce bans on diversity initiatives and other ideological restrictions. Faculty groups describe these attacks as an "intellectual reign of terror" and warn that new limits on hiring, shared governance, and academic freedom amount to one of the most sweeping state interventions in higher education in America's history.

Right-wing Christianity's longstanding grievance against public schools and universities gained new potency with the rise of the MAGA movement, which fused a faith-based crusade with growing economic resentment toward America's educated elite. Trump nodded to this sentiment with a memorable line from the campaign trail in 2016: "I love the poorly educated."

At that point, it was just an applause line for Trump, but a shift was underway in MAGA politics. Politicians, pundits, and operatives who had once benefited from the prestige of Ivy League educations reinvented themselves as anti-elite crusaders, trashing higher education and ridiculing the scientific community to strut their populist bona fides. Steve Bannon, J. D. Vance, Ted Cruz, and Ron DeSantis were among the MAGA contortionists who had passed through the gates of Harvard or Yale but now declared those institutions corrupted, hostile to faith, and detached from "real America." My GOP colleague Rep. Elise Stefanik morphed from a credential snob who rarely missed a chance to boast about her Harvard education to a born-again populist.

Conservative media fueled the anti-elite narrative by amplifying every campus controversy—DEI policies, accusations of "cancel culture" against conservative speakers, and student protests—until universities were transformed into a cultural and religious boogeyman. They became the embodiment of every "-ism" the Christian nationalist movement hated, from liberal elitism to secularism, multiculturalism, and the dreaded catch-all "wokeism."

After Trump's reluctant departure from the White House in early 2021, MAGA power players began scheming about escalating their attacks on universities. Two Ivy League dons led the way. In the fall of 2021, J. D. Vance signaled his support for a full-spectrum attack to strip universities of their societal influence in a speech titled, "The Universities Are the Enemy," which according to *The New York Times* seethed with "deep hostility to the entire academic enterprise." By the spring of 2024, Vance was praising Hungarian strongman Victor Orban's coercive takeover of his nation's universities as a model the US should emulate. Meanwhile, his fellow Yale alum Ron DeSantis used his sweeping interventions against Florida universities to position himself for a 2024 presidential campaign. Trump handily defeated DeSantis for the GOP nomination, but DeSantis helped cement the war on universities as a central grievance in the campaign.

Trump took up the theme and supersized it, vowing to defund "woke" universities and science programs and to impose sweeping federal changes across higher education. He pledged to fire "radical Left" accreditors who, in his words, had allowed colleges to be "dominated by Marxists, maniacs and lunatics," and he threatened that institutions that resisted his demands would face harsh financial penalties.

But this all-out war plan against the higher education and science establishment might have amounted to little more than campaign bluster if the Trump-appointed justices of the Supreme Court had not delivered a massive windfall in the summer of 2024. In *Trump v. United States*, the Court concocted a new presidential immunity doctrine that shielded Trump from prosecution for crimes during his first term, ruling 6–3 that presidents enjoy absolute immunity for core responsibilities and presumptive immunity for anything done in their official capacity. The dissenting justices warned that this breathtaking expansion of executive power stripped away the guardrails of accountability and effectively placed the president above the law, opening the door to all manner of abuse, corruption, and illegality.

For a strongman like Trump, the gift of absolute immunity was a license for impunity. What had once been unthinkable or legally unattainable suddenly gleamed as an open invitation to pursue vindictive or authoritarian impulses. The Court's ruling reset his calculus, removing any vestige of restraint: A second Trump presidency could now use any means necessary to neutralize people or institutions he saw as obstacles to his pursuit of absolute power.

Universities and scientists share a common trait with other targets of Trump's systematic attacks in his second presidency—the journalists, judges, law firms, civil servants, independent agencies, inspectors general, and watchdog agencies. They generally don't bend the knee to political power. They investigate, verify, adjudicate, educate, and equip the public with tools to resist manipulation. All of this complicates a strongman's ability to control the narrative—a potent check on his power.

So, immediately upon taking office, Trump launched a scorched-earth attack on universities and scientists, along with these other institutions. Within days it was clear that Trump 2.0 wasn't just sparring—he was out to crush them. Sweeping cuts, agency firings, funding freezes, and ominous notices of audits and investigations rained down across the higher-education and research landscape. The attacks rested on three pillars: ending "woke indoctrination," claiming to root out "waste, fraud, and abuse," and policing alleged systemic anti-Semitism.

Leading the blitzkrieg was a pseudo-agency Trump created by fiat: the Department of Government Efficiency, or DOGE. Led by billionaire Elon Musk and staffed with his private-sector loyalists, DOGE simply did whatever Musk wanted—ignoring laws, rules, and norms, and functioning as a shadow government. Trump reveled in the chaos, the compliant GOP Congress let it run, and courts moved too slowly to stop most of the damage.

Trump's Department of Education reinterpreted civil rights laws meant to prevent unlawful discrimination and began wielding them as tools of political leverage, threatening loss of accreditation and federal funding for universities that resisted Trump's sweeping political and cultural directives. Meanwhile, the Justice Department launched an anti-Semitism task force that operated as a parallel intimidation mechanism. Under these dubious authorities, the administration began shaking down hundreds of universities with audits and investigations, threatening to cancel federal support unless they agreed to end DEI, adopt new policies on student discipline, admissions, hiring, and other aspects of campus life, and submit to intrusive federal oversight.

More than sixty institutions—including Harvard, Columbia, Cornell, Princeton, and the University of Pennsylvania—were accused of tolerating anti-Semitism connected to pro-Palestinian demonstrations and hit with audits or funding suspensions. Harvard was singled out with a $2.3 billion federal funding freeze. Under pressure from the administration, the presidents of Columbia and University of Virginia were forced to resign—a chilling signal that Trump would topple noncompliant university leaders. Harvard was one of the few to refuse Trump's demands and fight back in court. Columbia simply capitulated. Most others tried to quietly resolve the administration's concerns under tremendous budgetary pressure.

Meanwhile, Trump and his allies in Congress proposed and ultimately enacted steep new taxes on large university endowments, framing them as corrupt hoards. And because elite universities often rely heavily on international students and scholars—not just for tuition, but for research labs, teaching, and global prestige—Trump weaponized the immigration system against them, including the unprecedented step of suspending entry of all new international students and scholars to Harvard and attempting to strip the university of its ability to enroll any foreign students. Visa revocations, travel bans, and mass removals of international students from the federal system that tracks and verifies their legal status unleashed turmoil across the higher education landscape.

The punitive zeal with which these coordinated attacks on higher education unfolded is impossible to overstate. Trump's education secretary boasted about it as "body-slamming" the "college cartel." University leaders described it as an unprecedented governmental intrusion into academic decision-making.

A similarly bleak scenario unfolded at the federal agencies that sustain America's scientific and research enterprise, starting with an abrupt order for NIH to "cease all external communications" and stop all grant reviews, and followed by DOGE's takeover of award decisions. This plunged billions in research funding that sustains the budgets for many universities and hospitals into total chaos. Because complex research cannot easily be paused without devastating impacts, much of it simply ended. Complex projects from pandemics preparedness to dementia research and HIV prevention were among those defunded.

At NSF, DOGE ordered layoffs for up to half the agency's staff, and more than two hundred peer-reviewed grant proposals were flagged for ideological "compliance" review while hundreds of others were canceled outright. The vaunted NSF merit-review system that has anchored America's scientific leadership for decades was summarily overridden, with already-approved proposals canceled without explanation.

America has seen previous religiously inflected political attacks on NIH and NSF. The Reagan administration slowed AIDS funding and research due to conservatives' discomfort with a disease they associated with homosexuality; both parties have restricted research on therapeutic uses of cannabis and psychedelics; and President George W. Bush restricted embryonic stem cell research for faith-based reasons. But these episodes were minor perturbations compared to the destruction Trump unleashed.

The damage goes far beyond research. Trump knew exactly what he was getting when he put Robert F. Kennedy Jr.—an anti-vaccine conspiracist whose own family had begged that he never be entrusted with power—at the helm of the Department of Health and Human Services. Trump chose a man who insists Lyme disease was a US military bioweapon, pedals the racist trope that Black people have stronger immune systems, claims vaccines cause autism, and once likened the CDC to Nazi death camps, to oversee the sprawling research and health portfolio of NIH, as well as the Food and Drug Administration (FDA), the Centers for Disease Control and Prevention (CDC), the Centers for Medicare and Medicaid Services, and the Office of the Surgeon General. This placed Kennedy in charge of everything from drug and vaccine policies, to public health, biomedical research, and our nation's response to pandemics.

After promising at his Senate confirmation hearing that he would follow established science, Kennedy quickly reverted to form and launched an unhinged spree of ideologically driven interventions that gutted core health and safety functions, including the nation's life-saving vaccine infrastructure. He hollowed out entire divisions at the CDC and the FDA, fired top vaccine and drug-safety scientists, sidelined federal offices responsible for outbreak surveillance, and injected inaccuracies, misinformation, and unsupported claims into regulatory decisions. Experts warned that his reckless actions left the nation's health infrastructure in "an unprecedented state of upheaval." His public promotion of false claims about vaccines and infectious diseases led to lower immunization rates and resurgent outbreaks of measles and pertussis.

America's premiere climate and environmental science agency, NOAA, was also decimated. Mass firings and office closures degraded the agency's ability not only to forecast weather, manage commercial fisheries, and ensure aviation and maritime safety, but also to support military readiness and national security. Adding insult to injury, new political loyalty tests were added for science-based job openings like meteorologist to ensure applicants' enthusiasm for Trump.

The attacks continued unabated, despite dire warnings from science and health authorities, including more than twenty Nobel laureates, about irreversible damage to America's entire scientific enterprise. Yet through it all, the Republican Congress shrugged, even when Trump's cuts threatened to shut down pediatric cancer research.

There's no mystery to why Trump would embrace and supercharge the Christian nationalist war on education and science. It was never theological for him—it was tactical. His affection for the "poorly educated" was not a joke or a gaffe. It was a recognition of a political truth he understood and exploited relentlessly: Ignorance, grievance, and conspiracism are fertile soil for authoritarian power. When Voltaire wrote that "those who can make you believe absurdities can make you commit atrocities," he surely had someone like Trump in mind. Like Jefferson,

Trump knows that an educated public and independent academic institutions are antidotes to despotism. But unlike Jefferson, Trump doesn't want to protect against a tyrant; he wants to become one.

Trump's self-serving anti-intellectualism, however, is only half the story. Because for most of the protagonists in the war on education and science, the fight is very much about religion. Right-wing Christian resentment of secular schools, universities, and scientific authority has simmered for decades, rooted in a biblical worldview that sees modern knowledge as a threat. That grievance found new expression in the parental-rights and homeschooling movements, the anti-science conspiracists who targeted public health, medical research, and climate science, and the crusade against universities.

I saw this up close as my devout Republican colleagues cheered Trump's wrecking ball against the university and science establishment even as it upended jobs and entire communities in their own congressional districts. Their reaction wasn't a reluctant concession to budget cuts, reforms, and political necessity; it was jubilation.

This is the point where our examination of the war on education and, especially, science turns from politics to psychology. The patterns on display—the rejection of evidence, the embrace of conspiratorial narratives, the moralization of misinformation—are well-studied phenomena. A robust body of peer-reviewed research has long shown that religiosity and science denial often travel together. The correlation between strong religious belief and skepticism toward scientific consensus on evolution, climate change, vaccines, and more is so well proven that it is essentially beyond debate. But a groundbreaking 2024 study from Stanford and Columbia reveals something even more potent than religiosity driving science denial: religious *intolerance*.

Published in *Proceedings of the National Academy of Sciences*, the study engaged over fifteen thousand participants across the US and dozens of other countries to test whether science denial correlates more strongly with religious absolutism than with mere religious belief. The answer: It does, overwhelmingly. The researchers found that "sectarian supremacy"—the belief that one's religion is the sole and exclusive truth—was a powerful predictor of science denial, independent of how devout someone is. As the study puts it: "From sectarian supremacism, it is a small step to also reject science, another rival belief system." Indeed, the study singled out white evangelicals, Trump's most loyal base, for the highest levels of science denial among Christian groups in the US, a trend researchers link directly to sectarian intolerance and lack of exposure to other belief systems.

In other words, the more someone believes their faith is the only truth and that it must dominate public life, the more likely they are to see science as a threat that must be neutralized. Jefferson saw this coming. And now, research confirms it.

Right-wing Christians are not wrong that science poses a threat to their fundamentalist biblical worldview. The conflicts are inherent. Science demands doubt, scrutiny, evidence, revision, and humility, while fundamentalism demands certainty, obedience, and scriptural supremacy. When science reveals new facts and explanations that refute the biblical script, their theology tells them they must treat it as heresy. It's therefore no wonder that the vast majority of elite scientists reject belief in God, including a whopping 92 percent of National Academy of Sciences members.

Yet the fact that religious fundamentalism is hardwired to attack science is precisely why science must be defended. The acclaimed astrophysicist Neil deGrasse Tyson, a Humanist, makes the point with a stark historical parable. From roughly the eighth through the fourteenth centuries, the Islamic world led humanity in mathematics, astronomy, medicine, and engineering, with Persian scholars at the forefront in institutions like the House of Wisdom in Baghdad, the birthplace of algebra, and the world's most advanced observatories. But that intellectual flourishing gradually collapsed as fundamentalist clerics began criticizing aspects of science and rational inquiry as arrogant intrusions into divine territory. As more rigid forms of religious orthodoxy gained influence, the space for critical inquiry narrowed: Scientific institutions withered and intellectual curiosity was recast as a threat to religious authority. The result was a steady civilizational retreat, as a culture that had once defined global knowledge production forfeited its scientific edge.

The point is not a critique of Islam—it is a warning of what happens in any society when extreme religious authority is allowed to override empirical reasoning: The engines of progress shut down. Scientific cultures can be undone when rational inquiry loses its protected place in public life. And today, the cost of allowing religious fundamentalism to override science is far steeper than when the Persianate Golden Era unraveled into religious entrenchment—or even in Jefferson's time, when the fight for critical inquiry and knowledge was fundamentally about liberty and individual rights.

As the top Democrat on the House Natural Resources Committee, much of my work in Congress centers on the worsening climate crisis. The symptoms are no longer abstract: Rising temperatures, collapsing ecosystems, vanishing biodiversity, and intensifying resource conflicts are already destabilizing agriculture and displacing communities. The World Health Organization warns that climate-related health impacts, including malnutrition, malaria, and heat stress, could soon claim an additional 250,000 lives annually. The number of deadly natural disasters and heat-related deaths has climbed steadily for more than a decade, and the pace of surface and ocean warming is outrunning our ability to adapt.

As terrible as that is, the climate crisis isn't the only existential threat we're sleepwalking into. Lost in the chaotic news cycles of Trump's first year was this harrowing story: In January of 2025, the Bulletin of the Atomic Scientists moved the hands of their Doomsday Clock to 89 seconds from midnight—the closest to global catastrophe since 1947. That shift was motivated by the rising risk of global pandemics. COVID-19 was a brutal reminder that civilization can be brought to its knees by a microscopic pathogen. Experts warn that even deadlier pandemics may be on the horizon, demanding not just cutting-edge science but global cooperation at the very moment when both are being recklessly undermined.

These two looming civilizational threats are compounded by a dark synergy: Climate change fuels pandemic risk. As ecosystems unravel and human-wildlife contact intensifies, the likelihood of zoonotic spillover—diseases jumping from animals to humans—rises sharply. Sixty percent of emerging pathogens originate in animals, and a third of those are linked to land-use changes, often driven by climate pressures. Climate destabilizes the biosphere; pandemics expose the fragility of our response systems. Together, they form a feedback loop of vulnerability. It raises the stakes of the war on science from epistemological and political to truly existential.

Fortunately, science isn't quietly yielding to religious extremism. In the two fields most relentlessly targeted by the war on science, climate and public health, researchers are fighting back with increasing urgency. At the forefront of that resistance are two experts at the top of their respective fields of climate science and global health, Dr. Michael Mann and Dr. Peter Hotez. Their 2025 book, *Science Under Siege: How to Fight the Five Most Powerful Forces That Threaten Our World,* is both a warning and a battle plan. Mann and Hotez have spent years on the frontlines of disinformation, enduring blistering attacks from MAGA-aligned science deniers. Both are Jewish, and the online vitriol against them often carries the stench of anti-Semitism. Mann shared with me that the most hateful attacks usually come from social media accounts with images or references to Jesus in the profile.

Science Under Siege exposes the machinery of science denial: how institutions like NIH, NSF, and NOAA are targeted for discrediting and defunding; the dark money pipelines that finance fake grassroots groups; the "credentialed contrarians" who cherry-pick data and mislead the public, often platformed by mainstream media under the guise of "balance;" and the viral spread of conspiracy and pseudoscience online. Their book offers a decoder ring for spotting anti-Enlightenment tactics and a call to arms for reclaiming the narrative.

Mann and Hotez emphasize the importance of building alliances across science, education, journalism, and policy expertise, that help ensure an informed and resilient citizenry. They underscore the importance of communicating science in ways that are clear, compelling, and relatable, especially in the age of social media and viral disinformation, because truth doesn't win by default. They stress that the fight over funding of public science must be seen as a civic emergency because agencies like CDC, NIH, NSF, EPA, and NOAA do more than just sustain jobs for scientists; they are democracy's immune system.

Mann, a member of the National Academy of Sciences and a friend, is one of my go-to advisors on climate policy. We share the unusual honor of being named Humanist of the Year by the American

Humanist Association—him in 2023, me in 2020. In a recent conversation, Dr. Mann pointed out that the great astrophysicist Carl Sagan once held the Humanist of the Year title, too, and he reminded me of Sagan's chilling warning, in his epic book, *The Demon-Haunted World*:

> I have a foreboding of an America in my children's or grandchildren's time . . . when the people have lost the ability to set their own agendas or knowledgeably question those in authority; when, clutching our crystals and nervously consulting our horoscopes, our critical faculties in decline, unable to distinguish between what feels good and what's true, we slide, almost without noticing, back into superstition and darkness.

Sagan's crystal-clutching metaphor was gentler than Jefferson's firebrand denunciations of "priestcraft" and "religious delirium," but the message was the same: Reason must be defended. Science, learning, and critical thinking are not elite luxuries—they are the foundation of liberty and increasingly a civilizational lifeline. Without them, democracy and perhaps civilization itself is a sandcastle in a rising tide.

The ancient fault line that defined Jefferson's life—the collision between faith and reason, dogma and science—is rumbling again. Christian nationalists are wielding Jefferson's razor in reverse, slicing away climate data, evolutionary theory, vaccines, and anything else that threatens their brittle biblical worldview. Their war on education and science gravely imperils the health of our planet, and the security and prosperity of future generations. In his own time, Jefferson fought back against these theocratic forces, and thankfully he prevailed.

Now it's our turn.

CHAPTER 9

DEFENDERS OF DEMOCRACY

For I was an hungred, and ye gave me meat:
I was thirsty, and ye gave me drink:
I was a stranger, and ye took me in:
Naked, and ye clothed me:
I was sick, and ye visited me:
I was in prison, and ye came unto me.

—SERMON ON THE MOUNT (MATTHEW 25:35–36)

ON THE FRIGID MORNING OF JANUARY 21, 2025, BISHOP Mariann Edgar Budde scanned the overflow audience of dignitaries that filled Washington's National Cathedral. She was about to preside over an American political ritual: the Inaugural Prayer Service. Forty feet in front of her, newly inaugurated President Donald Trump sat in the same front-row seat every president since Franklin Delano Roosevelt has occupied. From the ornate décor to the music performed by the organist and the cathedral choir, the trappings belied the reality that longstanding traditions were being shattered.

Normally, the cathedral defers to the inaugural committee's choice of preachers, as they did with Trump's first Inaugural Prayer Service in January of 2017. Not this time. As the first female bishop of Washington's Episcopal Diocese, Budde had built a reputation for speaking truth to power, including calling out Trump's hateful, divisive actions during his first presidency. She was appalled at the way he targeted vulnerable, marginalized people to whom her ministry is dedicated. Allowing a Trump-friendly preacher to sanctify his inauguration with an innocuous "let us pray for the nation and our new president" homily was unthinkable.

Bishop Budde would do it herself. She would give a sermon rooted in the teachings of Jesus Christ's longest continuous discourse: the moral manifesto known as the Sermon on the Mount. Found in the Bible's book of Matthew at chapters 5 through 7, this sermon is a sweeping call for humility, compassion, mercy, and a form of grace so disarming that it commands: "Love your enemies and pray for those who persecute you." For the millions of earnest Christians who still take these values to heart—and for a president who so brazenly flouts them—this would be the homily the moment demanded.

The man in the front row was shattering traditions, as well. Arguably the most irreligious person to ever win the presidency, Trump had twice been lifted to victory by overwhelming support from Christian nationalists who viewed him as something of a messiah. Trump's 2024 campaign was built on the foundation of the Cyrus anointing that had gotten it all started in 2016. But this campaign was even more drenched in religious fervor, as indicated by his endlessly promoted "God made Trump" video and $55 "God Bless the USA" Bibles. After Trump survived an assassination attempt, the narrative of his prophetic destiny was sealed. For millions of enraptured supporters, Trump's subsequent election victory was a mandate from the Almighty himself.

Thus, by the time Trump took his seat in the front row of the National Cathedral that morning, he had completed a transformation into a *religious* figure. He would lead the ascendant Christian nationalist movement in taking back America for God. That vision of God, however, was quite different from Budde's.

It wasn't just Trump's gaudy, merchandised version of faith that anguished Christians like Budde; it was the way he and his most fervent supporters trampled Christ's core teachings and modeled a harsh, punitive Christian variant that mocks the Sermon on the Mount as "wokeness" and replaces it with a hypermasculine, demonize-and-destroy creed.

As Bishop Budde met Trump's gaze and began to speak, two antithetical strains of Christianity were about to square off, with the bishop pitching for Team Compassion and Trump batting leadoff for Team Vengeance. She addressed Trump directly:

> In the name of our God, I ask you to have mercy upon the people in our country who are scared now. There are gay, lesbian, and transgender children in Democratic, Republican, and Independent families, some who fear for their lives . . . They may not be citizens or have the proper documentation, but the vast majority of immigrants are not criminals. They pay taxes and are good neighbors. They are faithful members of our churches and mosques, synagogues, and temples. I ask you to have mercy, Mr. President, on those in our communities whose children fear that their parents will be taken away and that you help those who are fleeing war zones and persecution in their own lands, to find compassion and welcome here.

Trump didn't take this rebuke sitting down. After the service, he blasted Budde as a "so-called bishop" and a "radical left hard-line Trump hater" whose sermon was "nasty" and "ungracious." His allies in Congress piled on, with one congressman demanding that Budde be "added to the deportation list." Twenty-two House Republicans cosponsored a resolution that chastised the bishop for "promoting political bias instead of advocating the full counsel of biblical teaching." Right-wing Christian leaders like Tony Perkins denounced the bishop as "pathetic," and televangelist Franklin Graham declared that the National Cathedral had been "taken over by gay activists." Some hard-line Christian nationalists considered the bishop's defiance tantamount to blasphemy, since God had anointed Trump for this moment.

For many Christians, however, a star was born. Bishop Budde was inundated with "thank you" messages from around the country. Democrats like Senator Chris Van Hollen praised her for reminding Trump "we are all God's children." Editorials in *The Washington Post*, *The New York Times*, and *The Guardian* lauded her courage and moral clarity. And dozens of Christian faith leaders validated the bishop's "timely and prophetic" message of grace and compassion as accurately reflecting Jesus' core teachings.

Bishop Budde's takedown of Trump was like a national Rorschach test for Christians. MAGA Christian nationalists were outraged, viewing her sermon as the kind of soft Christian values that no longer work in today's world. Mainstream and progressive Christians, however, welcomed the bishop's message as a beacon of true Christianity that might help reset the debate over what their faith stands for.

The dustup over Bishop Budde's sermon reminded me of something one of my favorite writers, Kurt Vonnegut, said in his final book, *A Man Without a Country*. In 2005 when the book was published, Christian nationalism wasn't a household term, but Vonnegut must have seen the storm clouds gathering. "For some reason," he wrote, "the most vocal Christians among us never mention the Beatitudes. But, often with tears in their eyes, they demand the Ten Commandments be posted in public buildings. And of course that's Moses, not Jesus. I haven't heard one of them demand the Sermon on the Mount, the Beatitudes, be posted anywhere." Vonnegut was foreshadowing a theological reckoning that seems to have finally arrived. A growing number of Christians are echoing his lament. And not just from the margins, but also from pulpits and seminaries, and in bestselling books, religious journals, documentary films, podcasts, and advocacy coalitions. Which brings us to a turning point in our story.

In the beginning of this book, we charted Christian nationalism's rise from its Moral Majority roots in the 1980s to January 6th and the dominion theology wielded by its fanatical faith leaders. We've exposed how Trump is lending these hard-liners unprecedented legitimacy, how Christian privilege has sharpened their blade and armored their advance, how their shadow theocracy is eroding the wall between church and state, and how their extreme beliefs are distorting foreign policy and imperiling our systems of secular education and science that not only safeguard American democracy but equip us to navigate existential global threats.

All of this may seem overwhelming, like extreme Christian nationalism is invincible and unstoppable. That is certainly what they want us to think. But beneath the swagger lies a brittle coalition strained by theological rifts, cultural fault lines, economic and philosophical differences, and clashing egos. It's an explosive mix primed for implosion. And as the embrace of Bishop Budde's message proves, one of the widening chasms is the growing number of Christians who are choosing the side of Team Compassion.

It turns out many Christians, including some prominent evangelicals, still believe that the Sermon on the Mount, not demonization and cruelty, should define their core values. These faithful dissenters are increasingly speaking out and mobilizing against Christian nationalism as a betrayal of Christ's gospel.

One of the most influential groups of faithful dissenters is Christians Against Christian Nationalism, a coalition launched in 2019 by the Baptist Joint Committee for Religious Liberty. It now includes more than forty thousand pastors, theologians, lay leaders, and congregants from every major denomination, preaching a unified creed: Christian faith should never be fused with American identity, and all people—of any faith or none—are equal in the public square. Like the minority Christian sects of our founding era, especially the Quakers and Baptists who were among the most passionate champions of church-state separation, these Christians have figured out that secular governance is critical to protecting *their* religious freedom.

At the helm of this group is Amanda Tyler, a constitutional lawyer and preacher's daughter from Austin, Texas. As executive director of the Baptist Joint Committee for Religious Liberty, she shows up at churches and school boards, testifies before Congress, and barnstorms the country talking to community groups and bookstore audiences about her faith-based manifesto, *How to End Christian Nationalism.*

Tyler's central message is that Christian nationalism is political ideology masked by religious rhetoric; that Christians must reject such distortions and reclaim the soul of their faith; and that to protect religious freedom, vigorous defense of church-state separation is more important than ever. Tyler and her pro-democracy Christian allies have the potential to be breakthrough messengers in a media and political landscape steeped in Christian privilege and hypersensitive to charges of "anti-Christian bias." Christians are more open to warnings and criticisms coming from their fellow believers, whose theologically grounded arguments cannot be dismissed as secular hostility to religion.

The stalwarts of Team Compassion are organizing effectively. And they're focused on equipping pastors and congregations with resources to resist the creep of Christian nationalism into their faith communities. One of Tyler's most prominent allies, journalist Tim Alberta, knows the importance of that pastoral support from bitter experience. A lifelong evangelical and son of a minister, Alberta's bestseller, *The Kingdom, the Power, and the Glory: American Evangelicals in an Age of Extremism*, illuminates the upheaval within evangelical communities nationwide. His elegy reveals how congregations once grounded in a theology of radical compassion have been overtaken by a harsh strain of Christianity centered on cultural dominance and scorched-earth politics. Alberta shares how this toxic shift even infected his father's congregation and the sacred space of his father's funeral. In early 2025 he completed a college lecture tour, "The Crisis in American Christianity," where he lamented the hijacking of his faith by nationalists who replace compassion with coercion and called for a fundamental recentering of Christianity on Jesus's moral teachings—including disentangling faith from partisan political identity.

Russell Moore is a prominent faith leader sounding the alarm from inside the evangelical power structure. Moore led the Southern Baptist Convention's Ethics & Religious Liberty Commission until his resignation in 2021 in response to relentless attacks by Trump loyalists. Moore's outspoken criticism of Trump, advocacy for racial justice, and calls for accountability on sexual abuse made him a target. But he did not go quietly. Moore now uses his platform as editor-in-chief of *Christianity Today* to deliver unflinching critiques of the moral abyss of Trumpism. He calls Christian nationalism "liberation theology for white people," denouncing the way it reduces Christianity to a cheap tribal identity marker instead of a transformative personal faith.

In a recent conversation, Moore told me the MAGA religious right is "flimsier than it looks." He admits their scorched-earth tactics have left many mainstream Christians "exhausted and demoralized," but he also sees cracks forming. One of those involves the increasingly racist and anti-Semitic rhetoric he sees coming out of Christian nationalist circles, especially from extremists on social media. According to Moore, this escalating bigotry is repelling many evangelicals.

Previous chapters in this book have examined the persuasive power of right-wing faith leaders, like Dutch Sheets, who have amassed huge followings with their violent preaching and hyper-partisan prophecies. But as both Alberta and Moore make clear, radicalization is not always a pulpit-down phenomenon. Like Alberta, Moore has seen many evangelical churches succumb to MAGA takeovers not because of radical pastors, but because of pressure from congregants. "It is almost always the people who are bringing social media information, Fox News information, and anti-democracy extremism into the churches," he says.

Moore and Alberta's experience validate the wisdom of Amanda Tyler's strategic focus on equipping pastors and congregations to resist MAGA takeovers. They are also sharing a crucial insight from evangelical frontlines—one that could be Christian nationalism's Achilles' heel. The movement's core strategy of pushing right-wing politics into churches happens to be a leading reason why millions are walking away from religion.

Data shows that a broad majority of Americans—including churchgoing Republicans—believe churches should steer clear of politics. Younger generations are particularly turned off by pastors blurring the line between gospel and partisan ideology. MAGA extremists may be exciting their declining base, but they are sailing headlong into a fading wind. Historian Jemar Tisby, himself a devout evangelical, put it bluntly: "People aren't leaving the church because we love too much . . . They're leaving because they see White Christian Nationalism and say, 'If that's Christianity, I want nothing to do with it.' And rightly so."

This clash between Team Compassion and Team Vengeance for the soul of Christianity seems to mirror the dualism within human nature itself: our capacity for radical empathy, kindness, and grace on the one hand; and our competing drive for tribal identity and righteous domination on the other. Team Compassion is betting that our hunger for peace and reconciliation will win out.

The contrast with Team Vengeance is stark. Having spent hours listening to NAR leaders like Sheets, and consulting religious scholars who dissect their sermons and prophecies, I'm struck by the same thing Vonnegut observed: They almost never mention the Sermon on the Mount, the manifesto of love, mercy, and compassion that is supposed to be the moral centerpiece of Christianity. As we've seen, NAR focuses on violent Old Testament stories, like Elijah's slaughter of 450 prophets of Baal, Joshua's brutal conquest of Jericho, David's beheading of Goliath, and the favorite, the grim saga of Jezebel, the archetypal "wicked woman" who corrupted the Hebrews until God raised up Jehu to throw her from a palace window, where she was trampled by horses and devoured by dogs.

David French, *The New York Times'* syndicated columnist, unpacked these competing visions of Christianity in his 2025 column, "Why Are So Many Christians So Cruel?" He argues that the allure of political power has led many Christians to lash their cruelty to the cross, becoming "the most dangerous kinds of people—a cruel person with a clean conscience." French is a devout evangelical who consistently calls on his readers to embrace a Sermon on the Mount theology rooted in compassion and reject Christian nationalism. Team Vengeance has responded to French's writings by targeting him and his family with personal attacks for refusing to support Trump, disparaging them as spiritual traitors, and driving them out of their own church.

Pro-democracy Christians are going to need tough skin. But if Tyler and her impressive allies can reach enough of their fellow Christians, the data suggests fertile ground for change. While Trump has enjoyed near-monolithic overall support from conservative Christians, polling shows that a significant majority of them also reject key aspects of his agenda such as cruelty to immigrants, anti-LGBTQ bigotry, and sweeping abortion restrictions. Moreover, Christians across the political spectrum overwhelmingly support the separation of church and state. Though the "Christian nation" chorus is loud and politically powerful, polling reveals most Christians reject the core tenets of Christian nationalism.

My former colleague Adam Kinzinger predicts an inevitable countermovement within conservative Christianity. "The human heart can only remain awash in anger and mistrust and hate for so long before you need to come to Jesus, so to speak," he told me. Kinzinger sees signs that the Sermon on the Mount is mounting a comeback: "In the churches I go to, you're seeing this kind of real rising up and understanding that Jesus is actually about taking care of people—that actually, the church is not called to be deeply engaged in government."

Another vulnerability for the Christian nationalist movement is the theological fissures between the three ascendant religious subcultures fueling the MAGA Christian coalition: Rad Trad Catholics, Reconstructionist Theo Bros, and NAR-aligned independent charismatic evangelicals. This uneasy alliance, rooted in a shared embrace of Trump and opposition to abortion, LGBTQ rights, and secular liberalism, masks fierce absolutism within each subculture. Each believes it possesses the only legitimate blueprint for Christian dominion, and that the others' doctrines are somewhere between misguided and heretical. Tensions have been temporarily muted by the unifying force of Trump, but make no mistake: They don't like each other, and their differences could easily flare into conflict.

The most glaring rift lies between fundamentalist Catholics and Protestants. Rad Trads exalt institutional authority and liturgical exactitude, demanding strict adherence to Catholic doctrine and ritual purity like the Traditional Latin Mass. They even criticize their own popes for lacking rigor and being too ecumenical. So, you can imagine their disdain for the techno-libertarian futurist schemes of the Theo Bros or for the charismatic freelancing of NAR, whose *Ekklesia* issue wild prophecies and exhilarate legions of independent prayer warriors with spirit mapping and demonic cosplay.

The Protestant factions don't care much for Catholics, either. NAR apostles have long disparaged "traditional," "sacramental," and "hierarchical" religions as "demonic strongholds" that must be broken for true

Christian revival. Theo Bro Pastor Joel Webbon goes even further, preaching that America's coming Christian kingdom will be distinctly Protestant, with Catholics relegated to second-class status. His unambiguous message to Catholics: "You're welcome to ride along, but this is Protestant territory. . . . You can be in the car, but you don't get to drive. The Protestants are driving."

Meanwhile, the Theo Bros have major problems with NAR's wild-eyed charismatics. CREC leader Doug Wilson not only scorns their prophetic theater and apostolic cosplay but condemns their embrace of women in church leadership as outright apostasy. Like Catholics, the Theo Bros insist on a framework of biblical patriarchy that relegates women to subordinate roles, whereas NAR elevates female pastors like Paula White and Cindy Jacobs as influential prophetic leaders. Wilson rebuked Trump's appointment of White as the official White House spiritual advisor, calling her "an erratic woman preacher who has been all over the map." This, in turn, prompted a sharp retort from NAR apostle Lance Walnau, who dismissed Wilson and his allies as "whackos." Just one big Protestant family rebuking each other as heretics.

Perhaps their most volatile fault line is Israel. NAR embraces Christian Zionism with fervor. This devotion is conditioned on mass Jewish conversion and eventual Christian dominion over Israel, but there's no denying that charismatic evangelicals have built real political partnerships with Jewish leaders around pro-Israel policies. By contrast, Rad Trads and Theo Bros are both wary of Israel. They reject Christian Zionism, and both groups are steeped in longstanding undercurrents of antisemitism. Among Rad Trads, that lineage runs from Nazi-loving Priest Father Coughlin to the neo-Nazi integralist Nick Fuentes. For Theo Bros, it shows up in R. J. Rushdoony's denunciation of Judaism as an "apostate" revolt against God's order and Pastor Joel Webbon's thinly veiled bigotry: "I hate Judaism but love Jews and wish them a very pleasant conversion to Christianity."

Yet more than any single theological flashpoint, it's likely to be these extremists' sheer intolerance and absolutism that eventually upends their coalition. NAR's *Ekklesia* are hardwired for purges, schisms, and internecine betrayal. We saw flashes of this after Trump's 2020 defeat, when the fallout over false prophesies sparked fierce battles about "prophetic standards" triggering public rebukes, cross-accusations of spiritual treason, and the shutdown of at least one ministry.

Absolutism and extreme intolerance have long coursed through right-wing Christianity, so much so that their endless rhetoric about freedom of religion should come with a disclaimer. In a revealing 2022 sermon, the prominent megachurch televangelist John MacArthur said the quiet part out loud: "I don't even support religious freedom. Religious freedom is what sends people to hell. To say I support religious freedom is to say I support religious idolatry."

That same rigid absolutism fueled the backlash against Moral Majority stalwart Colonel V. Doner when he dared question the movement's lack of compassion. It's why conservative evangelicals like Russell Moore, Adam Kinzinger, and Tim Alberta were ostracized. And inevitably, this self-consuming purity spiral will turn the uneasy theological bedfellows of Christian nationalism against each other, especially once MAGA is forced to evolve.

For now, the glue holding this shaky coalition together is Trump. His unique position, unaligned with any religious faction but appealing to all of them, allows the three groups to each claim him as their own, according to religion scholars Dr. Matthew Taylor and Dr. Bradley Onishi. Trump's potential GOP successors—Catholics like J. D. Vance, Marco Rubio, Ron DeSantis, and Greg Abbott, or evangelicals like Ted Cruz, Glenn Younkin, and Mike Pompeo—all carry distinct religious affiliations, and will therefore face a far tougher challenge bridging these doctrinal divides.

But vulnerability is not the same thing as defeat. Even if the three-legged stool of NAR, Theo Bros, and Rad Trads wobbles, and even if these factions never unite behind another Republican leader the way they have around Trump, the threat of Christian nationalism will still be with us. This movement won't just fade away: It has amassed too much power, too much money, and too much momentum in its war on secular democracy.

So, much as I admire the work of Christians Against Christian Nationalism and their faith-based allies, let's be very clear: They can't win this fight by themselves. Pro-democracy Christians need partners. Defeating the powerfully entrenched Christian nationalist movement requires a big-tent coalition—one that brings together not only other faith communities but also secular and nonreligious groups wherever possible.

A coalition spanning the full spectrum of shared opposition to Christian nationalism would be formidable enough to win, but building and sustaining it won't be easy. My conversation with Russell Moore highlighted some of the complexity. Moore, like Tim Alberta and many other evangelical allies in this fight, holds conservative views on abortion, and probably many other issues. Yet his vigorous opposition to Christian nationalism and commitment to church-state separation places him alongside secularists and Democrats in defense of democracy. Moore shared his discomfort with the way liberals sometimes dismiss or condescend to pro-life evangelicals, straining the threads of cooperation. He also cautioned that secular advocates sometimes frame church-state separation so aggressively they feed into the "naked public square" argument, alienating people of faith. Fortunately, Moore remains deeply committed to building pro-democracy coalitions across religious and ideological divides. But navigating these tensions and holding the big-tent coalition together will be an ongoing challenge requiring careful, thoughtful leadership.

There are promising signs of such a coalition taking shape. The February 2022 collaboration between the Baptist Joint Committee and the Freedom From Religion Foundation—a group representing atheists, humanists, and agnostics—on a comprehensive joint report regarding Christian nationalism's role in the insurrection was an important first step. Other joint initiatives have followed, like the Freedom Express Bus Tour in Pennsylvania led by interfaith leaders and Humanists to mobilize voters in the 2022 midterm election; the 2023 collaboration between grassroots advocacy group MoveOn and the faith-based Kairos Center which produced a seventy-five-page strategic blueprint titled *All of U.S.: Organizing to Counter White Christian Nationalism and Build a Pro-Democracy Society*; and several ongoing organizing, education, and media campaigns where the national multifaith group Interfaith Alliance is teaming up with the Secular Coalition of America and Americans United for Separation of Church and State.

Christians Against Christian Nationalism is making partnerships with interfaith and secular allies a top priority. Toward that end, Amanda Tyler tirelessly engages Christians and non-Christians alike in urgent conversations about defending church-state separation, including with my Congressional Freethought Caucus.

Speaking of which, I would be remiss not to spotlight the little caucus Jamie Raskin and I launched back in 2018 as a growing force in the pro-democracy fight against Christian nationalism. Until the Freethought Caucus, Congress had never had a working coalition of lawmakers dedicated to defending church-state separation. What began as just me, Raskin, and our cofounders Jerry McNerney and Mark Pocan, soon expanded to colleagues Pramila Jayapal, Dan Kildee, Rick Nolan, Hank Johnson, Eleanor Holmes Norton, and Sean Casten as word spread about our work. By 2026, our ranks had swelled to thirty-three members—more than the Republicans' so-called Freedom Caucus!—all of us passionate about defending religious freedom, resisting theocracy, and advancing our nation's core values, including civil rights, pluralism, rule of law, academic freedom, and the defense of science.

Some of the Freethought Caucus' work was mentioned in earlier chapters, such as highlighting the role of Christian nationalism in the January 6th insurrection and releasing a white paper to expose Speaker Mike Johnson's religious extremism. We work continuously to spearhead important bills and resolutions, lead hard-hitting coalition letters, file amicus briefs, and host impactful briefings and events to shape policy and public discourse. Leading secular and pro-democracy advocacy groups now recognize the power of this coalition and have become partners in our work. But perhaps our most vital contribution is simply normalizing religious diversity and pluralism in an institution that truly needs it. Unlike Congress broadly—a near-monolith of Christianity—our Freethought Caucus mirrors the religious mix of America: Christians, Jews, a Muslim, a Hindu, a Buddhist, some who decline to state, and me, the lone Humanist. We have broken important new ground and are here to stay.

As we appreciate all this progress and continue building momentum toward a powerful religious-secular coalition for democracy, let's also be clear that we cannot afford to backslide into a "believers only" paradigm of confronting Christian nationalism. To this point, the aftermath of Bishop Budde's moral takedown of Trump at the National Cathedral was a striking missed opportunity. Budde's sermon and the MAGA reaction to it should have sparked a unifying national conversation about the urgent threat we face and the imperative for Americans of all faith perspectives to rally together in defense of our shared values and democratic institutions. Instead, the ensuing national discourse left non-Christian America—34 percent of the population, 114 million people—watching from the sidelines as Team Compassion and Team Vengeance duked it out over which brand of Christianity should dominate our politics. To be clear, I know which side I am rooting for in their intra-faith struggle, but it should never distract from the North Star: saving democracy while fighting for every American's religious freedom.

The strategic importance of maintaining a united pro-democracy coalition that includes nonbelievers and secularists should be obvious: 30 percent of Americans now identify as nonreligious. "Nones" are now the single largest religious group in America, and we're growing fast. Embracing and including nonbelievers is a *mathematical* political necessity.

Moreover, nonbelievers and non-Christians bring a lot of talent and resources that pro-democracy Christians should welcome in this fight. One example is the fearless and brilliant advocacy work of secular litigators like Rachel Laser and Andrew Seidel at Americans United for Separation of Church and State. These badass lawyers wage legal battles against Christian nationalist powerhouses like the Alliance Defending Freedom, taking on the toughest cases—including in the Supreme Court—and often winning landmark victories. They scored a federal court injunction against Texas's outrageous Ten Commandments mandate for public school classrooms, for example.

Other leading secular groups such as the Secular Coalition for America, Center for Freethought Equality, and American Atheists are steadily building capacity as well. In recent years, they have evolved from niche interest groups into influential political forces representing millions of nonreligious Americans. They're racking up impressive legislative wins, like Colorado's 2023 Patient's Right to Know Act, which guarantees transparency when health-care services—such as abortion or tubal ligation—are denied for nonmedical reasons like religion.

The Center for Freethought Equality and allied organizations are also working at every level of government to recruit, track, and support secular elected officials. Slowly but surely, this will bridge the disconnect between our increasingly diverse, nonreligious population and institutions like Congress which do not yet reflect that diversity.

Some creative secularists are also harnessing the power of wit and humor to defend pluralism. Lucien Greaves, through his spoof organization The Satanic Temple, uses satire to expose the hypocrisy of Christian nationalist overreach. Beneath the kitschy trappings—"666 Wedding Packages," Pizzagate-themed fundraisers, and open-mic satanic comedy nights—the "Temple" promotes basic civic values of empathy, reason, and pluralism. It's more aligned with the Sermon on the Mount than much of what we hear from Team Vengeance. Greaves' genius lies in triggering moral panic from theocrats, prompting them to overreach in ways that backfire in court and thus expose the asymmetry of Christian privilege. In that way, satire can shift the debate about religious freedom and strengthen church-state separation.

Building a full-spectrum coalition to save democracy doesn't mean all these groups have to think alike or share the same space. The provocative antics of The Satanic Temple would be a disaster at one of Amanda Tyler's prayer meetings. And many devout Christians would be poorly suited to mobilizing non-Christian communities. Different groups can work in different lanes using different tactics. But we should all be rowing in the same direction, and amplifying each other's efforts wherever possible through litigation, legislation, grassroots organizing, and media campaigns. Unleashing the full power of these diverse, and sometimes improbable, allies has the potential to reach many millions of Americans and activate the awesome power of public opinion—the ultimate key to winning this fight against extreme Christian nationalism.

If we build and sustain this interfaith-secular coalition, we can defeat America's most dangerous political movement. We can prevent these fanatics from dismantling our democracy and fundamental rights and begin disentangling the Christian nationalist project from our public institutions and laws. We can ensure religious neutrality in the public square so that everyone is welcome on equal terms and freedom of conscience is respected. But there's one more thing we will all need.

Winning this urgent, uphill fight requires the right mindset—the intangible but indispensable key to persevering and ultimately winning. At this great inflection point, we must acknowledge the reality that the United States is facing a fascist specter with disturbing parallels to Europe in the late 1920s and early 1930s, and that Christian nationalism is a driving force behind it. Our moment is different, but we can draw guidance from those who resisted fascism in its darkest hour.

Antonio Gramsci, imprisoned by Mussolini, inspired the Italian resistance with his prolific writings from a small prison cell where fascists tried to break him physically and psychologically. The clarity, resilience, and unyielding determination that sustained him are captured in his letters, including this famous exhortation to his brother:

> A man ought to be deeply convinced that the source of his own moral force is in himself—his very energy and will, the iron coherence of ends and means—that he never falls into those vulgar, banal moods, pessimism and optimism. My own state of mind synthesizes these two feelings and transcends them: my mind is pessimistic, but my will is optimistic. Whatever the situation, I imagine the worst that could happen in order to summon up all my reserves and will power to overcome every obstacle.

Gramsci's ethic—pessimism of the intellect, optimism of the will—was a call to confront brutal political realities without illusion, while summoning the resolve to keep fighting and to win.

Which reminds me, improbably, of Admiral James Stockdale, who some remember for his awkward 1992 vice presidential campaign moment, when he opened the debate by asking, "Who am I? Why am I here?" Before he was Ross Perot's running mate, however, Stockdale was a serious war hero, imprisoned and tortured in a Vietnamese POW camp alongside John McCain. Years later, he reflected on what enabled some prisoners to survive while others didn't. The key, now known as the Stockdale paradox, was essentially the same ethic that sustained Gramsci. He advised that "You must never confuse faith that you will prevail in the end . . . with the discipline to confront the most brutal facts of your current reality."

Meeting the brutal facts of our current reality and saving democracy from Christian nationalism requires a lot from us. It requires us to rally a pro-democracy coalition big enough to meet the scale of the threat. And this moment demands that we maintain the clarity of Gramsci's pessimism of the intellect and optimism of the will—or Stockdale's paradox, take your pick. But if we hold fast to that clear-eyed resolve, and put our faith in each other, then the story of this era will not be the fall of pluralism, democracy, and the America we love. It will be the story of people who refused to be intimidated, who linked arms across lines of belief and identity, and chose to stand together when it mattered most.

CONCLUSION

THERE IS A POPULAR STORY ABOUT GEORGE WASHING-ton at Valley Forge, during the bleak winter of 1776 when his troops were starving, freezing, and demoralized. Legend has it that Washington went alone into the woods, knelt in the snow, and prayed for divine intervention. Immortalized in Arnold Friberg's 1975 painting *The Prayer at Valley Forge*, Washington's prayer has become a visual catechism for those who stubbornly promote a "Christian nation" narrative of our founding. But like so many retrofits of American history, it's fiction crafted from wishful mythmaking.

What actually happened at Valley Forge is more radical and more revealing of the Enlightenment values on which America was founded. In that freezing crucible of despair, Washington didn't turn to scripture—he turned to reason. He ordered that his beleaguered troops receive a dramatic reading of Thomas Paine's freshly published pamphlet *The American Crisis*, which began with those searing words: "These are the times that try men's souls . . ."

Paine, whose writings helped birth the American republic, was among the most important of our founders. His blockbuster *Common Sense* was a moral indictment of monarchy, a soaring articulation of natural rights and republican values, and an injunction for revolution that would later echo in Jefferson's Declaration of Independence. Paine wielded his pen like a revolutionary torch, igniting public imagination and infusing the rebellious colonists with moral clarity, courage, and inspiration when it mattered most. It is no exaggeration to say there would not be a United States of America without Paine: He was the one who proposed that name for our new nation.

Yet the story of Thomas Paine reveals how uncomfortable America has always been with the messy intersection of religion and politics, especially when the narrative doesn't flatter the faithful. After the war, Paine was so filled with revolutionary zeal that he decamped to Paris, where he wrote *The Age of Reason* in 1794. The book, part of Paine's full-throated campaign to infuse secular ideals into the French Revolution, was an irreverent critique of the fallacies, supernaturalism, and corruption at the heart of revealed religions like Christianity.

Though it became a huge bestseller, *The Age of Reason* ignited fierce debate. A chorus of Christian clergy denounced the book as blasphemy and churned out savage attacks on Paine as an atheist and anarchist whose French entanglements hinted at Illuminati-tinged subversion. The backlash was so great that Thomas Jefferson, Paine's friend and fellow deist, urged him not to publish the third volume of the book because of the damage it would cause to Paine's reputation.

But Paine, ever the provocateur, ignored Jefferson's advice and reignited a debate that sealed his fate as an outcast in the country he helped birth. Paine became our forgotten founder. A century after his death, President Theodore Roosevelt dismissed him as a "filthy little atheist."

Paine's fall from Revolutionary hero to cultural exile is because he picked a very public fight with Christianity. Other founders shared his skepticism about biblical miracles and supernaturalism, but they were discrete about it. Jefferson, for example, reserved his harshest religious critiques for private correspondence and only shared his redacted "Jefferson Bible" with close friends. But Paine launched a frontal assault on the Christian worldview in a bestselling book. And unlike Jefferson—the president and powerful Virginia aristocrat—Paine was just an itinerant writer. He was expendable. So the clergy destroyed his reputation and buried his legacy by equating his dissent from Christianity with disloyalty to America. It was an early expression of what we now recognize as Christian nationalism.

Christian nationalism has always been with us. But that throughline has brought us to a moment unlike anything in modern history. Today's Christian nationalist movement is not content to destroy reputations or merely prop up colonial-era blasphemy laws and religious tests. Their aim, as this book has shown, is to explode the wall of separation between church and state so that Christianity can take its rightful place as America's governing creed.

Christian nationalists have tried this before. After the Civil War, leaders of eleven Protestant denominations blamed the bloodshed on God's wrath at America for leaving Him out of the Constitution. They formed the National Reform Association and, in 1876, delivered thirty-five thousand petition signatures urging Congress to amend the Constitution by declaring the United States a Christian nation under the authority of God and Jesus Christ. Even devout lawmakers balked at such an open assault on the First Amendment, and the effort failed. But the "Christian Amendment" proposal kept coming back—during the revivalism of the 1890s, the fundamentalist surge of the early twentieth century, and again in the Christian nationalist fervor of the Cold War. The amendment never advanced, yet the National Reform Association still exists today, claiming to pursue the same goal, making it the longest-running religious lobbying campaign in American history.

But today's Christian nationalist movement isn't interested in another quixotic attempt to amend the Constitution, which would require approval by two-thirds of Congress and three-quarters of the states. What makes this movement so different is that it no longer seeks to persuade fellow Americans. It demands the hard certainty of conquest.

These pages have charted the rise of America's most dangerous political movement, its impacts, and the fight to save our democracy. Now that you better understand the threat of Christian nationalism, how it operates, and where to look for it, you'll see its manifestations and interconnections in many places—more than I could cover in a single book. We've brushed up against important nuances I hope others will continue to explore, and I may yet return to them myself. Fault lines of race, gender, and class, for example, run throughout much of the Christian nationalist movement. The broad spectrum of Christian nationalism should continue to be analyzed—not just the violent extremists who fomented insurrection on January 6th, but people like your Aunt Mabel who simply goes to church, votes for Christian candidates, and would never dream of overthrowing the government. Add to this the worrisome rise of Christian nationalist billionaires like Peter Thiel who fuse prophecy with a bizarre crypto-utopian ambition that may already be shaping American policy in Latin America and Greenland. We should keep our eyes on all of this and more as this story continues to unfold.

The most important point of this book, however, is that the reckoning with Christian nationalism is unavoidable. Ready or not, this movement is forcing us to make urgent choices about our governing structures and civic values—choices that could determine whether secular democracy and pluralism endure. To borrow one of Paine's iconic phrases, "the times have found us."

It's fair to wonder whether a society numbed by parallel crises can meet such a huge moment. Between the ugliness of our politics, the daily struggles of our affordability crisis, the relentless churn of social media, and the tragic treadmill of our news cycles compounded by disinformation and algorithms that manipulate us—there are layers of chaos and complexity before we even get to the vexing challenge of Christian nationalism.

America certainly won't summon the clarity and courage to confront this danger unless a lot of people grasp what we stand to lose and are willing to shoulder the burden and discomfort of joining the fight to save democracy. We are once again faced with times that "try our souls" as we contemplate our next steps.

Here's the good news: We don't need to invent a whole new governing paradigm to meet this moment. Our founders, Paine included, gave us the most important thing of all: a secular government. It's the ultimate guardrail against the age-old forces of religious tyranny. Our job is simply to defend it with enough vigor that it can work.

The theocrats of our era fail to appreciate how deeply church-state separation is rooted—not just in our Constitution but in the very idea of America. A century before our founding, Roger Williams planted the radical seed by chartering Rhode Island as a model of religious tolerance and secular government. Then during the revolution, Baptists,

Quakers, Catholics, Jews, and dissenters of every kind, all of whom had felt the lash of colonial theocracies, joined forces to fight for the American cause, cementing religious liberty as a debt owed to those who had suffered for conscience and then helped win our freedom.

By the time of the Constitutional Convention, the imperative of secular governance was both moral and practical, as dozens of religious sects jostled for influence across the colonial landscape. Our founders knew what the Enlightenment had only recently articulated: The only durable antidote to sectarian bloodshed was religious neutrality through a government that refused to pick a prophet, bless a creed, or enforce a theology: a republic where people could worship, or not, however they pleased. That is why our deeply religious nation chose to bind itself to a secular Constitution.

All these years later, with hundreds of sects now painting the fresco of religious diversity in America, the importance of keeping government secular is greater than ever. Beyond the First Amendment imperative, the practical necessity is why church-state separation has stood the test of time and remains broadly popular today.

But it's also important to understand we are at a low point in the modern arc of church-state separation. In 1960, John F. Kennedy gave a landmark speech assuring Protestant ministers he was committed to "absolute" separation of church and state—a secular vision where there are no religious voting blocks, and public policy is never guided by any "ecclesiastical source." A generation later, Ronald Reagan openly courted evangelicals as a religious voting bloc and winked at church-state separation in a 1980 speech that declared: "I know you can't endorse me. But I want you to know that I endorse you." Scholars point to this as a turning point where evangelicals began to take over the GOP, and pandering to their religious doctrine became an electoral necessity. By 2016, Donald Trump didn't just court conservative Christians as a voting bloc—he embraced their most extreme ambitions and elevated Christian nationalism to his governing ideology. In three generations, we have gone from a president promising "absolute" separation to one who mocks church-state separation ("let's forget about that") and presides over an administration that routinely presents Christianity as our de facto state religion.

That is our tattered political inheritance and the trajectory we must correct. Stopping the backslide won't be easy, but despite all the damage to the wall of separation between church and state, it refuses to fall. Courts continue upholding meaningful lines against theocratic overreach; public opinion remains overwhelmingly supportive, including among Christians and even a majority of evangelicals; and across the religious landscape, clergy and faith leaders are defending it with growing clarity. These are not small things. They are reminders that even under sustained attack, the constitutional architecture of religious freedom and governmental neutrality is resilient.

I have a theory about why that is, which I trace back to one of my environmental heroes, the great evolutionary biologist and entomologist, E. O. Wilson. Wilson spent much of his career studying ants and their cooperative behavior, which caused him to marvel about humans. Because *Homo sapiens*, like ants, is one of the few creatures that have evolved with instincts for both individual survival and broader group survival through behaviors like cooperative care of others' offspring, living in extended groups of unrelated individuals, and division of labor. This "eusociality" is wired into animals like ants and bees through their DNA, but humans get there simply by using our big, problem-solving brains. Wilson, a fellow Humanist, concluded that the essence of humanity, and the key to our long-term survival, lies in our ability to harness that brainpower to prevent our evolutionary drive toward individual survival from overriding our cooperative, empathetic capacities that made civilization possible in the first place.

I believe that Jesus Christ was describing that very same tension—between self-interest and community—when he preached the Sermon on the Mount, long before scientists like Wilson described these values in evolutionary terms. It's what the Jewish tradition of *tikkun olam* teaches—to "repair the world" through justice, generosity, and care for the vulnerable. The same goes for the Qur'anic emphasis on *rahma* (mercy), communal responsibility, and the moral duty to protect the weak. And in Hinduism, the intertwined principles of *ahimsa* (non-harm) and *seva* (selfless service) call believers to compassion, restraint, and active care for others. The moral vocabulary across these and other religious traditions affirms something very basic that mirrors evolutionary science: Humanity is best served when we show each other kindness, mercy, and respect regardless of our differences.

That's why the values of radical tolerance, inclusion, and freedom of conscience will never go away. Roger Williams's Rhode Island experiment, the Enlightenment, our secular Constitution—these are just the cooperative genius of our species, finding and re-finding our civilizational imperative. And defending church-state separation—the key to our fight to save democracy from Christian nationalism—is, at its core, simply about living peacefully and cooperatively with each other.

That gives us a lot to work with: a harmonic convergence of religion, philosophy, and hard evolutionary science all pointing toward keeping church and state separate. However, I realize that rationalism alone, no matter how much I urge the equanimity of Admiral Stockdale's paradox and the emotional discipline of Antonio Gramsci's pessimism of the intellect and optimism of the will, isn't always enough. At some point, we all need some old-fashioned hope. So, I leave you with this.

Our great founder Thomas Paine, and his Revolutionary torch of critical reasoning, truth, and justice, is at long last receiving overdue recognition. Thanks to legislation authored by Jamie Raskin and championed by our Congressional Freethought Caucus and leading secular advocacy groups, the Thomas Paine Memorial—an outdoor space near the Capitol for education and reflection—was congressionally authorized in 2022. It won't be built under a Trump administration steeped in hostility to Paine's Enlightenment values, but it will be built. And when it is, it will stand as a place where people of all faiths and none can gather to celebrate a religion-neutral public square—where faith is respected as a personal choice and never wielded by the state to favor or coerce anyone.

But the best testament to Paine's legacy would be more than a monument. Let us build a new civic patriotism grounded in our shared humanity, where secular and religious Americans choose to treat one another with the radical empathy and compassion of the Sermon on the Mount, which you don't have to be Christian to embrace. If I've learned anything from my odyssey with religion—from my Christian youth, to the spiritual drifting that ultimately landed in Humanism, to the wonderful complexity of having a Catholic wife, ultra-Orthodox Jewish sister, two agnostic brothers, and dear friends at every point on the spectrum of faith—it is the importance of stretching beyond narrow comfort zones to find the universal values that are always there to unite us.

We don't need to agree on everything, but right now we must come together as fellow Americans who agree on the most important thing: Our beleaguered democracy remains the best system of government the world has ever seen, and it belongs to all of us. Let us be worthy of it by confronting the myths, defending the facts, and honoring the Enlightenment inheritance that made pluralistic democracy possible. And as we do, let us remember Thomas Paine's words that echo across the centuries: "The mind once enlightened cannot again become dark."

ACKNOWLEDGMENTS

I never contemplated writing this or any book until the fall of 2023 when it struck me: My oddball status as Congress's only open nonbelieving member gives me some unique insights and a perspective some people might find interesting. Throw in my complicated personal history with religion and the unusual work I do in Congress to defend church-state separation at a moment of maximum peril for our democracy and, well . . . maybe I should at least try writing a book!

Getting from that germ of an idea to a finished book, published by a great company like W. W. Norton, has been an odyssey of intense work, false starts, emotional highs and lows, and a cutting-room floor littered with drafts that seemed promising until they weren't. Persevering through all of that and ending up with *No Prophets*—a book that is authentic, unique, and something I'm very proud of—would never have been possible without the help of some extraordinary people.

My wife, Susan, was amazingly supportive throughout. She endured my disappearances into the writer's cave for days at a time, my middle-of-the-night bursts of inspiration, and my grumpiness as deadlines loomed. Her common-sense feedback on all aspects of the book was invaluable, but mostly I appreciate her trust that all the stress and disruption was for something that deeply matters—and that eventually I would stop being a grumpy first-time author, and some normalcy would return to our lives.

This book would probably not have happened if my kindred spirit Jamie Raskin hadn't urged me to write it, and then offered strategic advice along the way—such as insisting that I include a chapter on

Israel, which I initially resisted. He also honored me by writing a beautiful and generous Foreword. Jamie's courage, brilliance, decency, and moral clarity inspire me every day and I'm so grateful to have him as a friend and close ally in Congress.

This book is, in many ways, an extension of my role in cofounding and leading the Congressional Freethought Caucus, a labor of love since 2018. In addition to Jamie, a handful of intrepid colleagues took a chance by joining us in the early years: Jerry McNerney, Dan Kildee, Pramila Jayapal, Mark Pocan, and the late Rick Nolan. Later came stalwarts like Sean Casten, Susan Wild, and Don Beyer, and now we have a new generation, including Laura Friedman, Emily Randall, and Yasamin Ansari, bringing us to thirty-two members strong. The Freethought Caucus is here to stay, and I'm especially proud that it reflects the full spectrum of faith diversity that is America.

My Freethought Caucus work has been supported over the years by dedicated congressional staffers who believed in the importance of our mission to promote policy based on facts, science and reason, and to defend secular governance. Critical support came from Ben Miller, Joe Sheehy, Mary Hurrell, Quentin Dupouy, Greg Barranco, Tyler Mentzler, Melissa Andrade, Jenny Callaway, Shane Trimmer, Morgan McCue, Julia Diamond, Jennifer Goedke, Jordan Sciascia, Anthony Montoya, Courtney Callejas, and Logan Ferree.

I owe a special debt of gratitude to Sarah Levin, one of the sharpest secular advocates in American politics and a key collaborator in much of my church-state separation work. Sarah's sage advice helped refine several concepts and themes in this book. Two other secular leaders, Roy Speckhardt and Ron Millar of the American Humanist Association, deserve special mention. Years ago, Kurt Vonnegut's writings planted the seed that I might be a Humanist—that I could embrace an affirmative moral framework rather than defaulting to labels like agnostic or atheist, which felt reductive and incomplete to me. Roy and Ron were the trusted sherpas guiding me through the rollout of my decision to publicly identify as a Humanist in 2017 which, as we suspected, wasn't career-ending after all.

One of the most ambitious aspects of this book is tackling complex matters of theology, history, and science, which I never could have done without the help of several really smart subject matter experts who were remarkably generous with their time. Four of them—religion scholars Matthew Taylor, Bradley Onishi, Julie Ingersoll, Lauren Griffin—were indispensable in helping me to understand the theology and religious dynamics explored in several chapters, with Taylor and Onishi in particular serving as sounding boards and technical advisors. Another expert, constitutional lawyer and historian extraordinaire Andrew Seidel, gave critical advice and feedback along the way. Chapter 8 benefited from the scholarly input of science gurus Dr. Michael Mann and Dr. Ana Unruh-Cohen. And I'm deeply grateful for the insights and comments graciously provided by Russell Moore, and my congressional colleagues Raskin, Adam Kinzinger, Bennie Thompson, and Pete Aguilar. And to my former colleague from Santa Barbara, Lois Capps, and the great folks at UCSB's Capps Center for helping me access archives that were critical to my research.

My agent, Jane Dystel, took a chance on me when others didn't see a path for this book, and guided me through the arduous process of refining my ideas into a serious proposal and then navigating the publishing journey. Which thankfully brought us W. W. Norton, and an amazing editor named Caroline Adams. From the start, Caroline believed in the importance of this book and my unproven ability to write it. We made a good team!

To the many friends and family members who over the years have waxed philosophical with me about religion, spirituality, and our place in the universe—believers and nonbelievers alike—thank you for the dialogue, good counsel, and for sharing (or at least indulging) my endless curiosity about these matters.

Finally, I will forever be grateful to the wonderful people of California's Second Congressional District, who entrusted me to represent them in Congress and have stood with me all these years, not because of religious labels but because of our shared universal values which matter so much more.

NOTES

INTRODUCTION

2 **That day, thousands:** details archived at Jerichomarch.org.

3 **Experts define Christian Nationalism:** Dr. Robert P. Jones interview, Center for American Progress, August 8, 2024.

4 **Among the unsettling examples:** People for the American Way, "The Jan. 6 Insurrection Should Have Been No Surprise—and Neither Should the Next Right-Wing Coup Attempt," Right Wing Watch, accessed January 11, 2026; "2020 Election 'No Less Than a Civil War,' Claims Pro-Trump Anti-Abortion Extremist Frank Pavone," People for the American Way, Right Wing Watch, July 20, 2022, article by Peter Montgomery and video links archived at peoplefor.org.

6 **Flanked by a row:** Sarah Posner, "How the Christian Right Helped Foment Insurrection," January 30, 2021, Revealnews.org.

6 **Right-Wing Watch posted footage:** "Prophets Gather at Trump's Washington Hotel to Unleash Angel Armies on His Deep State Enemies," People for the American Way, Right Wing Watch, March 1, 2018, article by Peter Montgomery and video links archived at peoplefor.org.

7 **Slaughter every living thing "both man and woman . . .":** Bible, Book of Joshua, Chapter 6 (Joshua spared the life of a Canaanite prostitute who was working as a spy for the Hebrews).

7 **Kinzinger laughed uneasily:** author interview with Adam Kinzinger, July 25, 2025.

7 **"We fight. We fight like hell":** See transcript of speech at, e.g., Julia Jacobo, "This Is What Trump Told Supporters Before Many Stormed Capitol Hill," ABC News, January 7, 2021.

9 **Then, at last, Trump surfaced:** "President Trump Video Statement on Capitol Protesters," C-SPAN, January 6, 2021.

10 **I wasn't surprised:** Private email from Speaker Pelosi to House Democrats, January 6, 2021.

CHAPTER 1: NOT YOUR PARENTS' CULTURE WAR

17 **a prescient book:** Michelle Goldberg, *Kingdom Coming: The Rise of Christian Nationalism* (W. W. Norton, 2007).

17 **Two groundbreaking books:** Katherine Stewart, *The Power Worshippers: Inside the Dangerous Rise of Religious Nationalism* (Bloomsbury, 2020); A. L. Whitehead and

S. L. Perry, *Taking America Back for God: Christian Nationalism in the United States* (Oxford University Press, 2020).

18 **About 30 percent of Americans:** Public Religion Research Institute, "Support for Christian Nationalism in All 50 States," Washington, DC, 2024.

20 **He railed against modernity:** Susan F. Harding, "American Protestant Moralism and the Secular Imagination: From Temperance to the Moral Majority," *Social Research* 76, no. 4 (2009): 1277–306.

21 **In a 1982 essay:** Walter H. Capps, "Falwell on Location," University of California, Santa Barbara, 1982.

23 **Falwell even invited:** Edward M. Kennedy, "Truth and Tolerance in America," Speech delivered at Liberty Baptist College, Lynchburg, VA, October 3, 1983, *American Rhetoric.*

25 **America's monolithic white Christian:** Pew Research Center, "Christianity in the United States," Wikipedia summary citing Pew Religious Landscape Studies, 1990–2020; Public Religion Research Institute, "2020 PRRI Census of American Religion."

26 **At its peak in:** "The Patriot Movement: Past & Present," Rural Organizing Project, accessed December 23, 2025.

26 **their ideology endured, metastasizing:** "Antigovernment General," Southern Poverty Law Center, n.d., accessed December 23, 2025.

26 **NAR combined a decentralized:** "New Apostolic Reformation," Wikipedia, accessed December 23, 2025.

28 **Doner recounts a chilling:** Colonel V. Doner, *Christian Jihad: Neo-Fundamentalists and the Polarization of America* (Samizdat, 2012), 189 (quoting Third Wave youth pastor Becky Fischer).

CHAPTER 2: BREAKING FAITH

32 **A landmark study:** Andrew Whitehead et al., "Make America Christian Again: Christian Nationalism and Voting for Donald Trump in the 2016 Presidential Election," *Sociology of Religion* 79, no. 2 (2018):147–71.

33 **The bigger reason:** Lauren Markoe, "White Evangelicals, Catholics and Mormons Carried Trump," Religion News Service, November 9, 2016.

33 **thousands of churches:** "Statistics and Reasons for Church Decline," Richard J. Krejcir, ChurchLeadership.org, accessed December 23, 2025.

33 **White was hosting celebrity:** John Fea, "From Prosperity Televangelism to the White House," *Christianity Today*, May 29, 2025.

34 **That's when prophet Lance Walnau:** Daniel Burke, "How Trumpism Has Pushed a Fringe Charismatic Theology into the Mainstream," Religion News Service, May 6, 2024; Ed Gaskin, "Politics and Prophecy: The Biblical Basis for the Trump–Cyrus Analogy," *The Times of Israel* (blog), May 22, 2025; "POTUS Shield: Trump's Dominionist Prayer Warriors and the Prophetic Order of the United States," People for the American Way, Right Wing Watch, August 2, 2017.

34 **Sheets put it bluntly:** Dutch Sheets, "You're Not Voting for a Personality, You're Voting for That Supreme Court," video, 5:38, posted October 24, 2016, facebook.com, accessed 2/3/2026.

35 **This sea change:** Rockefeller Center for Public Policy, "Leadership Lessons from Former White House Chief of Staff Andrew Card," Rockefeller Center, Dartmouth College, November 2016.

35 **She publicly boasted:** Katie Zezima, "Trump's Spiritual Adviser Says the President Is a 'Man of Repentance,'" *USA Today*, September 9, 2017.

36 **It was dubbed:** People for the American Way, "POTUS Shield."

38 **Newspapers across the:** January 7, 1990, articles in Associated Press: "Ohio Cult Leader Charged in Slayings of Family of Five," *New York Times*: "Bodies of Five Found in Ohio Barn; Cult Leader Held," and *Washington Post*: "Cult Prophet Accused of Mass Murder."

38 **The RLDS community:** "The Avery Family," Block Parole, accessed December 23, 2025.

39 **He later was convicted:** Watchman Fellowship, "Fire in the Sky," Internet Archive Wayback Machine, archived July 20, 2011; "Arson Charges Filed Against Man in Church Fire," *Lawrence Journal-World* (Lawrence, KS), January 3, 1990.

41 **"Put you down for 'heathen'":** KPIX CBS News Bay Area, "Bay Area Lawmaker Jared Huffman Holds His Own During Interview on '*The Colbert Report*,'" video, 0:38, posted September 25, 2014.

41 **"No other trait":** Michael Lipka, "Americans Are Somewhat More Open to the Idea of an Atheist President," Pew Research Center, May 29, 2014.

42 **Her story ran on:** Michelle Boorstein, "This Lawmaker Is Skeptical That God Exists. Now He's Finally Decided to Tell People," *Washington Post*, November 9, 2017.

CHAPTER 3: THREE ROADS TO THEOCRACY

45 **Taylor and other:** Matthew D. Taylor, *The Violent Take It by Force: The Christian Movement That Is Threatening Our Democracy* (Broadleaf, 2024), 2.

46 **Harrison Buttker made headlines:** James Farrell, "Here's Harrison Butker's [*sic*] Controversial Commencement Speech in Full," *Forbes*, May 15, 2024; Joe Bukuras, "Saddened by Restrictions, NFL Star Speaks Out in Defense of Traditional Latin Mass," Catholic News Agency, February 14, 2022.

47 **Father Coughlin declared:** Clyde Haberman, "Today in History: The Father Coughlin Story," PBS—Exploring Hate, March 9, 2022.

49 **The CIC doesn't bother:** Catholic Identity Conference, "Home," Catholic Identity Conference, accessed December 23, 2025.

49 **Posobiec continued:** Alex Woodward, "Far-Right Influencer Calls for 'End of Democracy' at CPAC as Republicans Downplay January 6," *Independent*, February 23, 2024.

49 **They were called out:** James Martin, "The Capitol Rioters Invoked Jesus. What Will the Churches Do?," *America Magazine*, January 12, 2021.

50 **Two years later:** "Archbishop Carlo Maria Viganò Calls for 3 Days of Fasting for Protection of January 6 Defendants," *Epoch Times*, December 2022.

50 **neo-Nazi agitator Nick Fuentes:** Clark Mindock, "Charlottesville Student Nicholas Fuentes Leaves Boston University After Death Threats Over Immigration Views," *Independent*, August 17, 2017.

50 **"Pretty good stuff":** "'I'm a 12th-Century Man': White Nationalist Nick Fuentes Longs for the Days of Catholic Monarchy, Crusades, and Inquisitions," People for the American Way, Right Wing Watch.

50 **In 2022, he urged:** Nick Fuentes, quoted in "Nick Fuentes Calls for a White Uprising," Media Matters for America, February 2, 2022, "Nick Fuentes Says He Wants Donald Trump to Become a Dictator," Media Matters for America, December 2, 2022, "Nick Fuentes Says He Wants to Get Rid of Congress," Media Matters for America, December 5, 2022.

51 **He promoted and:** Anti-Defamation League, *"Nicholas J. Fuentes: Five Things to Know," ADL*, July 20, 2021, Archived at the Internet Archive Wayback Machine.

51 **It may have happened:** Lara Sukster Mosheyof, "From Memes to Murder: The Far-Right 'Groyper' Movement Tied to Charlie Kirk Suspect," *JFeed*, October 3, 2025.

51 **These junior varsity:** See, e.g., Dr. Taylor Marshall status on X.

51 **FBI—whose hiring:** Stanford historian Prof. Lerone Martin has studied the FBI's longstanding conservative Christian bias, describing an agency culture "saturated with Christian conservatism," Lerone A. Martin, "The FBI's Culture and Recruiting Have Long Favored Conservative Christianity," *Washington Post*, February 23, 2023; and David Wise, *Spy: The Inside Story of How the FBI's Robert Hanssen Betrayed America* (Random House, 2003).

52 **The internal memo:** Matthew J. Cressler, "Yes, the FBI Is Problematic. So Are Catholic Nationalists," *U.S. Catholic*, March 3, 2023.

52 **pugnacious Catholic League:** Having been on the receiving end of the league's vitriol, I can attest to their propensity for equating dissent with persecution and never missing a chance to accuse adversaries of anti-Catholic bigotry or finding ties to scary Jews like George Soros, as perusing their many public statements confirms; see Catholic League for Religious and Civil Rights, "Our Mission," catholicleague.org, accessed February 4, 2026.

52 **The FBI cowered:** Bill Donohue, "Biden's FBI Lied About Spying on Catholics," Catholic League, catholicleague.org, accessed June 4, 2025.

52 **In October 2025:** "Tucker Carlson's Interview with Antisemite Nick Fuentes Exposes Rift Among Republicans," PBS NewsHour, February 9, 2024.

53 **Crusades is Hegseth's template:** "Pete Hegseth and His 'Battle Cry' for a New Christian Crusade," Reader Supported News, December 6, 2024.

53 **A Pavlovian chorus:** John Brown, "Pete Hegseth Leads Prayer to 'King Jesus' During Pentagon Event," *Christian Post*, May 22, 2025.

54 **The Hegseth family:** Mike Baker and Ruth Graham, "Pete Hegseth and His 'Battle Cry' for a New Christian Crusade," *New York Times*, December 5, 2024; Pete Hegseth, interview on God's Men of Influence podcast, "How God Moved Us to Tennessee," May 2024; Pete Hegseth, remarks at TPUSA Faith Nashville event, June 2024; Pete Hegseth and David Goodwin, "The Battle for the American Mind" (HarperCollins, 2022); Jonathan Edwards Classical Academy, "Mission and Vision," jecanashville.org, accessed February 3, 2026.

54 **Founded In 1998:** Kiera Butler, "A Christian Nationalist TheoBro Church Is Coming to DC," *Mother Jones*, May 15, 2025; Ian Ward, "Doug Wilson: The New Right's Favorite Pastor," *Politico*, May 23, 2025.

55 **Wilson didn't invent:** Ward, "Doug Wilson"; author interviews with Bradley Onishi and Julie Ingersoll.

55 **Toward that end:** R. J. Rushdoony, "The Institutes of Biblical Law" (Presbyterian and Reformed, 1973), 3–4.

56 **Reconstructionism profoundly impacted:** R. J. Rushdoony, "The Law of Divorce," *Pocket College*, transcript RR130AJ65, accessed 2025; R. J. Rushdoony, "Molech Worship and Baptism," Chalcedon, March 1, 2003. Rushdoony compared public schools to child sacrifice and "Molech worship." Conservative Protestants' hostile pivot against public education starting in the 1950s was no coincidence. Historically, when parochial schools were almost entirely Catholic, evangelicals and other protestants had fiercely opposed public funding—enshrining their stance in Blaine

Amendments across thirty-eight states. Mid-century desegregation and civil rights pushed white evangelicals to flee integrated schools, founding private Christian academies. Reconstructionism emerged in tandem with this movement, offering theological justification for what was surely a racial and cultural backlash.

57 **Wilson got the gig:** Ward, "Doug Wilson."

57 **Wilson coyishly presents:** Doug Wilson, "I Am a Paleo-Confederate," Quotes, dougwilsonsays.com, accessed December 23, 2025.

58 **Wilson chuckles:** Ward, "Doug Wilson."

58 **Webbon dedicated an episode:** Kyle Mantyla, "Christian Nationalist Pastor Joel Webbon Says Jews Cannot 'Serve in Public Office in My Nation,'" People for the American Way, Right Wing Watch, December 2, 2024; Kiera Butler, "Did Christian Nationalist Leaders Prompt Mike Johnson's Epstein Flip-Flop?," *Mother Jones,* July 22, 2025.

58 **Another Wilson acolyte:** Stephen Wolfe, *The Case for Christian Nationalism* (Canon, 2022).

59 **futuristic fever dream of:** Gil Duran, "Trump's Weird New 'Freedom Cities' and the Network State Cult," *Nerd Reich,* August 13, 2024; Theo Burman, "What Are 'Freedom Cities'? Billionaire CEOs' Plan Could Reshape America," *Newsweek,* March 12, 2025; Kiera Butler, "The Ultra-Christian Tech Bros Have Been Mingling at Mar-a-Lago," *Mother Jones,* January 14, 2025.

59 **New Foundings CEO:** David Jeans, "Anti-Woke Venture Capital: New Founding," *Forbes,* December 23, 2025.

59 **Exalting authoritarianism as:** Nate Fischer (@NateAFischer), "national divorce must be on the table. . . ." X, August 31, 2023.

60 **Longtime residents of:** Phil Williams, "Meet the Out-of-State Investors Funding a Christian Nationalist Community in Tennessee," NewsChannel 5 Investigates, WTVF Nashville, accessed December 23, 2025.

60 **Ingersoll explains:** author interview with Julie Ingersoll, 7/30/2025.

61 **Wilson has begun describing:** Doug Wilson et al., "Transcript: Interview with Doug Wilson on Christian Nationalism," christoverall.com, October 18, 2023.

61 **But it was CREC:** "CREC HotSpot Project," All Saints Presbyterian Church, Fort Worth, allsaintskirk.com, accessed December 23, 2025.

62 **They're jostling for position:** Southern Poverty Law Center, "SPLC Releases Annual Year in Hate & Extremism Report, Decodes the Far-Right's Plan to Undo Democracy," *SPLC Press Center,* June 4, 2024.

63 **Sheets interpreted the:** Dutch Sheets, "Running with the Horses," January 1, 2021, givehim15.com, accessed December 23, 2025.

63 **As Dr. Matthew:** Taylor, *The Violent Take It by Force,* 216.

64 **Wagner launched NAR:** Amy S., "C. Peter Wagner: 'NAR Is Not a Cult!,'" bereanresearch.org, September 21, 2015.

64 **"God has prepared":** "Sheets: Christians Must Take Back Government in 2015 Because 'We Are God's Governing Force on the Earth,'" People for the American Way, Right Wing Watch, January 2015.

65 **Sheets make his theocratic:** Discernment Research Group, "At First It May Seem Like Totalitarianism," *Herescope,* June 20, 2007.

65 **Among the demonic networks:** Sean McCloud, "Objects as Demonic Subjects in Spiritual Warfare Handbooks," *Societas Magica Newsletter* no. 29 (Fall 2013); Cindy Jacobs, "Deliver Us from Evil: Putting a Stop to the Occultic Influence Invading Your

Home and Community" (Regal, 2001), 198; Taylor, *The Violent Take It by Force*, 99; Colonel V. Doner, *Christian Jihad: Neo-Fundamentalists and the Polarization of America* (Samizdat, 2012), 202.

66 **In this fantastical:** Jack Jenkins, "Survey: More Than a Quarter of White Evangelicals Believe Core QAnon Conspiracy Theory," religionnews.com, February 11, 2021.

66 **NAR apostle Mary Glazier:** Doner, *Christian Jihad*, 202.

66 **Theologian Dr. Steve:** Steve Snow, "Prophets, Demons, and Witch Hunts," *Journal of Religion and Society* (2016): 18.

66 **Experts estimate that:** R. Douglas Geivett and Holly Pivec, *Counterfeit Kingdom: The Dangers of New Revelation, New Prophets, and New Age Practices in the Church* (B&H, 2022).

67 **The only formal:** Taylor, *The Violent Take It by Force*, 220.

67 **And it's why, Onishi:** author interview with Bradley Onishi, June 20, 2025.

68 **Peter Wagner later cowrote a book:** Peter Wagner et al., *Destiny of a Nation: How Prophets and Intercessors Can Mold History* (Wagner Institute, 2001).

68 **dozens of NAR:** Julia Duin, "The Christian Prophets Who Say Trump Is Coming Again," *POLITICO Magazine*, February 18, 2021.

68 **a "blue plate special":** Dutch Sheets, "America Will Not Eat the 'Blue Plate Special,'" November 13, 2020, YouTube, accessed December 23, 2025.

68 **Sheets spearheaded NAR's parallel:** For example, Sheets tapped an NAR-aligned pastor in Michigan to launch Jericho Marches there, stating: "We decree, the results of the 2020 election will not be tainted with fraud. All fraud will be swiftly exposed and severely dealt with. Those elected will be quickly known and acknowledged. We take authority over all these things in Jesus' name, amen." Life Song Church memo, 12-13-20-Jericho-March.pdf.

69 **At each stop:** Taylor, *The Violent Take It by Force*, 226.

69 **"No chicken legged":** "Pray for the Nation from Arizona," YouTube, accessed December 23, 2025.

69 **According to Taylor:** Matthew D. Taylor and Bradley Onishi, "Evidence Strongly Suggests Trump Was Collaborating with Christian Nationalist Leaders Before January 6th," *Religion Dispatches*, January 6, 2023; Taylor, *The Violent Take It by Force*, 234; Chuck Pierce, "Election Prophecy Update," Glory of Zion International, November 2020; Dutch Sheets, "January 6, 2021," Give Him 15, January 6, 2021.

70 **"We declare peace over":** Taylor, *The Violent Take It by Force*, 235.

71 **Indeed, the institute's:** Jeff Sharlet, "On the 'Violent-Prayer-a-Day' Christian Education of Dr. Vance Boelter, Alleged Killer of Minnesota Democrats," *Religion Dispatches*, June 16, 2025.

71 **"This is not what":** Christ for the Nations Institute, "Press Release—The Minnesota Tragedy and the Shooting Suspect, Mr. Vance Luther Boelter," cfni.org, June 14, 2025.

72 **61 percent believe in:** Stephanie McCrummen, "The Army of God Comes Out of the Shadows," *The Atlantic*, February 2025.

72 **dozens of members of Congress:** Matthew D. Taylor, "Mike Johnson, Polite Extremist," *The Bulwark*, October 30, 2023.

CHAPTER 4: FOUNDING FICTION

73 **Trump's executive order:** Donald J. Trump, "Establishment of the Religious Liberty Commission," *White House*, Executive Order, May 1, 2025.

73 **Trump mused aloud:** Rebecca Schneid, "What Exactly Is Trump's Religious

Liberty Commission—and Why Have Some Experts Raised Concerns?" *TIME,* May 11, 2025.

74 **As if that wasn't:** Mark Wingfield, "No, Dan Patrick, God Did Not Write the U.S. Constitution," Baptist News Global, August 8, 2022.

75 **progressive faith leaders:** Faith in Action, "Faith Leaders Denounce Commission Eroding Separation Between Church and State," press release, May 1, 2025, faithinaction.org, accessed January 11, 2026.

75 **The Interfaith Alliance:** Faith in Action, "Faith Leaders Denounce Commission"; Interfaith Alliance, "Christian Leaders Unite to Denounce Anti-Christian Bias Task Force," June 14, 2025, interfaithalliance.org.

75 **Chairman Patrick gaveled:** All quotes of commissioners and speakers are from the transcript of the Commission on Religious Liberty Hearing, first hearing, June 16, 2025.

78 **Robert Boucher, a:** Jonathan Boucher, *A View of the Causes and Consequences of the American Revolution, with an Historical Preface* (G. G. and J. Robinson, 1797), 534.

78 **As constitutional attorney:** Andrew L. Seidel, *The Founding Myth: Why Christian Nationalism Is Un-American* (Union Square, 2019), 62, Kindle.

79 **The rationalist search:** Facing History & Ourselves, "Religion in Colonial America: Trends, Regulations, and Beliefs," facinghistory.org, updated March 14, 2016.

79 **As Seidel concludes:** Seidel, *Founding Myth,* 90.

80 **In the same letter:** Jefferson to Roger C. Weightman, June 24, 1826, in *Works of Thomas Jefferson,* vol. 12, 477.

80 **With unusually specific language:** Supreme Court Justice Joseph Story, who served from 1812 to 1845, was among those who observed the obvious intent of this provision: "It had a higher objective: to cut off for ever every pretense of any alliance between church and state in the national government," J. Story, *Commentaries on the Constitution,* vol. 3, sec. 1841 (Hilliard, Gray, 1833), 705.

81 **He described its protections:** Thomas Jefferson, *Autobiography* (1821) in *The Founders' Constitution,* vol. 5, Amendment I (Religion), doc. 45, University of Chicago Press.

81 **Puritan theocracy rebuked:** Mass Moments, "Roger Williams Banished," massmoments.org, accessed January 11, 2026.

82 **Jefferson famously described:** Thomas Jefferson, Letter to the Danbury Baptist Association, January 1, 1802, Americans United for Separation of Church and State, au.org.

83 **Patrick calls him:** Dan Patrick, *The Second Most Important Book You Will Ever Read* (Brown, 2002), 133.

83 **Multiple historians and:** Southern Poverty Law Center, "Christian 'Historian,' Denounced as a Propagandist, Sees Book Withdrawn," *Intelligence Report* no. 148 (November 11, 2012); Barbara Bradley Hagerty, "The Most Influential Evangelist You've Never Heard Of," NPR, August 8, 2012; Chris Rodda, "Debunking David Barton's *Jefferson Lies,*" *History News Network,* September 21, 2013.

83 **He's greeted like:** Bob Allen, "Huckabee Defends Praise of Revisionist Historian," *The Christian Century,* April 19, 2011.

83 **Johnson calls Barton:** *The WallBuilders Show,* "Episodes," wallbuilders.com, accessed December 23, 2025; Mike Hixenbaugh, "Meet the Evangelical Activist Who's Had a 'Profound Influence' on Speaker Mike Johnson," *NBC News,* October 26, 2023.

84 **Johnson vouched for:** Jack Jenkins, "Blowback Continues to Grow over Johnson Misattributing a Prayer to Jefferson," Religion News Service, January 8, 2025.

84 **I was the first:** Michelle Boorstein and Sarah Pulliam Bailey, "Johnson Attributes Prayer to Thomas Jefferson, but There's No Proof He Said It," *Washington Post*, January 4, 2025.

85 **The Public Religion:** Public Religion Research Institute (PRRI), "Christian Nationalism Across All 50 States: Insights from PRRI's 2024 American Values Atlas," prri.org, February 4, 2025.

85 **In Perry's words:** PRRI, *Christian Nationalism and Patriotism: A Post-Fourth of July Conversation*, video, 44:50, YouTube, posted August 2024.

85 **Among self-identified:** PRRI, *Christian Nationalism and Patriotism*.

86 **"They see it in cataclysmic":** Zack Stanton, "It's Time to Talk About Violent Christian Extremism," *Politico Magazine*, February 4, 2021; Mehdi Hasan, "Capitol Siege Has Been a 'Success' for Recruiting Extremists, Former DHS Staffer Says," LAist (republishing NPR reporting), January 12, 2021.

87 **In his prolific writing:** Richard John Neuhaus, *The Naked Public Square: Religion and Democracy in America* (Eerdmans, 1984).

88 **literally his full-time job:** GLAAD, "Ryan T. Anderson," glaad.org, updated April 21, 2023.

88 **Metaxas casts court decisions:** Michelle Boorstein, "Eric Metaxas, Trump's Favorite Evangelical Author, Has a New Mission," *Washington Post*, September 12, 2020.

90 **It also includes early:** Facing History & Ourselves, "Religion in Colonial America: Trends, Regulations, and Beliefs," facinghistory.org, last updated March 14, 2016; and Frederick Wertz, "Reformed Dutch and German Churches of Manhattan and the Bronx," New York Genealogical & Biographical Society, April 27, 2018.

90 **At the time of the Revolution:** John R. Vile, "Established Churches in Early America," *The First Amendment Encyclopedia*, Middle Tennessee State University, last updated February 21, 2025.

90 **The rationale: "Christianity":** Sir William Blackstone's *Commentaries on the Laws of England*, vol. 4, 1769.

91 **Blasphemy laws slowly:** "What the History of U.S. Blasphemy Laws and the Fight for Religious Freedom Can Teach Us Today," *First Amendment Encyclopedia*, Middle Tennessee State University, posted October 25, 2023.

91 **This prompted a lawsuit:** *Kalman v. Cortes*, 723 F. Supp. 2d 766 (E.D. PA, 2010).

91 **Blatantly unconstitutional blasphemy:** MCLS § 750.102; 21 Okl. St. § 901; S.C. Code Ann. § 16-17-520.

91 **Silverman litigated all:** In *Torcaso v. Watkins Silverman v. Campbell*, 486 S.E.2d 1 (S.C. 1997).

92 **For example, Holly Hollman:** Holly Hollman, "Faith-Based Advocacy and Understanding the Separation of Church and State," faithandleadership.com, June 13, 2023, accessed January 11, 2026.

CHAPTER 5: CHRISTIAN PRIVILEGE

94 **Senator Lindsay Graham:** Olafimihan Oshin, "Audio: Graham Knocked Trump in Wake of Jan. 6 Attack," *The Hill*, May 11, 2022.

95 **caught on a hot mic:** Paul McLeod, "Liz Cheney Removed from Leadership for Refusing to Bow to Trump," *BuzzFeed News*, May 12, 2021.

95 **Cheney's response was:** Zak Hudak et al., "Liz Cheney Removed from House GOP Leadership," CBS News, May 13, 2021.

95 **Meanwhile, McCarthy faced:** Olivia Beavers, "GOP Leader's Jan. 6 Call to Trump

Draws Scrutiny in Commission Fight." *The Hill*, May 12, 2021; Steve Benen, "GOP's McCarthy Haunted by His Failed Jan. 6 Committee Strategy." MaddowBlog, MSNBC, December 20, 2022.

95 **Katko and Thompson announced:** Jordain Carney, "McConnell Says He Opposes 'Slanted' Jan. 6 Commission Bill," *The Hill*, May 19, 2021.

97 **Hodges testified:** "WATCH: Officer Daniel Hodges Testifies on What Happened in the Jan. 6 Attack," PBS NewsHour, video, 17:33, YouTube, posted July 27, 2021.

97 **Peter Manseau, historian:** Mike Altman et al., "Uncivil Religion: January 6, 2021," Department of Religious Studies, University of Alabama, and the Smithsonian's National Museum of American History.

97 **"This committee must investigate":** Andrew L. Seidel, "Christian Nationalism and the Capitol Insurrection," written testimony submitted to the US House Select Committee to investigate the January 6th attack on the United States Capitol, July 2022.

98 **Attached to their letter:** Jack Jones, "Major Christian Leaders Asked Jan. 6 Committee to Investigate Christian Nationalism," Religion News Service, November 3, 2022.

98 **Amazingly, the report:** US House of Representatives, Select Committee to Investigate the January 6th Attack on the United States Capitol, *Final Report of the Select Committee to Investigate the January 6th Attack on the United States Capitol* (Government Publishing Office, 2022).

99 **Nothing about the three:** Jonathan Merritt, "The New Apostolic Reformation Drove the January 6 Riots. So Why Was It Overlooked by the House Select Committee?," Baptist News Global, January 6, 2023; Paul Burke, "Evidence Strongly Suggests Trump Was Collaborating with Christian Nationalist Leaders Before January 6th," Religion Dispatches, January 6, 2023; "How Christian Nationalism Fueled the Capitol Riot," *New York Times*, video, 8:39, YouTube, posted January 19, 2021; Jonathan Edwards, "Radical Beliefs in 'Spiritual Warfare' Played a Major Role in Jan. 6, an Expert Argues," Yahoo News, December 27, 2022; Matthew D. Taylor, *The Violent Take It by Force: The Christian Movement That Is Threatening Our Democracy* (Broadleaf, 2024), 115.

99 **Dec. 16: "We're getting ready":** Michelle Boorstein, "'I Needed to Be There': The Christian Case for the Capitol Riot," *Washington Post*, February 19, 2021.

100 **Chairman Bennie Thompson:** All quotes from committee members are from author interviews.

103 **"We'll be praying":** Aris Folley, "House Democrat Calls It Unconstitutional to Cite God in Hearing Oaths," *The Hill*, September 19, 2019.

103 **They believed vital:** Josh Dawsey and Jacqueline Alemany, "Liz Cheney's Break with the GOP Was Years in the Making," *Washington Post*, November 23, 2022.

103 **To their credit, Kinzinger and Raskin:** Jack Jenkins, "Despite Ample Evidence, Christian Nationalism Mostly Absent from Final Jan. 6 Report," Religion News Service, December 23, 2022.

104 **The Smithsonian's Peter:** Daniel Burke, "Christian Nationalism Mostly Absent from Final Jan. 6 Report," Religion News Service, December 23, 2022.

104 **Instead of being:** Matthew D. Taylor and Bradley Onishi, "Evidence Strongly Suggests Trump Was Collaborating with Christian Nationalist Leaders Before January 6th," religiondispatches.org, accessed January 11, 2026.

104 **Buzzfeeed's litigation revealed:** Jason Leopold and Ken Bensinger, "The Capitol

Police Said the Jan. 6 Unrest Was on Capitol Grounds. They Knew It Wasn't," *BuzzFeed News*, August 26, 2021.

105 **Social scientists who:** L. Z. Schlosser, "Christian Privilege: Breaking a Sacred Taboo," *Journal of Multicultural Counseling and Development* 31, no. 1 (2003): 44–51; Robert A. Pape and Keven Ruby. "Understanding American Political Violence: The January 6th Insurrection in Context," *American Psychologist* 80, no. 1 (2025): 1–17; Warren J. Blumenfeld et al., eds. *Investigating Christian Privilege and Religious Oppression in the United States. Transgressions: Cultural Studies and Education*, vol. 37 (Brill, 2009); National Council for the Social Studies, "White Christian Privilege: Race and Religion in America," Webinar event page, October 7, 2021.

105 **Special Agent Robert:** E. Shannon and A. Blackman, *The Spy Next Door: The Extraordinary Secret Life of Robert Philip Hanssen, the Most Damaging FBI Agent in U.S. History* (Little, Brown, 2002).

105 **Over a two-decade:** "Robert Hanssen," Wikipedia, last modified June 2023.

106 **He even confessed:** Amy Welborn, "Hanssen's Sin," Catholic Exchange, February 25, 2002.

106 **But his betrayal:** CBS News, *Agent of Betrayal: The Double Life of Robert Hanssen*, hosted by Major Garrett, podcast series, 2020–2023.

106 **Under the second:** Andrew Goudsward and Sarah N. Lynch, "FBI Scales Back Staffing, Tracking of Domestic Terrorism Probes, Sources Say," *USA Today*, March 21, 2025.

107 **Terrorism is defined:** Gus Martin, "What Is Terrorism?" in *Terrorism and Homeland Security* (Sage, 2012).

107 **His preaching invokes:** David Edwards Bennett, "'It Could End Up Bad': Pastor Behind 'Patriot Church' Movement Threatens Violence If Trump Is Not Made President Again," Raw Story, October 16, 2024; and Lydia O'Connor, "These Pastors Are Telling People Trump Is Still President—and Are Ready for 'War,'" *VICE News*, February 25, 2021.

108 **staging partisan political rallies:** Will Sommer, "We Spent a Wild Weekend with the Gun-Worshipping Moonie Church That's Trying to Go MAGA," *VICE News*, October 14, 2022.

108 **such as Florida's Rep. Randy Fine, who fits in:** *J. Weekly* (Jewish Telegraphic Agency), "Rep. Randy Fine's Incendiary Comments on Muslims Alarm Many Jews—Without Denting His Standing on the Pro-Israel Right," January 2, 2026; Ashleigh Fields, "Randy Fine's Comments on Muslims, Ilhan Omar Draw Backlash from Democrats," *The Hill*, July 9, 2025.

CHAPTER 6: THE SHADOW THEOCRACY

115 **Colonial America's military:** "Continental Navy," Wikipedia, accessed August 22, 2025; Don Loeser, "Flags of the American Revolution: Military Units," loeser.us, accessed December 23, 2025.

115 **Sheetz published a:** Dutch Sheets, 2015. *An Appeal to Heaven: What Would Happen If We Did It Again?* (Charisma House, 2015); FlashPoint, "Mario Murillo: Prophetic Word for America," video, YouTube, posted January 17, 2021.

115 **Today, you can buy:** Dutch Sheets Ministries, "Appeal to Heaven Flag (3 × 5)," product page, accessed December 23, 2025.

116 **Supreme Court Justice:** Jared Huffman, "I Want to Thank Samuel Alito for Flying His Flags," Daily Beast, May 29, 2024.

116 **Johnson is the member:** Michael Blanding, "Mike Johnson Attended Seminars

Led by a Christian-Nation Speaker with Far-Right Ties," *Mother Jones*, October 26, 2023; see also Brian Kaylor, "Church Scrubs Sermons by Speaker Johnson but I Saved Them," Public Witness, November 9, 2023.

116 **In the weeks:** Summer Concepcion, "Mike Johnson Played Key Role in Efforts to Overturn 2020 Election," NBC News, October 25, 2023.

116 **God began speaking to him:** Asawin Suebsaeng and Patrick Reis, "Mike Johnson Compares Himself to Moses at Christian-Nationalist Gala," *Rolling Stone*, December 7, 2023.

117 **The Declaration of Independence:** Mike Johnson, "Speaker-Elect Mike Johnson Floor Speech," October 25, 2023, speaker.gov/speeches.

117 **"I've always flown":** Asawin Suebsaeng, "Mike Johnson's Christian Nationalist 'Appeal to Heaven' Flag Problem," *Rolling Stone*, November 20, 2023.

117 **Very close ties to NAR:** Charlie Sykes, "Mike Johnson: The Polite Extremist," *Bulwark*, October 26, 2023; Timothy Carscadden, "Congratulations to Louisiana's newest . . . ," Facebook, February 3, 2015.

117 **"Well, go pick":** Matt Berg, "New House Speaker Tells Hannity: 'Go Pick Up a Bible Off Your Shelf and Read It—That's My Worldview,'" Mediaite, October 26, 2023.

118 **Johnson rejects church-state:** Will Hall, "Mike Johnson: Faith, Family & Freedom Motivate Run for Seat in U.S. Congress," *Baptist Message*, September 30, 2016.

118 **"The church is supposed:** "Fact Check: Boebert Says the Church Is Supposed to Direct the Government," WRAL News, July 15, 2022.

118 **And the only reason:** Lauren Sforza, "Speaker Johnson: Separation of Church, State 'a Misnomer,'" *The Hill*, November 14, 2023.

119 **President Ulysses S. Grant:** Jeremiah Chaplin, ed., *Words of Our Hero, Ulysses S. Grant* (D. Lothrop, ca. 1885).

119 **Johnson's vision of:** Documentation for extensive discussion of Johnson's record on these issues is provided in the Congressional Freethought Caucus white paper, "Speaker Johnson: Christian Nationalism in the Speaker's Office?," US House of Representatives, 2023, PDF, accessed January 11, 2026.

119 **If you're hearing echoes:** Southern Poverty Law Center, "Alliance Defending Freedom," SPLC Extremist Files.

120 **The mission of ADF:** Mike Johnson, "Justices Take Swipe at American Values," *Shreveport Times*, July 8, 2003; "Alliance Defending Freedom," Southern Poverty Law Center, n.d.

120 **booster of "Covenant Eyes":** James Kirchick, "The Creepy History of Mike Johnson's Favorite Anti-Porn App," *New Republic*, October 27, 2023.

120 **He urges school:** Mike Hixenbaugh, "Meet the Evangelical Activist Who's Had a 'Profound Influence' on Speaker Mike Johnson," NBC News, October 26, 2023; Robert Downen, "Meet the Christian Nationalist from Texas Advising Mike Johnson," *Texas Tribune*, November 3, 2023.

121 **Twice a year:** WallBuilders, "Pastors and Ministry Leaders!" WallBuilders's [*sic*] Substack, 2023.

121 **Several board members:** Jonathan Larsen, "Speaker Mike Johnson to Allow Privately Run National Prayer Breakfast into the Heart of the Capitol," Religion Dispatches, February 1, 2024.

122 **NAR apostle Jim Garlow:** Matthew D. Taylor, "Mike Johnson, Polite Extremist," *Bulwark*, October 30, 2023; see also Peter Montgomery, "The Religious Right's Rhetoric Fueled the Insurrection," *American Prospect*, February 5, 2021.

123 **And lo, a great multitude:** Molly Olmstead, "The National Prayer Breakfast's Mysterious Schism," *Slate Magazine*, February 2, 2023. For more information about the National Gathering for Prayer and Repentance, see Mark Wingfield, "Museum of the Bible to Host Wednesday Morning Event to Pray for God's Judgment on America," Baptist News Global, January 31, 2023. For Dutch Sheets's prayer at the 2024 event, see "National Gathering for Prayer and Repentance 2024—Prayer by Dutch Sheets," video posted by Peggy Connett, January 31, 2024, YouTube.

124 **When Jesus said:** On the Prayer Chapel, see Brian Kaylor, "Mike Johnson Violates Spirit of Congressional Chapel," Religion News Service, June 5, 2025.

125 **"We have ministers":** Katherine Stewart, *The Power Worshippers: Inside the Dangerous Rise of Religious Nationalism* (Bloomsbury Publishing, 2020), 41, Kindle.

125 **His weekly White:** Drollinger lists thirty-six House members and fifteen senators—all Republican—as official "sponsors" of the Bible study. See "Capitol Ministries Weekend with Ralph Drollinger," Capitol Ministries.

126 **He railed against:** "Capitol Ministries State Director Leaves, Joins New Christian Group," *Capitol Weekly*, 2009.

126 **Capitol Ministries cut ties:** "Capitol Ministries State Director Leaves."

127 **This allowed Drollinger:** Nina Burleigh, "Trump Cabinet Spiritual Adviser Shares His Views, and Some Find Them Spooky," *Newsweek*, October 31, 2017.

127 **"These guys are faithful":** Molly Redden, "White House Bible Study Group Leader Defends Trump's Child Separation Policy," ThinkProgress, July 12, 2018; Stewart, *Power Worshippers*.

127 **Trump's deputy Press:** Brett Samuels, "White House Slams Pastor Leading Cabinet Bible Studies for Linking Homosexuality, Coronavirus," *The Hill*, April 23, 2020.

128 **"discipleship Bible study":** "Through God of the Impossible, European Ministries Have Quickly Gone from None to 20 Nations," Capitol Ministries, accessed January 11, 2026.

128 **"'Oh yes, you do'":** Ralph Drollinger, "Should You Argue from the Bible in a Secular Capitol?," Capitol Ministries, December 22, 2024.

128 **She went further:** Stewart, *Power Worshippers*.

129 **Garlow's *Well Versed Ministries*:** Well Versed Ministries, "Government," wellversedworld.org, 2025; Stewart, *Power Worshippers*.

129 **Prophetic pastors like:** Rhoda Gayle, "Sean Feucht Leads Members of Congress Into Worship Inside the US Capitol," Christian Learning & News (GOD TV), July 27, 2022.

129 **Tony Perkins's Family:** Southern Poverty Law Center, "Family Research Council," SPLC Extremist Files.

129 **For example, Awake America:** Awake America Ministries, "Home," awakeamerica .org, 2025.

129 **Faith and Law ministry:** Faith and Law, "Home," faithandlaw.org, 2025.

130 **laid out in Project 2025:** Molly Redden et al., "'Put Them in Trauma': Inside a Key MAGA Leader's Plans for a New Trump Agenda," Government Executive, govexec.com, October 28, 2024; Global Project Against Hate and Extremism, "Ready or Vought: Project 2025's Mastermind Takes His Shot," globalextremism.org, December 2, 2024.

130 **Among his Project 2025:** Heritage Foundation, *Project 2025*, heritage.org, accessed January 11, 2026.

131 **Led by former:** Military Religious Freedom Foundation, "About," militaryreligious freedom.org, n.d.

131 **A prominent academy:** Author interview with the alumnus.

131 **He even gave:** TYT Investigates, "Sean Duffy Put On BLAST Over Video Showing Jesus Painting Being Moved 'Out of the Basement,'" video, YouTube, 2025.

131 **That same sense of:** Lauren Irwin, "Transport Chief Prioritizes High Birth, Marriage Rate Areas," *The Hill*, February 3, 2025.

CHAPTER 7: CHRISTIAN ZIONISM

134 **"Scripture teaches us":** "US Speaker Johnson Makes Landmark Visit to West Bank Settlement of Ariel," *Times of Israel*, December 18, 2023.

138 **With ultra-Orthodox families:** Lee Cahaner and Gilad Malach, *Statistical Report on Ultra-Orthodox Society in Israel 2024*, chap. 6, "Health," Israel Democracy Institute, February 19, 2025, en.idi.org.il/haredi, accessed January 11, 2026.

139 **Harold Camping's breathlessly:** "Harold Camping," Wikipedia, last modified December 31, 2025.

139 **televangelist Jerry Fallwell:** "Apocalypse Not: Other Times the World Was Supposed to End—and Didn't," *U.S. News & World Report*, December 20, 2012.

140 **Lindsey elevated this worldview:** Lifeway Research, "Evangelical Attitudes Toward Israel: Research Study Report," Lifewayresearch.com, December 2017.

140 **thirty million members worldwide:** Friends of Zion Museum, "Friends of Zion," fozmuseum.com, accessed January 11, 2026.

140 **There are now an estimated:** Douglas Youvan, "There Are More Christian Zionists in the U.S. than Jews in the World," ResearchGate, 2024.

140 **For scale, the America:** Christians United for Israel, "Christians United for Israel," cufi.org, accessed January 11, 2026; American Israel Public Affairs Committee (AIPAC), "About AIPAC," aipacpac.org, accessed January 11, 2026.

141 **The math says:** Public Religion Research Institute, "2024 PRRI Census of American Religion," prri.org, accessed January 11, 2026 (showing relative percentages of white evangelicals and Jews); Pew Research Center, "White Protestants and Catholics Support Trump, but Voters in Other U.S. Religious Groups Prefer Harris," pewresearch.org, September 9, 2024 (showing overwhelming support among white evangelicals for Trump, and overwhelming opposition among Jews).

141 **They believe that:** T. Sturm, "Christian Zionism and the Apocalyptic Landscape of Gaza," Contending Modernities (blog), University of Notre Dame, January 24, 2024.

141 **Sometime between now:** Billy Graham ministries notes, for example, that upon Christ's return, "living unbelievers and the wicked dead now raised to life will be judged at the great white throne judgment. They will then be cast into the lake of fire, while the saved will live forever with Christ in a new heaven and earth (Revelation, chapters 19–22)." Billy Graham Evangelistic Association, "What Is the Rapture?," billygraham.org, accessed January 11, 2026.

141 **This expectation of mass:** Christ Over All, "Reformation and Re-Embracement: A Brief History of the Puritan Hope for Israel," christoverall.com, accessed January 11, 2026.

142 **AIPAC's messaging emphasizes:** American Israel Public Affairs Committee (AIPAC), "About AIPAC," aipacpac.org, accessed January 11, 2026.

142 **For example, CUFI:** Fox News, "Evangelical Leaders Praise Trump's Continued Support for Israel amid War with Iran," foxnews.com, accessed January 11, 2026.

142 **Televangelist Franklin Graham:** Fox News, "Evangelical Leaders Praise Trump's Continued Support."

143 **Just as Esther:** Lou Engle Ministries, "The Call," louengle.com, accessed January 11, 2026.

143 **In this worldview:** Dutch Sheets Ministries, "June 17, 2025," dutchsheets.org, accessed January 11, 2026.

143 **These aren't sightseeing:** Pierce and Jacobs both discuss these trips in their books, among other places. See C. Pierce, *Interpreting the Times* (Charisma House, 2012); C. Jacobs, *Possessing the Gates of the Enemy* (Chosen Books, 2018).

143 **Some, like Pastor:** IHOPKC Israel, "Wes Hall 2017—God's Plan for Israel's Future," video, YouTube, 2017.

144 **It's a theological playbook:** Holly Pivec, "The NAR's Obsession with Israel," Spirit of Error (blog), hollypivec.com, April 2013.

144 **Christian scholar Holly:** Pivec, "The NAR's Obsession with Israel."

145 **"Those who bless Israel":** Middle East Eye, "Ted Cruz' Bible Reference on Israel Scrutinized by Tucker Carlson," video posted by @middleeasteye, tiktok.com, accessed January 11, 2026.

145 **Stefanik testified that:** Al Jazeera, "Trump's UN Ambassador Pick Says Israel Has Biblical Right to West Bank," aljazeera.com, January 21, 2025.

145 **"There's no such thing as":** Al Jazeera, "Trump's UN Ambassador Pick Says Israel."

145 **Friedman justified his proposal:** Jacob Kornbluh, review of David Friedman, *One Jewish State: The Last, Best Hope to Resolve the Israeli-Palestinian Conflict*, forward.com, accessed January 11, 2026.

145 **In the spring of 2025:** Jacob Kornbluh, "What Is the New 'Judea and Samaria Caucus' in Congress All About?" forward.com, accessed January 11, 2026.

146 **With this kind of maximalist:** Amelie Botbol, "Faith Under Fire: Netanyahu Calls Out Efforts to Divide Christians and Israel in US," foxnews.com, accessed January 11, 2026; "Netanyahu Vows 'Complete Solidarity' with Christians Persecuted in Iran," *Times of Israel*, accessed January 11, 2026.

146 **Prominent rabbis have:** "Dispensationalism, Christian Zionism, and Their Role in Antisemitism in the U.S.," *Times of Israel* (blogs), accessed January 11, 2026; Steven Gardiner, "End Times Antisemitism," Political Research Associates, July 9, 2020.

146 **Emerging surveys show:** Diana Chandler, "Evangelical Support for Israel Constant, but Future Shift Indicated, New Study Finds," Baptist Press, accessed January 11, 2026; "Declining Support of Young Evangelicals for Israel," Tel Aviv University, accessed January 11, 2026.

CHAPTER 8: THE DUMBING OF AMERICA

149 **The demonstration was:** "Moms for America Statement on Low Confidence in Public Schools," Moms for America, press release, July 15, 2022.

150 **The speech was:** "Illinois Congresswoman Says 'Hitler Was Right on One Thing,'" NBC Chicago, accessed January 11, 2026.

150 **"May God have mercy":** "Rep. Mary Miller Criticized for Post Targeting Sikh Chaplain," WQAD News 8, accessed January 11, 2026.

150 **This, after all:** Steven Spearie, "Rep. Mary Miller Blasts Study That Finds Her 'Polarizing Rhetoric' Among Most Inflammatory," *State Journal-Register*, updated October 25, 2022.

150 **"God controls the climate":** Right Wing Watch, "Rep. Mary Miller Says 'Climate Change Is a Sham' Because 'God Controls the Climate,'" video, 0:44, YouTube, posted April 10, 2025.

151 **From that point in:** "US Rep Moves to Amend Constitution to Include Parental Rights," Home School Legal Defense Association, November 11, 2025.

151 **In her district:** "2024 American Values Survey: Religion Findings," Public Religion Research Institute, December 2024.

151 ***The New York Times:*** Spearie, "Rep. Mary Miller Blasts Study."

152 **Exhibitions like *Slavery*:** "Institutional Evolution: How Monticello Faced and Interpreted a Legacy of Slavery," American Alliance of Museums, September 1, 2013.

152 **That's why he challenged:** "Thomas Jefferson to Peter Carr, August 10, 1787," Library of Congress, loc.gov.

152 **In letters to his friend:** "To John Adams from Thomas Jefferson, 12 October 1813," *Founders Online*, National Archives, founders.archives.gov.

153 **Jefferson's Northwest Ordinance:** "Morrill Act (1862)," National Archives, archives .gov, accessed January 11, 2026.

153 **Perhaps Jefferson's proudest:** "The Founders' Secular Vision," *UVA Magazine*, accessed January 11, 2026.

153 **Their preferred method:** Andrew L. Seidel, *The Founding Myth: Why Christian Nationalism Is Un-American* (Union Square, 2019), 62–63, Kindle.

153 **Puritan Minister Cotton Mather's:** Frederic D. O'Brien, "1721 Two Hundred Seventy-Five Years Ago," *American Heritage* 47, no. 7 (November 1996).

153 **Jefferson rebuked this kind:** "Thomas Jefferson to Bengamin Rush, 23 September 1800," *Founders Online*, National Archives, founders.archives.gov.

153 **likened religious science denial to witchcraft:** "Thomas Jefferson to José Corrêa da Serra, 11 April 1820," *Founders Online*, National Archives, founders.archives.gov.

154 **He mocked blind faith:** Thomas Jefferson, *Jefferson on Freedom: Wisdom, Advice, and Hints on Freedom, Democracy, and the American Way* (Skyhorse, 2011), 39.

154 **And he declared that:** "Thomas Jefferson to Horatio G. Spafford, 17 March 1814," *Founders Online*, National Archives, founders.archives.gov.

154 **In an 1814 letter:** "Thomas Jefferson to John Adams, 24 January 1814," *Founders Online*, National Archives, founders.archives.gov.

154 **Tim Dwight, the:** Timothy Dwight, *The Duty of Americans, at the Present Crisis* (Thomas and Samuel Green,1798).

154 **In a letter thanking:** "Thomas Jefferson to Joseph Willard, 24 March 1789," *Founders Online*, National Archives, founders.archives.gov.

155 **Its fingerprints are everywhere:** See National Institutes of Health, "Budget," nih.gov, accessed February 4, 2026. Among other things, NIH co-led the Human Genome Project, unlocking personalized medicine and gene therapies. See National Human Genome Research Institute, "The Human Genome Project," genome.gov, accessed February 4, 2026. Long-term NIH support for mRNA research enabled Operation Warp Speed to deliver life-saving COVID-19 vaccines and cutting-edge cancer treatments. See Elie Dolgin and Heidi Ledford, "mRNA COVID Vaccines Saved Lives and Won a Nobel—What's Next for the Technology?," *Nature* (October 3, 2023). The Framingham Heart Study, funded since 1948, identified key cardiovascular risk factors and helped drive a 52 percent drop in premature heart attacks since 1999. See National Heart, Lung, and Blood Institute, "Framingham Heart Study," nhlbi.nih.gov, accessed February 4, 2026. NIH-backed immunotherapy research led to PD-1 inhibitors, doubling five-year survival rates for many cancers. See National Cancer Institute, "PD-1 and PD-L1 Inhibitors," cancer.gov, accessed February 4, 2026. Even the blockbuster weight-loss drug Ozempic traces its origins

to NIH-funded studies of reptilian metabolism. Indeed, between 2010 and 2019, NIH-supported research underpinned over 99 percent of FDA-approved drugs. See Fred D. Ledley et al., "NIH Funding for Drug Development: 2010–2019," *JAMA Health Forum* 4, no. 5 (2023).

155 **NSF has catalyzed:** See US National Science Foundation, "NSF by the Numbers," nsf.gov, accessed January 11, 2026.

155 **The unique resources:** US universities—many NSF-funded—dominate the list of the top fifty global innovation leaders. See "Clarivate Identifies Top 50 Universities Powering Global Innovation," press release, clarivate.com, January 30, 2025.

155 **why we consistently boast:** Helen Pearson et al., "Exclusive: The Most-Cited Papers of the TwentyFirst Century," *Nature* 640, no. 8059 (April 2025): 588–92.

155 **and why our scientists:** "List of American Nobel Laureates," Wikipedia, accessed January 11, 2026.

158 **Homeschooling and "parental rights":** "By Focusing on the Family, James Dobson Helped Propel US Evangelicals Back into Politics, Making the Religious Right into the Cultural Force It Is Today," The Conversation, June 6, 2023; "How 'Parents' Rights' Became a Rallying Cry for Conservatives," *Washington Post*, June 11, 2022.

158 **The next phase escalates:** BlitzWatch, Press Releases: Congressional Prayer Caucus Foundation, WallBuilders, and National Legal Foundation, "Project Blitz Playbook 2018–19."

159 **Second- and third-tier:** "Project Blitz," Wikipedia, accessed January 11, 2026.

159 **Barton fundraised for:** "Ten Commandments in Texas," Texas Values, accessed January 11, 2026.

159 **Louisiana and Arkansas passed:** BrieAnna J. Frank, "Federal Judge Bars Arkansas Public Schools from Displaying the Ten Commandments," *USA Today*, August 6, 2025, updated August 7, 2025; Kaleigh Begneaud, "Another Arkansas School District Added as Defendant in Ten Commandments Lawsuit," MSN News, October 28, 2025.

159 **Florida's censorious "Parental":** Katerina Fernandez, "Undermining Education: How Florida's Censorship Laws Disrupt Inclusivity and Contradict Human Rights Standards," *Immigration and Human Rights Law Review*, University of Cincinnati, October 27, 2024.

159 **Florida has also:** "Florida Has Become the Shining Example for Censorship in Schools," *Florida Today*, June 23, 2025.

159 **The state's sweeping voucher:** Independent Lens, "Hundreds of Voucher Schools Teach Creationism in Science Classes," pbs.org, accessed January 11, 2026.

159 **The 2022 "Stop WOKE":** "Controversial PragerU Curriculum Approved for Florida Classrooms—But It's Unclear Where It Will Be Used," WUFT News, August 7, 2023.

160 **Texas has done:** "Texas House Rejects School Vouchers Again, Signaling Continued Resistance to Diverting Public Education Funds," *Texas Tribune*, April 17, 2025.

160 **Parental primacy is now:** "Texas Proposition 15, Parental Rights Amendment (2025)," ballotpedia.org, accessed January 11, 2026.

160 **Florida launched a barrage:** "Report of the Special Committee on Academic Freedom and Florida," American Association of University Professors, accessed January 11, 2026; "Academic Freedom Under Scrutiny: Legal and Educational Implications of Florida's Higher Education Reforms," *Harvard Undergraduate Law Review* (spring

2025); "Florida Educators File Federal Lawsuit to Challenge Florida's SB 266, Defending Academic Freedom," ACLU of Florida, accessed January 11, 2026.

160 **Faculty groups describe:** "Texas Senate Bill 37 Would Give State Leaders More Power Over University Governing Boards," *Texas Tribune*, May 24, 2025; "Texas Lawmakers Create Overseer to Make Colleges Follow State Directives," Inside Higher Ed, August 11, 2025; "Higher Ed Bills in the 2025 Texas Legislature," AAUP–Texas, accessed January 11, 2026; "Report of the Special Committee on Academic Freedom and Florida," American Association of University Professors, accessed January 11, 2026.

160 **"I love the poorly":** "Donald Trump: 'I Love the Poorly Educated,'" *USA Today*, February 24, 2016.

161 **In a speech titled:** "Trump's New War on 'Woke' Academia," *New York Times*, February 14, 2025.

161 **By the spring of 2024:** "J. D. Vance Praises Viktor Orbán's 'Smart Decisions' in 'Face the Nation' Interview," CBS News, accessed January 11, 2026.

161 **He pledged to fire:** "Trump Says He'll 'Fire the Radical Left' from Colleges, Focus on 'Defending American Tradition' if Elected," Fox News, accessed January 11, 2026.

163 **Justice Department launched:** "Trump DOE Funding Threat Over DEI: A Guide for Colleges," Davis Wright Tremaine, April 2025.

163 **Most others tried:** "39 Ways Universities Are Trying to 'Trump-Proof' Themselves," *Forbes*, April 16, 2025.

163 **Visa revocations, travel bans:** "Impact International 2025: Surge in Scrutiny of Student Visas," VisaVerge, accessed January 11, 2026.

163 **Trump's Education Secretary:** "Trump's New War on 'Woke' Academia," *New York Times*, February 14, 2025.

163 **University leaders described:** "Inside Trump's Pressure Campaign on Universities," *Deccan Herald*, updated April 14, 2025.

164 **This plunged billions:** "US Universities Brace for Sweeping Federal Overhaul," *Nature* (December 18, 2025); "How Trump's Policies Are Reshaping Cancer Research Funding," *New York Times Magazine*, September 14, 2025.

164 **Because complex research:** Annie Waldman et al., "The Scientific Research Lost Amid the Trump Administration's NIH Cuts," ProPublica, June 12, 2025.

164 **The vaunted NSF merit:** "DOGE's Orders Threaten NSF Grants and Proposals," *Chemical & Engineering News*, April 18, 2025; "The Administration's New Science Strategy: Power, Punishment, and the Future of Federal Research," *The Atlantic*, February 2025.

164 **Trump chose a man:** "RFK Jr.'s History of Medical Misinformation Raises Concerns Over HHS Nomination," Brookings Institution, accessed January 11, 2026.

165 **public promotion of false:** "2025 Healthcare Year-Ender: A Tumultuous Year of Policy Shifts and Medical Uncertainty," United Press International, December 17, 2025.

165 **Mass firings and office:** "DOGE Job Cuts Hit NOAA, the Agency in Charge of the Weather Service," *Newsweek*, Feb. 27, 2025; "Why DOGE's Sharp Cuts to NOAA's Forecasting Efforts May Affect Your Company," Inc.com, March 4, 2025.

165 **Adding insult to injury:** "At Work, the National Weather Service Isn't Ready to 'Explain or Agree' with Trump," ABC News, accessed January 11, 2026.

165 **dire warnings from science:** "Trump's Budget Slashes Science Funding," American

Physical Society, June 2025; "National Advocacy Update: March 7, 2025," American Medical Association, accessed January 11, 2026.

165 **shut down pediatric cancer:** "How Trump's Policies Are Reshaping Cancer Research Funding," *New York Times Magazine*, September 14, 2025.

166 **A robust body of:** E. H. Ecklund et al., (2017), "Religious People and Public Attitudes Toward Science in the United States," *Public Understanding of Science* 26, no. 7 (2017): 794–812 (Higher religious commitment correlates with skepticism toward scientific consensus, especially on evolution and climate change); J. P. Hill, "Rejecting Evolution: The Role of Religion, Education, and Social Networks," *Journal for the Scientific Study of Religion* 53, no. 3 (2014), 575–94 (Evangelical Protestants with high religiosity are significantly less likely to accept evolution, even when controlling for education); D. M. Kahan et al., "The Polarizing Impact of Science Literacy and Numeracy on Perceived Climate Change Risks," *Annals of the American Academy of Political and Social Science* 658, no. 1 (2012), 36–66 (Religious identity, especially among conservative Christians, predicts rejection of scientific consensus on climate change and vaccination); M. C. Nisbet and E. M. Markowitz, "Public Opinion on Stem Cell Research: Consistency and Change," *International Journal of Public Opinion Research* 26, no. 4 (2014): 456–65 (Intensity of religious belief strongly predicts opposition to embryonic stem cell research, independent of political ideology); B. T. Rutjens and S. van der Linden (2018), "Science Skepticism Across the Globe: The Influence of Religious and Political Ideology," *Social Psychological and Personality Science* 9, no. 6 (2018): 678–86 (Strong religiosity correlates with lower trust in medical science and higher vaccine hesitancy).

166 **The researchers found:** "The Changing Landscape of U.S. Science Policy: Implications for Research Institutions," *PNAS Nexus*, April 2024.

167 **Majority of elite scientists:** "The Impact of U.S. Science Policy Shifts on Research Productivity," *Journal of Biomedical Science* (2013).

168 **The number of deadly:** "Humanity Is Facing Two Existential Threats: Climate Change and Pandemics," *Africa Climate Reports*, June 2023; "New Study Reveals How Climate Change Is Accelerating the Spread of Infectious Diseases," *ScienceDaily* (May 14, 2024).

168 **closest to global catastrophe:** "Countries Are Neglecting the Existential Threat of Pandemics. Bold Leadership Is Necessary," *Bulletin of the Atomic Scientists*, January 2025.

169 **form a feedback loop:** "Humanity Is Facing Two Existential Threats: Climate Change and Pandemics."

169 **Their 2025 book:** Michael E. Mann and Peter J. Hotez, *Science Under Siege: How to Fight the Five Most Powerful Forces That Threaten Our World* (PublicAffairs, 2025).

170 **Sagan's haunting warning:** C. Sagan, *The Demon-Haunted World: Science as a Candle in the Dark* (Random House, 1995), 25.

CHAPTER 9: DEFENDERS OF DEMOCRACY

173 **"In the name of our God":** "Episcopal Bishop Urges Trump to 'Have Mercy' on LGBTQ Communities and Immigrants," PBS NewsHour, accessed January 11, 2026.

173 **After the service:** "National Cathedral Bishop Responds to Trump After Sermon Draws Strong Reaction," CBS News, accessed January 11, 2026.

173 **Twenty-two House Republicans:** "H.Res.59—119th Congress: Cosponsors," US Congress, accessed January 11, 2026.

173 **Right-wing Christian leaders:** Jack Jenkins, "After Eyebrow-Raising Sermon to Trump, Bishop Budde Beset by Criticism and Praise," *National Catholic Reporter*, January 23, 2025.

174 **a star was born:** Jenkins, "After Eyebrow-Raising Sermon."

174 **"I haven't heard one":** Kurt Vonnegut, *A Man Without a Country* (Seven Stories, 2005).

175 **One of the most:** "Baptist Joint Committee for Religious Liberty," Wikipedia, accessed January 11, 2026; Christians Against Christian Nationalism, christiansagainstchristiannationalism.org, accessed January 11, 2026.

175 **As executive director:** Amanda Tyler, *How to End Christian Nationalism* (Broadleaf, 2024).

176 **A lifelong evangelical:** T. Alberta, *The Kingdom, the Power, and the Glory: American Evangelicals in an Age of Extremism* (HarperCollins, 2023).

176 **In early 2025:** Jeannette Cooperman, "Finally, an Explanation for the Paradox of MAGA Christianity," *Common Reader*, February 11, 2025.

177 **He calls Christian nationalism:** "Russell Moore on the Future of American Christianity," WNYC Studios, New Yorker Radio Hour, accessed January 11, 2026.

177 **The movement's core strategy:** "Politics and Faith: Why Many Are Leaving Evangelical Churches," Faith on View, accessed January 11, 2026; "'The Great Dechurching': Why So Many Americans Are Leaving Their Churches," NPR News, January 24, 2024.

177 **Younger generations are:** "Most Americans Oppose Churches Endorsing Political Candidates," Public Religion Research Institute, accessed January 11, 2026.

177 **"They're leaving because":** Brian Kaylor, "Supporting Church-State Separation with Faithful Challenges to Christian Nationalism," Word&Way, April 10, 2025.

178 **He argues that:** "Opinion: Christmas, Jesus, Power and Humility," *New York Times*, December 22, 2024.

178 **While Trump has enjoyed:** "Religion and Views on LGBTQ Issues and Abortion," Pew Research Center, February 26, 2025.

179 **Though the "Christian nation":** "Christianity's Place in Politics and Christian Nationalism," Pew Research Center, March 15, 2024.

179 **NAR apostles have:** C. Peter Wagner, *Confronting the Powers: How the New Testament Church Experienced the Power of Strategic-Level Spiritual Warfare* (Regal, 1996), 75–76, where Wagner teaches traditional, sacramental, and hierarchical Christian systems (including Catholic, Orthodox, and mainline Protestant churches) are "religious strongholds" that must be "pulled down."

180 **Theo Bro Pastor:** Webbon calls for codification of the Five Solas of protestant theology, which declare that salvation comes by *grace alone*, through *faith alone*, in *Christ alone*, revealed in *Scripture alone*, and for the *glory of God alone*. "Joel Webbon's 'Christian Nation' Will Be Distinctly Protestant," People for the American Way, Right Wing Watch, accessed January 11, 2026.

180 **Wilson rebuked Trump's:** "Trump's Choice to Run White House Faith Office Sparks Theological Turf War," Religion News Service, February 21, 2025.

180 **Rushdoony's denunciation of Judaism:** Rousas John Rushdoony, *The Institutes of Biblical Law*, vol. 1 (Ross House, 1973).

180 **Webbon's thinly veiled bigotry:** "The Christian Nationalist 'TheoBros' Have, Uh, Thoughts About Antisemitism," *Mother Jones*, December 2024.

180 **We saw flashes:** "Statement on NAR, Christian Nationalism Answers Few

Questions but Exposes Growing Rifts in the Movement," Religion Dispatches, accessed January 11, 2026; "Jeremiah Johnson Apologizes for Trump Prophecy, Shuts Down Ministry," *Christianity Today*, March 10, 2021.

181 **"I don't even support religious freedom":** Mark Silk, "When Religious Freedom Is for Me, Not for Thee," Religion News Service, January 20, 2022.

182 **February 2022 collaboration:** "New Report Details the Influence of Christian Nationalism on the Insurrection," Religion News Service, February 9, 2022.

182 **Other joint initiatives:** Jeff Brumley, "Interfaith Coalition Launches Bus Tour Against Christian Nationalism," *Christian Century*, October 19, 2022.

182 **Advocacy group MoveOn:** "All of Us: A Vision for a More Inclusive and Secure Future," *Nexus Project*, June 2023.

182 **Interfaith Alliance is:** "Our Vision," Interfaith Alliance, accessed January 11, 2026.

184 **They scored federal court:** "Court Blocks Texas Ten Commandments Law," Americans United for Separation of Church and State, accessed January 11, 2026.

184 **They're racking up:** "Atheists Applaud Colorado Patients' Right to Know Act," American Atheists, October 1, 2024.

185 **In that way, satire:** "The Satanic Temple," Wikipedia, accessed January 11, 2026.

186 **Antonio Gramsci, imprisoned:** "Pessimism of the Will," *Viewpoint Magazine*, May 28, 2020.

186 **The Stockdale paradox:** Jim Collins, "The Stockdale Concept," jimcollins.com, accessed January 11, 2026.

CONCLUSION

188 **crafted from wishful mythmaking:** "Barton Presents Legend as Fact at Capitol Prayer Event," People for the American Way, Right Wing Watch, accessed January 11, 2026.

189 **Paine's friend and fellow Deist:** Patrick Wallace Hughes, "Antidotes to Deism: A Reception History of Thomas Paine's The Age of Reason, 1794–1809," PhD diss., University of Pittsburgh, 2013; "Thomas Paine: Age of Reason," *U.S. History*, accessed December 28, 2025.

190 **longest-running religious lobbying:** "National Reform Association," nationalreformassociation.weebly.com, accessed January 11, 2026.

192 **John F. Kennedy gave:** John F. Kennedy, *Address to the Greater Houston Ministerial Association*, September 12, 1960, John F. Kennedy Presidential Library and Museum.

192 **"know that I endorse you":** Matthew A. McIntosh. "From Pews to Power: How Evangelicals Took Over the Republican Party in the 20th Century," Brewminate, October 3, 2025.

192 **de facto state religion:** See, e.g., US Department of Homeland Security (@DHSgov), "Merry Christmas, America. We are blessed to share a nation and a Savior," X (formerly Twitter), December 24, 2025.

FURTHER READING

Alberta, Tim. *The Kingdom, the Power, and the Glory: American Evangelicals in an Age of Extremism*. Harper, 2023.

Doner, Colonel V. *Christian Jihad: Neo-Fundamentalists and the Polarization of America*. Prometheus, 2007.

Du Mez, Kristin Kobes. *Jesus and John Wayne: How White Evangelicals Corrupted a Faith and Fractured a Nation*. Liveright, 2020.

Mann, Michael E., and Peter J. Hotez. *Science Under Siege: How to Fight the Five Most Powerful Forces that Threaten Our World*. PublicAffairs, 2025.

Onishi, Bradley. *Preparing for War: The Extremist History of White Christian Nationalism—and What Comes Next*. Fortress Press, 2023.

Seidel, Andrew L. *The Founding Myth: Why Christian Nationalism Is Un-American*. Sterling, 2019.

Sharlet, Jeff. *The Family: The Secret Fundamentalism at the Heart of American Power*. Harper, 2008.

Speckhardt, Roy. *Justice-Centered Humanism: How (and Why) to Engage in Public Policy for Good*. Humanist Press, 2021.

Stewart, Katherine. *Money, Lies, and God: Inside the Movement to Destroy American Democracy*. Bloomsbury, 2025.

Stewart, Katherine. *The Power Worshippers: Inside the Dangerous Rise of Religious Nationalism*. Bloomsbury, 2019.

Taylor, Matthew D. *The Violent Take It by Force: The Christian Movement That Is Threatening Our Democracy*. Broadleaf, 2024.

Throckmorton, Warren, and Michael L. Coulter. *Getting Jefferson Right: Fact Checking Claims About Our Third President*. Salem Grove, 2012.

Tyler, Amanda. *How to End Christian Nationalism*. Broadleaf, 2024.